# In Defense of the Founders Republic

# In Defense of the Founders Republic

## Critics of Direct Democracy in the Progressive Era

Edited by
Lonce H. Bailey and Jerome M. Mileur

Bloomsbury Academic
An imprint of Bloomsbury Publishing Inc

B L O O M S B U R Y
NEW YORK • LONDON • NEW DELHI • SYDNEY

**Bloomsbury Academic**

An imprint of Bloomsbury Publishing Inc

| | |
|---|---|
| 1385 Broadway | 50 Bedford Square |
| New York | London |
| NY 10018 | WC1B 3DP |
| USA | UK |

**www.bloomsbury.com**

**BLOOMSBURY and the Diana logo are trademarks of Bloomsbury Publishing Plc**

First published 2015

**Library of Congress Cataloging-in-Publication Data**
A catalogue record for this book is available from the Library of Congress.

ISBN: HB: 978-1-6235-6030-0
PB: 978-1-6235-6577-0
ePUB: 978-1-6235-6257-1
ePDF: 978-1-6235-6260-1

Typeset by Integra Software Services Pvt. Ltd.
Printed and bound in the United States of America

*In memory of my father, Larry Bailey, a foot soldier for the*
*legendary political boss James Michael Curley. As a kid, he tucked*
*me into bed with stories of Boston politics that undoubtedly inspired*
*me in my career and in this book.*

*LHB*

*To my parents, who passed a love of baseball,*
*politics, and school to their son.*

*JMM*

# Contents

# Acknowledgments

The development of this project was possible through the work and contributions of many people, most of whom are contributors to this book. We thank the contributors for working together to help develop these ideas through a series of panels at the Northeastern Political Science Association meetings. In addition to the contributors, we greatly benefited from readings and editorial advise generously offered by Alison Dagnes and Michael Hannahan. We would also like to thank the departments of political science at Shippensburg University and the University of Massachusetts Amherst for their long-standing support. The editorial insight and guidance at Bloomsbury Academic has been outstanding. In particular, Matthew Kopel helped us think through the project more fully and usher it into production. Our Production Editor James Tupper also deserves our deep thanks for bringing it into its final form along with Michelle Chen and Rajakumari Ganessin. We could not have completed this without everyone's time, effort, and contributions and we will always be grateful.

1

# Introduction: Progressivism and its Critics

Lonce H. Bailey
*Shippensburg University*

There has been a revival of scholarly interest in the Progressive Era over the past several decades. The role of Progressive reforms in the development of the American national state has been widely explored, as have questions about their philosophical or ideological coherence as they have played out in the twentieth century's two subsequent periods of liberal reform. There is general agreement about the *governmental* legacy of Progressivism: a much enlarged and more bureaucratic, managerial, and technocratic national state with a more robust presidency at its center, a larger role for public opinion in day-to-day governance, a diminished role for representative institutions in politics and government, and more opportunities for direct citizen intervention in government at the state and local levels. There is general agreement as well about its *political* legacy: political parties were weakened in elections and governance, direct primaries and candidate-centered campaigns gained prominence, democracy and political process became more important in political debates and constitutionalism less so, women gained the vote, groups became more prominent, and private money more important. Progressivism, and the liberalism that followed it, has had its critics on both the Left and Right, political as well as academic, but other than "big government," these criticisms have centered, to a remarkable degree, on public policy rather than institutional issues. Basic constitutional questions were raised to which responses from reformers were more often assumed or asserted than explored or analyzed. What does *popular government* mean? What is the role of *citizens* and of public *opinion* in a democracy? What is the role of *representation* and of executive *leadership* in a democratic system? What is the role of mediating *institutions* in legislative bodies and elections? What is the effect of reform on *constitutional* government?

These questions were widely and hotly contested in the final decades of the nineteenth and early ones of the twentieth century, but for the most part, these debates have passed from view as Progressivism has become hegemonic in American government, politics, and the academy. Rarely have the consequences of the political reforms of the Progressives been subjected to serious examination. Nothing better illustrates the broad acceptance of these reforms than the broad and uncritical acceptance of direct democracy and direct government as essential to politics and government in a democracy. These reforms, as the political sociologist Arthur Lipow observes, have "proven to be peculiarly resistant to critical historical analysis [and] remarkably free from serious ideological or organized challenge. In short," he continues, "the reforms themselves, as well as the underlying ideological assumptions have come to be regarded as part of the natural political order in the United States."[1] Similarly, John Epperson writes that, "unfortunately," the arguments of those opposed to direct-democracy reforms have "been ignored or lost in the rush to 'purify' American political parties," adding that those who were critics of Progressivism in its time "point to issues and problems which have not received the attention they deserve."[2] Lipow agrees, noting that "the cogent and prophetic views of [Progressivism's] critics have simply gone down the memory hold. For the most part [the critics] have been derided as blinkered conservatives."[3]

Progressivism has left America with a distinctive and, in the case of the direct primary, a unique understanding of democracy as a political system in which citizen participation directly controls both politics and governance. In both cases, institutions are measured not by whether they encourage deliberation or virtue (the aims of the Constitution's framers), but rather by how well they facilitate and how completely their products reflect the immediate will of the people. Today, direct democracy (or "participatory democracy" as it has been better known since the 1960s) is accepted by academic and political commentators and by democracy reformers as a "self-evident truth." It is almost universally assumed, or thought to be common knowledge, that the more fully citizens are directly involved in their own governance, the closer government and politics come to realizing the democratic ideal. Left behind and largely forgotten are many of the republican ideas and ideals in the framers' design for constitutional government, including the central importance of a representative system of democracy. Left behind as well is the ancient understanding of democracy as a class-based system of governance, displaced by the view that it is a process or method. It is the older understanding of democracy that informed the minds of the framers and that lies at the heart of James Madison's lament about factions in *Federalist* 10.

## The framers' choice

The first generation of Americans who designed the Constitution in the late eighteenth century, like the generation that remade it early in the twentieth, were products of their time, intellectual and political. The framers inhabited a world of Newtonian mechanics and Lockean liberalism, for whom the most immediate and important historical experience was as colonists who had overthrown their master to create a nation thought by them to be something entirely new in the history of nations. Their overarching goal was to establish a popular government that guaranteed an ordered liberty in a stable political regime. They found this in a republican frame of government characterized by a representative system of democracy. The Progressives lived in a different world that was dominated by the new Darwinian science of evolution and a philosophical pragmatism that cast reality as a collection of processes. For them, the defining historical experience was the Civil War with its violent disruption of the framers' constitutional order and a new industrial economy that enriched the few, impoverished the many, and left a new and troubling social and cultural diversity in its wake. Their aim was to craft popular government into a true democracy in which citizens would act directly as individuals to give direction to politics and government.

In creating a new nation, the American founders were of necessity preoccupied with establishing order and giving stability to their foundling. Experience under the Articles of Confederation added to these concerns and led to a Constitution that created a more energetic central power better able to govern the former colonies and, at the same time, secured the liberty for which the revolution had been prosecuted. They sought a government of limited powers, based on the will of the governed, but one that could achieve an effective union of what had been largely independent states. To this end, they designed an institutional arrangement of separate powers for three separate and coequal branches of government, as well as a division of power between the national government and its component states. With the addition of a Bill of Rights, this seemed a structure that could act aggressively when necessary and yet be easily prevented from taking unnecessary actions. Their invention included a dimension of direct democracy in the popular election for the lower house of the legislature but insulated other offices (the upper house of the legislature, the executive, and the supreme court) from the direct reach of the people in what the framers deemed a mixed government in which all social interests were represented. In addition, it was calculated to produce a moderate politics, deliberative in style that would frustrate selfish interests and encourage reasoned accommodation of competing interests while still honoring the foundational democratic concept of majority rule. They saw the activity of politics as the ultimate protection of liberty.

The framers believed in popular government but feared the pure democracy of direct majority rule. In their view, unrestrained majorities could become a mob and be as great a threat to liberty as any tyrant. They were republicans in the Aristotelian mold, who believed that the best form of popular government was rule by enlightened self-interest. This was most likely to be achieved through representative institutions, but even they required restraints which the framers found in the system of checks and balances built into their Constitution. Indeed, there was no issue greater in the first seven decades of governance under the Constitution than the question of power between the branches and levels of government, as well as between the government and the governed. In these formative years, executive power grew, largely through the veto, and the people's power grew, primarily through the emergence of a two-party system. The Civil War resolved the question of national power by clearly establishing the supremacy of the central government over the states.

From its ratification through the Civil War, the Constitution shaped the character and content of politics and government in America with no formal change in its content save for an amendment modifying the operation of the Electoral College. Like the Newtonian universe, the Constitution with its firmament of checks and balances seemed a permanent and unchanging system, fixed forever as the frame of government for the nation. For many, the document acquired a near-sacred quality whose worship defined what it meant to be an American. The Progressives, however, did not share the reverence of earlier generations for the Constitution. Under the influence of Darwin, they saw it as an organism in the body politic which, like all living things, had to adapt to changing conditions if it were to survive. Abraham Lincoln released this spirit of revisionism in his speech at Gettysburg when he dated the founding of the nation with the *Declaration of Independence* and, in doing so, elevated equality, a word to be found nowhere in the Constitution, to share center stage with liberty as the founding principles of the nation. Despite the clear reservations of the framers, the Progressives took this as evidence that democracy was a founding principle of the nation, every bit the equal in importance to liberty, but unlike liberty, it was a principle that had not been fully realized in the political development of the nation.

## The Progressive reforms

The Progressive Era was something new in American history. It was the first period of broad-ranging reform of the framers' constitutional system and the politics it had produced that the nation had known. Released from the romance with the Founding by the Civil War and faced with the economic ills and social injustices of new industrial and banking systems, the program of the reformers was twofold: it aimed at the use of government to reign in the influence of great wealth and of the unfettered capitalism that created the money power; and it sought to break the hold on politics of the party bosses and their machines whose collaboration with the robber barons underlay the wrongs of the economic system. Their reforms were concentrated for the most part on the state and local levels of government, but ultimately the changes they brought about affected government and politics at all levels across the nation and changed the character of the Framers' Constitution.

None of the Progressive reforms were more contentious than the enlarged role of government in the economy. Conservatives decried it as socialism, while academics and the new Muckraking journalists backed it as necessary and just. From the academy, there came statistical analyses that, among other things, documented collusion between railroads and banks to drive up shipping costs for farmers, while the new magazines published explosive accounts of the working conditions in meat packing and other industries that exposed workers to unsanitary and unhealthy conditions and exploited women and children. Social workers drew attention to the conditions of poverty of those, many of them recent immigrants, who inhabited the urban slums. Meanwhile, the laissez-faire philosophy embraced by both political parties, albeit for different reasons, and the preeminence of legislatures controlled by party bosses and moneyed interests resisted change, aided by a constitutional system of checks and balances which made it easier to block action than to take it.

Progressives championed direct forms of citizen government as one way to bypass the legislature. They urged adoption of the initiative through which voters could enact statutes and constitutional amendments of their own design without legislative interference, and its companion, the referendum, by means of which voters could reject laws and constitutional provisions of which they disapproved. They also endorsed the recall by which elected officials and judges could be removed from office by the voters. These direct government reforms won approval in many states, though not all. None was adopted at the national level. The reformers also embraced civil-service reform, a merit system intended to replace patronage in public employment, a blow aimed directly at political parties and party leaders in the legislature and weakened their hold on the membership in both. They sought as well to regulate lobbying and private contributions as they viewed them as corrupting influences in legislatures. Civil-service reform and the regulation of lobbying and political money found approval at the federal as well as the state level, but public sector unions and free speech provisions in the First Amendment have diminished the effect of these reforms.

To the American framers, the legislature was the first branch of government, and the House of Representatives with direct and frequent elections the most democratic branch. Not so for the Progressives, who looked to the executive as the one office for which all had been able to vote and which was therefore the most representative of the public. It was to the executive they looked for leadership and sought to give him not only added powers, but also the assistance of an administration chosen by merit and populated by experts. This vision of the executive was also connected to a more dynamic and expanded understanding of the role of public opinion in both democratically influencing the executive and in allowing the executive to influence and communicate directly with the people. Under this understanding, the new position and enhanced role of the executive in the constitutional frame of state and national governments was perhaps the most important single achievement of the reform era.

The Progressives succeeded in greatly enlarging the scale and scope of government at the state and national levels, expanding its role in regulating the economy, ameliorating social ills resulting from industrialization, urbanization, and immigration, preserving the nation's natural environment, and more. This transformation in the character of government was, if anything, more controversial than was the political agenda of the reformers, for it drew a determined opposition from Old Guard Republicans and conservative Democrats intent on preserving both limited government and property rights in the new corporate America. But, these reforms are not the focus of this volume. It is instead the direct-democracy political reforms of the Progressives that are of primary interest here.

Of these so-called direct-democracy reforms, the most controversial was the adoption of a state-sponsored primary that extended to all state and local offices. Primaries had been first used by political parties in the years preceding the Civil War where the growth of cities had made it impossible for all residents to come together to make nominations. They were private party elections unregulated by statute in the administration of which government had no role. By the end of the nineteenth century, some cities had adopted ordinances establishing primary elections that were conducted with government oversight. The Progressives championed the adoption of primaries for all statewide and legislative offices, as well as for the state's representatives to Congress. It spread slowly to states across the country and came gradually to include municipal elections and, since the 1970s, has become for practical purposes the method by which presidential candidates are nominated.

None of the political reforms of the Progressives have had a greater impact on the Framers' Constitution than the adoption and growth of the direct primary. It succeeded in the goal of denying the bosses control over party nominations and has effectively eliminated party bosses altogether from American politics. In doing this, it has also transformed American politics, greatly weakening the parties as a representative and mediating institution and reducing their role to little more than that of a fund-raiser for candidates who win party nominations. Parties have been all but eliminated in many municipalities where the Progressive call for nonpartisan elections has won support. The reformers sought to make candidates the focus of voter choice, and in this, they have succeeded far more than they could have imagined and perhaps more than they desired. In many ways, we are still coming to terms with the effects of such candidate-centered elections and the politics it created.

Of their other political reforms, the initiative and referendum has won widespread but far from universal acceptance. Twenty-four states have one or both, eighteen of these being west of the Mississippi River.[4] Before the 1970s, the importance of the initiative was limited for the most part to states that had it, but in the decades since it increased significance for national politics as well. Progressives intended the initiative as a way for voters to bypass slow-moving and unresponsive legislatures and enact legislation that would deal effectively with the social and economic problems of their time. Their intent may not have been liberal in the New Deal sense, but it was almost surely not conservative in the way the initiative has been used recently to attack the size and capacity of government. The recall, which enabled voters to remove elected officials by popular vote, has not received as wide acceptance as the direct government reforms. It has been used most frequently at local levels of government, often for the removal of judges who have rendered unpopular decisions. None of these Progressive reforms have been adopted by the federal government.

The only Progressive reform to be adopted at the national level was the Seventeenth Amendment which provided for the popular election of US Senators. Consistent with their view of direct democracy, this change derived primarily from the desire to weaken the power of state legislatures, and therefore the party machines that controlled them, that had previously made the choice of Senators. The ballot was also spread more widely after World War I by ratification of the Nineteenth Amendment which gave the vote to women. This was consistent in spirit and purpose with Progressivism, but credit for the amendment's success goes primarily to women's organizations who had pressed the cause for almost a century. There was also a strain in Progressivism that sought to limit access to the ballot to new immigrant groups, and of course reformers did nothing to bring the vote to racial minorities in the South.

## The book

There is a rich literature on the effect of Progressive reforms on the development of the American national government and politics, the rise of an administrative state with the presidency at the center, the growth in the size of government and the reach of public policy, and the expanded role of citizens and experts in its direction and management. This literature has focused on the intent of the Progressives, the content of their reforms, and the consequences for the nation's governance. Little attention, however, has been paid to the debates that attended these reforms. There were anti-federalists as well as federalists at the time of the Constitution's ratification, and the thought of both has been explored often and at great length. There is no comparable record for the Progressive Era. The critics of Progressive reforms—the anti-progressives, so to speak—have largely passed from historical accounts of the time. Insofar as attention is given to them, they are usually characterized as conservatives defending a status quo of capitalists and party bosses exploiting the masses, indifferent to the public good, turning America into something its founders had not intended. This depiction may be correct for some of the critics, but others offered a spirited defense not of the economic and political status quo but of the principles and logic of the Framers' Constitution that had governed the nation for a century. The recovery of their thought, especially their criticism of direct-democracy and direct-government reforms which is the focus of this volume, sets the Progressive Era in a larger frame that lends credence to the contention that the period was less a time of mere reform and more one that constituted a second founding of the nation. A more complex understanding of the debates and conflicts of the time will broaden our view of this important reform picture and its resultant consequences.

Jeffrey Sedgwick's essay on James Madison, the principal architect of the Framers' Constitution, examines the analysis and arguments that lay behind its design. He explores Madison's view of human nature and science and his understanding of the republican ideal that informed and guided the work of the framers. In a finely nuanced essay, Sedgwick explains the connections Madison makes between the activity of politics and individual liberty and his fear of unfettered democracy that could lead to factions and, worse, to a tyranny of the majority. He shows how experience with politics that the Constitution created led Madison to support political parties as essential institution in a representative system of popular government. Madison was something of a "godfather" for the critics of Progressivism. Many of them drew upon him by name, as they countered the arguments of reformers by recalling those made by the framers in defense of the Constitution they had authored.

The five essays that follow Madison deal with critics of Progressivism, all of whom were figures of national prominence in the early decades of the twentieth century and all of whom have been seen as conservatives. There can be no doubt that Nicholas Murray Butler and Joseph G. Cannon were philosophically or ideologically conservative and believed that American government and politics as they operated at the turn of the twentieth century were in need of little, if any, reform. William Howard Taft, Elihu Root, and Henry Jones Ford, however, were decidedly more moderate in their views. All were intimately associated with Progressive presidents, Taft and Root with Theodore Roosevelt and Ford with Woodrow Wilson, with whom they shared the belief in a more activist and expansive state but had deep reservations about many of the Progressive political reforms. The Socialists Eugene Debs and Victor Berger could not be mistaken for conservatives and were in many ways the fiercest foes of the direct primary for the destructive effects they foresaw it having on political parties, which they believed were essential for an authentic mass-based politics.

The penultimate essay focuses on two states that were prominent in the movement to political reform, both of which produced leaders who earned national reputations as champions of direct democracy. In Wisconsin, Robert La Follette led the successful fight for the nation's first statewide primary system. He was opposed both politically (within the Republican Party) and philosophically by Emanuel Philipp, a moderate conservative in the style of Taft and Root whose criticisms were principled but also grounded in the evidence of the state's experience with the effect of the primary on a once-vibrant party system. In Oregon, William U'Ren led the fight for the initiative and referendum. Unlike Wisconsin where Philipp emerged as a vigorous antagonist for La Follette, no individual emerged in Oregon to oppose U'Ren who for a decade reigned as the most influential figure in the state's politics. The "Oregon Plan," as the initiative and referendum were called, came to be embraced by many western states, California the most prominent among them.

The Butler and Ford essays present perhaps the most comprehensive critiques of Progressivism. Best known as president of Columbia University, Butler was a lifelong Republican and an active public intellectual. He was a regular delegate to National Conventions of the GOP, twice sought the party's presidential nomination, and served briefly as Taft's running mate in 1912, replacing James Sherman who died six days before the election. A political scientist by training, Butler's assessment of the Progressive reforms rested on his belief that political institutions developed from simple to more complex forms and were grounded in natural law and universal truths that came to us through centuries of experience and historical reflection. If there was an intellectual leader among the critics of reform, Butler could lay a strong claim for the title.

Ford was a journalist, whose book on the history of political parties in America and numerous scholarly articles led to his joining the political science faculty at Princeton University where he became an associate and ally of Woodrow Wilson, serving in his administration as both governor and president. Like Taft and Root, Ford was sympathetic to the Progressive call for a more activist government, but often harsh in his condemnation of the political reforms they proposed. Like Wilson, he believed in a strong party system, and while he had no illusion about corruption, he was resolute in defending the party as an institution against the evil effects of the direct primary. He argued for the central importance of politics in a democracy and for accountability in government, faulting reformers for their disdain for the former and easy disregard for the latter.

Taft was of course Roosevelt's choice as a successor and shared many of his convictions about reform, but had a more complex view of Progressivism and, as Paul Rego shows, was not the politician TR was. He was very much in the tradition of his mentor as a trust buster but did not share his enthusiasm for other policies, such as that for protecting public lands. He did not share TR's view of the president's constitutional authority and did not have his predecessor's taste for independent action taken on his own initiative. Taft was much more of a party-government man and far more willing than Roosevelt to deal with party leaders in Congress. The most violent rupture in their association, however, came when TR endorsed the use of the recall in case of judges and judicial decisions. For Taft, an independent judiciary was sacrosanct and should be protected from the passions of public opinion, and he came to view direct-democracy reforms, such as the initiative, referendum, and recall, as undermining the representative democracy that was fundamental to the Framers' Constitution.

Joseph Cannon, speaker of the House of Representatives during Taft's time in the White House, was a determined supporter of party government and a fierce foe of direct forms of politics and governance. As Doug Harris observes, Cannon took not only strong but highly principled stands for the role of parties in representative government and for the integrity and clarity of majorities as the expression of the popular will. Drawing on Cannon's speeches in the House, Harris shows that Uncle Joe, as the Speaker was called by friend and foe alike, held a coherent view of the importance of organization in politics as enabling voters to more easily and clearly assign responsibility for actions taken and to know whom to hold responsible for their decisions. Like other critics, Cannon believed in party government, though his enforcement of it may not have been what other critics had in mind.

Elihu Root, who twice served in Roosevelt's cabinet as secretary of war and state and later as a US senator from New York, was among the most respected men of his time. He shared many of the Progressive views as to the problems the nation faced—the accumulation of wealth and power in a few hands and the corrupting effect this had on politics—but also saw their direct-democracy and direct-government reforms as an irresponsible attack upon representative institutions. As Robert Lacey's chapter details, he argued for the reform of existing institutions, not their abridgment, and believed that citizens were best able to play a responsible public role by passing judgment on the actions those chose to serve in public office. He fought the direct election of Senators, which he thought undermined the framers' constitutional structure of government, and argued for reforms such as the short ballot as the best way to weaken party bosses and provide for more responsible government by simplifying accountability.

In many ways, Eugene Debs and Victor Berger might be seen as outliers among the critics of the Progressive political reforms. In their argument for social democracy, they were ideologically in a different realm of politics, but practically the differences were not as great as the enemies of Socialism insisted. They condemned the direct primary for its destructive effects on a party system organized by programs of governance and preferred reform much like that urged by Wilson, Ford, and Root. For them, parties were the nonviolent path to changing an economic system that they saw as crushing the working class. They were more sympathetic to the direct government reforms than were other critics, and while many of the latter shared the Socialist desire to improve conditions of life for the poor, they did not agree that public ownership of the means of production was the answer.

The case studies of Wisconsin and Oregon attest to the enthusiasm for direct-democracy and direct-government reforms and also to the fact that, as a reform movement, Progressivism found its home in state and local government, not at the national level, though the consequences of these reforms have been as profound in national politics and governance as they have for any state or locality. It is also clear from these essays that while for the most part they were conservatives, their conservatism was located not in the radical individualism of the Social Darwinists but in the tradition of the English statesman, Edmund Burke, upon whom many drew by name. The critics not only shared the framers' belief in representative democracy but also their view of change, believing that reform properly grew from experience and experimentation, not from abstract and untested theories. For them, the political and institutional reforms urged by the Progressives represented an abrupt and radical departure from the constitutional arrangements of the framers, and it is remarkable how prescient their predictions were about the consequences of the reformers' program. Today, we have the political system designed by the Progressives, and while it may be said this is not what they intended, it may not be said that they were not warned.

# Notes

1  Arthur Lipow, *Political Parties and Democracy* (Chicago: Pluto Press, 1996), 13.

2  John W. Epperson, *The Changing Legal Status of Political Parties in the United States* (New York: Garland, 1986), 152–153.

3  Lipow, *Political Parties*, 16.

4  National Conference of State Legislatures, "Elections and Campaigns: Initiative and Referendum States." www.ncsl.org. http://www.ncsl.org/research/elections-and-campaigns/chart-of-the-initiative-states.aspx (accessed August 15, 2014).

# 2

# James Madison: Architect of the First Founding

Jeffrey Leigh Sedgwick
*University of Massachusetts Amherst*

Political reform always arrives with a backstory or narrative against which debates are carried on. Progressive reforms calling for direct democracy and direct government challenged the republican principles embodied in the founders' Constitution, so much so that their critics saw them as constituting a second founding. To understand the debate between the two sides requires therefore an understanding of the essential characteristics of the first founding that the reformers sought to change. These are fourfold: the superiority of science and of empirical evidence born of experience over speculative theory; the imperfect and imperfectable nature of man; the emphasis on stability with the institutional arrangements to secure it; and the sanctity of the Constitution as the embodiment of the will of the American people. The most articulate and sophisticated architect of the nation's first founding, which established the first modern republic, was James Madison of Virginia.

This essay lays out Madison's thinking behind the creation of America's first constitutional order. It is not done to render a judgment in the contest between the Progressives and their critics, but rather to clarify the contours of the battlefield over which they fought. Madison clearly articulates the foundations of the modern republic in juxtaposition to both the ancient republics of Greece and Italy and the politics of state and confederation governments of his time. His analysis and arguments detail the contours and characteristics over which the Progressive reformers and their critics chose to fight some 125 years later.

## The new science of politics: The lamp of experience

The elevation of science and of empirical evidence over abstract theory in the first founding is seen most clearly in *The Federalist Papers* published anonymously in New York newspapers from September 1787 through May 1788 and distributed nationally soon thereafter in book form. In *Federalist* number ten, Madison addresses the topic, "The Union as a Safeguard against Domestic Faction and Insurrection," in which he draws upon historical experience rather than theory as a guide. In this essay, Madison referred to the spirit of parties which caused them to ignore both justice and the rights of minorities:

> Complaints are everywhere heard from our most considerate and virtuous citizens, equally the friends of public and private faith, and of public and personal liberty, that our governments are too unstable, that the public good is disregarded in the conflicts of rival parties, and that measures are too often decided, not according to the rules of justice and the rights of the minor party, but by the superior force of an interested and overbearing majority ... It will be found, indeed, on a candid review of our situation, that some of the distresses under which we labor have been erroneously charged on the operation of our governments; but it will be found, at the same time, that other causes will not alone account for many of our heaviest misfortunes; and, particularly, for that prevailing and increasing distrust of public engagements, and alarm for private rights, which are echoed from one end of the continent to the other. These must be chiefly, if not wholly, effects of the unsteadiness and injustice with which a factious spirit has tainted our public administrations.[1]

Madison thus suggests that the experience of pre-constitutional politics in the United States was quite similar to the experience of politics in ancient Greece and Italy: our governments were unstable; they too disregarded the public good, justice, and the rights of minorities. All of these problems, as in ancient republics, were traced back to factions born of partisanship. Significantly, he located the deficiencies of ancient republics in their purely democratic, as opposed to republican, character:

> It may be concluded that a pure democracy, by which I mean a society consisting of a small number of citizens, who assemble and administer the government in person, can admit of no cure for the mischiefs of faction. A common passion or interest will, in almost every case, be felt by a majority of the whole; a communication and concert result from the form of government itself; and there is nothing to check the inducements to sacrifice the weaker party or

an obnoxious individual. Hence it is that such democracies have ever been spectacles of turbulence and contention; have ever been found incompatible with personal security or the rights of property; and have in general been as short in their lives as they have been violent in their deaths.[2]

Here Madison has taken the genus of free government (or government based on consent of the governed) and divided it into two species: pure or direct democracy and republicanism. The former was necessarily small so that citizens could be personally involved in the administration of government; the latter large and necessarily based on representation. The promise of his "new science of politics" was that it could avoid the inconveniences of ancient, purely democratic republics as well as the similar defects observed among the pre-constitutional states.

The preference of the ancients for small republics that were purely democratic in character was grounded in the political theory of Aristotle and carried into modernity by Montesquieu. In Book I of *The Politics*, Aristotle considered the proper size of the political community and concluded that it must be small enough to cultivate and support friendship. It must also be small enough to take advantage of shame since shame is a uniquely human capacity which disciplines a citizen. But shame operated only in a small community where everyone knew one another. Aristotle argued that a political community must be based on trust (shame and friendship) for where trust was absent, the community must use force or coercion to achieve discipline. Montesquieu also argued in *The Spirit of the Laws* that "it is in the nature of a republic that it have only a small territory; without that it can scarcely continue to exist."

In his observation based on the experience of ancient republics, Madison took a swipe at theoretical speculation: "Theoretic politicians, who have patronized this species of government [i.e. pure democracy], have erroneously supposed that by reducing mankind to a perfect equality in their political rights, they would, at the same time, be perfectly equalized and assimilated in their possessions, their opinions, and their passions."[3] Some years later, in his party press essays, Madison again criticized speculative or abstract theorists like Montesquieu:

Montesquieu was in politics not a Newton or a Locke, who established immortal systems, the one in matter, the other in mind. He was in his particular science what Bacon was in universal science: He lifted the veil from the venerable errors which enslaved opinion, and pointed the way to those luminous truths of which he had but a glimpse himself.[4]

In short, historical experience trumped speculative theory in teaching that the political and social arrangements that produce perfect political and social equality cannot and do not produce assimilation of interests, opinions, or passions.

We may pause for a moment to consider a peculiar vulnerability of a politics grounded on the modern scientific method of skeptical observation of evidence, particularly historical evidence. We may ask if such science is a fixed and constant standard by which to guide or anchor government and politics. One can appreciate the attraction that science of a particular form held for Madison and his collaborators in designing modern republicanism for the extended representative democracy that America was to become. Their scientific paradigm was Newtonian in character and explained how stability could be achieved in a system where every component part was in constant motion as in the planetary system. The *Declaration of Independence* had posited equality of rights among Men, especially with regard to life, liberty, and the pursuit of happiness as fixed truth. But, under these very conditions, Americans would become, if they were not already, a restless, striving, entrepreneurial folk. Reconciling that motion with political stability was a major conceptual problem for which Newtonian science provided a welcome solution: checks and balances or offsetting centrifugal and centripetal forces playing off against one another.[5]

In the second half of the nineteenth century, however, the modern scientific paradigm shifted from Newton's physical science of gravity to Charles Darwin's biological science of natural selection. Darwinian science served better to explain change than stability and, indeed, urged change in order to survive. Darwin's emphasis on adaptation in the service of survival found a receptive audience in America, especially among hundreds of thousands of young boys in blue and gray who had witnessed the price for their leaders' failures to adapt military tactics to new technologies such as rifled musket barrels and minie balls. With the paradigmatic shift in science during the second half of the nineteenth century, the cornerstone upon which the Founders' republican government rested, with its separation of powers among distinct branches of government, elaborate system of checks and balances, rule of law with judges serving for good behavior, and representation of the people through deputies of their own election, all in the name of stability, came under assault. That assault was the core of Progressive reform.

## Faction and the imperfect nature of man

If faction, whether of interest, opinion, or passion, was the source of the instability that bedeviled ancient republics, as well as the pre-constitutional politics of eighteenth-century America, then why not simply eliminate the causes of faction as a solution? In reply, Madison observed that there were but two methods of eliminating the causes of faction: destroying liberty, which was essential to the existence of faction; or giving to every citizen the same opinions, passions, and interests.[6] Madison quickly disposed of the first with the observation that the cure was worse than the disease, for the whole purpose of eliminating faction was to preserve liberty. With regard to the second, Madison observed that it was impractical because Man was fallible:

> As long as the reason of man continues fallible, and he is at liberty to exercise it, different opinions will be formed. As long as the connection subsists between his reason and his self-love, his opinions and his passions will have a reciprocal influence on each other; and the former will be objects to which the latter will attach themselves.[7]

Madison does not say that all human beings were dominated by their self-love; he merely asserted that there was a connection. The point was that all must come to grips with self-love, both individually and collectively in a political body and, in turn, that self-love implied that the origin of faction lay in the individual self, the unique body. Removing the cause of faction required overcoming the fact of separate human bodies.

The magnitude of this task, he argued, should not be underestimated, for the connection between human reason and self-love was both durable and omnipresent:

> The latent causes of faction are thus sown in the nature of man; and we see them everywhere brought into different degrees of activity, according to the different circumstances of civil society. A zeal for different opinions concerning religion, concerning government, and many other points, as well of speculation as of practice; an attachment to different leaders ambitiously contending for pre-eminence and power [has], in turn, divided mankind into parties, inflamed them with mutual animosity, and rendered them much more disposed to vex and oppress each other than to co-operate for their common good.[8]

This argument applied to both individuals and groups. Hence, it undermined both the hope that "enlightened statesmen" would be able to mediate the resulting conflict and the proposition that a group, whether majority or minority, would be able to mediate. "The inference to which we are brought," Madison concluded, "is, that the *causes* of faction cannot be removed, and that relief is only to be sought in the means of controlling its *effects*."[9]

There was an additional aspect to this point: these different sources of factions corresponded to different types of politics. Factions borne of differences in opinion produced an abstract, speculative politics prone to civil strife between true believers and heretics. Factions borne of differences in passion produced a politics dominated by charismatic leadership prone to demagogic appeals and fanaticism designed to arouse the intense feelings of citizens.

Significantly, Madison did not attach a dysfunctional type of politics to factions based on interests despite acknowledging that "the most common and durable source of factions has been the various and unequal distribution of property."[10] Indeed, he observed that:

> Those who hold and those who are without property have ever formed distinct interests in society. Those who are creditors, and those who are debtors, fall under a like discrimination. A landed interest, a manufacturing interest, a mercantile interest, a moneyed interest, with many lesser interests, grow up of necessity in civilized nations, and divide them into different classes, actuated by different sentiments and views. The regulation of these various and interfering interests forms the principal task of modern legislation, and involves the spirit of party and faction in the necessary and ordinary operations of the government.[11]

There is a significant turn in this argument between the first two sentences and the last two: the former referred to factions based on interests falling into a simple dichotomy—the rich versus the poor or creditor versus debtor—while the latter two amended this simplistic dichotomy to suggest that there would be a great number of interested factions, none of which, by itself, was likely to achieve majority status and thus control the levers of power. This observation was Madison's great contribution to republican government since it illuminated the pathway from oppressive majority faction to compromise, moderation, and stability. It was for this reason that Madison chose to cultivate a materially based, interest-centered type of politics.[12]

Subsequently, in *Federalist* number fifty-one, Madison made a further comment on human nature and its imperfection:

> It may be a reflection on human nature, that such devices [checks and balances or ambition made to counteract ambition] should be necessary to control the abuses of government. But what is government itself, but the greatest of all reflections on human nature? If men were angels, no government would be necessary. If angels were to govern men, neither external nor internal controls on government would be necessary.[13]

The defects of government that give rise to abuse of power were rooted not in government but in human nature of which government was but a reflection. This reminder that men were not angels, that human nature was not perfect, came in the context of an essay laying out additional precautions against faction, particularly majority factions that were able to seize power in free government through the principle of majority rule.

The initial precautions, laid out in *Federalist* numbers nine through twelve, stressed enlargement of the orbit of government, representative instead of direct democracy, and the spread of commerce to fracture society into such a multiplicity of interests that no faction was likely to find itself a majority and thus be able to seize the levers of government power.[14] In *Federalist* fifty-one, however, these geographic, participatory, and economic arrangements were shown to be insufficient protection; institutional, auxiliary precautions were necessary as well.

This essay introduced the notion that the government structure itself (i.e., its institutional arrangement) required careful attention. Not only should the legislative, executive, and judicial departments be separated, but they should also be clothed with sufficient means to keep one another in their proper places. In addition, the principle of federalism, or of a compound republic, offered a second security against one department or one level of government aggrandizing its powers at the expense of the others, thus upsetting the delicate balance of checks and balances.

That Madison felt multiple layers of security against faction were necessary is testimony to his concern over the imperfection of human nature and the persistence of faction or partisanship borne of fallible reason and self-love. Indeed, it must have come as a shock to some readers to come across the following: "In framing a government which is to be administered by men over men, the great difficulty lies in this: you must first enable the government to control the governed; and in the next place oblige it to control itself."[15] That the first priority of any government is to restrain the people and only then restrain itself was further evidence that Madison located the source of political instability in human nature and sought the solution in political and social institutions.

## Stability and the institutional arrangements that secure it

Madison's reliance on inductive reasoning from historical experience (the new science of politics) and his analysis of human nature as fallible led him to the form and character of a republican government capable of protecting the natural rights of life, liberty, and the pursuit of happiness for majority and minority alike. Stability was a consistent theme running through his thought. He believed that an improper reliance on speculative theory had caused others wrongly to prefer direct democracy despite its manifest instability and incivility. Their insufficiently skeptical view of human nature led them to locate the cause of instability in deficient social and political institutions rather than in human nature itself. Theory had encouraged democratic reformers to embrace social and political structures that only magnified the impact of human imperfection on public affairs. At the same time, Madison did not reject popular arrangements in favor of non-popular ones such as hereditary monarchy or aristocracy, because rulers, being human, are imperfect as well.

Indeed, the first solutions Madison offered for the problem of instability were geographic, participatory, and economic: stability would be served by enlarging the orbit of government, substituting representative for direct democracy, and encouraging rather than repressing commerce. At the same time, it was clear that these devices were but part of the solution. Institutional arrangements also made a significant contribution. Madison began the discussion of institutions as early as *Federalist* number ten where he noted that representative democracy afforded the opportunity

> to refine and enlarge the public views, by passing them through the medium of a chosen body of citizens, whose wisdom may best discern the true interest of their country, and whose patriotism and love of justice will be least likely to sacrifice it to temporary or partial considerations. Under such a regulation, it may well happen that the public voice, pronounced by the representatives of the people, will be more consonant to the public good than if pronounced by the people themselves, convened for the purpose.[16]

The tentative or conditional quality of his argument here is striking. Madison said that the wisdom of the representative "*may* best discern the true interest of their country" and that it "*may* well happen that the public voice, pronounced by the representatives of the people, will be more consonant to the public good ..." (Italics added). He conceded that the effect might be the opposite, especially if the elected representatives were to act as nothing more than a corrupt cabal. Madison's tentativeness in this passage suggested that the fallibility of human nature was such that we dare not trust alone in the virtue of rulers, be they elected representatives or hereditary monarchs and aristocrats.

In a large society, and especially one centrally concerned with commerce and the pursuit of self-interest, each representative sent to the legislature would have to represent a larger, more diverse constituency than in a smaller, more homogeneous nation. To be successful, each representative would have to cultivate the skill of coalition-building, which ordinarily involves finding the common thread or the good present in each of several partial, conflicting claims to public recognition. Once assembled as a group, each representative would find himself but one among many, each pressing for his or her constituency's interests and advantage. Again, the problem of coalition-building would appear. The moderation of claims through compromise and the brokering of interests would again be indispensable prerequisites to political success.

As different interests confront one another, they would need to justify or legitimate themselves and their claims. The word "justify" is the important one, for one legitimates his or her claims on the public by linking them to a principle of justice. Consequently, the clash of interests within and between the two chambers of the legislature would encourage deliberation about the nature of justice as each of many interests struggled for advantage and recognition. Thus, the possibility existed that periodically the legislature would rise above simple moderation to a rough approximation of reasoned discourse on principles of justice. What began as the raw assertion of interest may, in the proper institutional setting, be transformed into a deliberative debate over the meaning of justice in a complex, heterogeneous society.[17] No such possibility existed in direct democracy.

A similar argument could be made about the system of checks and balances, both between the levels of government and among the three branches at each level. Since the Constitution separated powers and instituted a system of checks and balances in a compound republic, it encouraged confrontation between branches and levels of government, each ambitiously contending for dominance. But, this confrontation would not only produce moderation, Madison argued, but also encourage the articulation of a principled defense of each division's position and power.

The importance of institutional devices to supplement the wisdom, love of justice, and patriotism of representatives formed the backbone of the argument in *Federalist* number sixty-three. Here, Madison discussed the Senate of the United States and the way in which its institutional structure made a critical contribution to the success of the proposed Constitution:

> As the cool and deliberate sense of the community ought, in all governments, and actually will, in all free governments, ultimately prevail over the views of its rulers; so there are particular moments in public affairs when the people, stimulated by some irregular passion, or some illicit advantage, or misled by the artful misrepresentations of interested men, may call for measures which they themselves will afterwards be the most ready to lament and condemn. In these critical moments, how salutary will be the interference of some temperate and respectable body of citizens, in order to check the misguided career, and to suspend the blow meditated by the people against themselves, until reason, justice, and truth can regain their authority over the public mind?[18]

As an institution, the Senate, one half of a bicameral legislature different in structure from the House of Representatives, would provide such a check. "The people can never wilfully betray their own interests," Madison argued, "but they may possibly be betrayed by the representatives of the people; and the danger will be evidently greater where the whole legislative trust is lodged in the hands of one body of men, than where the concurrence of separate and dissimilar bodies is required in every public act."[19] The "temperate and respectable" character of the Senate stemmed from its distance from the people and their fleeting impulses; this distance, in turn, was a product of small size, lengthy term of office, and the indirect method of election of Senators by state legislatures.

The smaller size of the Senate meant that "a sensible degree of the praise and blame of public measures may be the portion of each individual;" hence the small size of the Senate concentrated responsibility rather than diffusing it. The six-year term of office assured "that the pride and consequence of its members may be sensibly incorporated with the reputation and prosperity of the community." In other words, a lengthy term of office gave Senators an incentive to address objects that depended on a "succession of well-chosen and well-connected measures, which have a gradual and perhaps unobserved operation."

In addition, indirect election by state legislatures prevented the Senate from becoming a ruling cabal. For this to happen, the Senate would have first to become corrupt itself, then corrupt the House of Representatives, and finally corrupt the numerous state legislatures that were responsible for the selection of its members.

It may seem ironic that a popular government required institutions of deliberately varying degrees of distance from, rather than closeness to, the people. Here again, Madison referred to the fallibility of man. To those who would complain of the undemocratic nature of the small, indirectly elected Senate serving for lengthy terms of office before returning to face the voters, he replied "that liberty may be endangered by the abuses of liberty as well as by the abuses of power; that there are numerous instances of the former as well as of the latter; and that the former, rather than the latter, are apparently most to be apprehended by the United States."[20]

This reference to "abuses of liberty" pointed in the direction of public opinion, especially since Madison was at pains to juxtapose the "cool and deliberate sense of the community" and the "temperate and respectable character" of Senators with "irregular passion," "illicit advantage," or "artful misrepresentations" afoot among the public. One may wonder then what the role of public opinion should be in popular government if it is so beset by wild passions, pursuit of illicit advantage, and artful misrepresentations. To check and discipline opinion, Madison called for one more institution he thought indispensable to the survival of republican government: the political party.

## Political parties and public opinion

In Madison's party press essays, written a half decade after the Constitutional debates, he argued that "Public opinion sets bounds to every government, and is the real sovereign in every free one,"[21] but then added nuance to this view by observing that, while there were instances where government must obey public opinion, there were also instances in which public opinion, being unsettled, would be influenced by the government. He cited the demand for a Constitutional Bill of Rights as an example of a demand that was a fixed and settled point in public opinion to which the government had to defer.

Madison went on to note that, in an extensive republic such as ours, it was difficult to decide what was truly settled in public opinion and what was counterfeit or pretense. Moreover, what was wrongly presumed to be settled opinion on a controversial subject had an undeserved authority over the citizenry, especially as each individual came to lose himself and his identity in the mass. Neither of these dynamics was conducive to liberty, leading Madison to conclude:

> Whatever facilitates a general intercourse of sentiments, as good roads, domestic commerce, a free press, and particularly a circulation of newspapers through the entire body of the people, and Representatives going from, and returning among every part of them, is equivalent to a contraction of territorial limits and is favorable to liberty, where these may be too extensive.[22]

For Madison, public opinion was and had to be authoritative over government when it was settled. But, public opinion was often unsettled and in need of a good tutor or exchange of sentiments to weed out irregular passion, illicit advantage, or artful misrepresentations. This could be facilitated by infrastructure improvements that brought citizens into contact with one another for business or pleasure, by a free press that educated the citizenry on the alternatives debated within the government, and by the back and forth travel of representatives between the corridors of power and the private citizens who elected them.

Madison later penned another brief essay entitled, "Parties," which he began by noting that parties were unavoidable in every political society, but that their harm could be diminished by thoughtful and deliberate policy:

1. By establishing a political equality among all;
2. By withholding *unnecessary* opportunities from a few, to increase the inequality of property, by an immoderate, and especially an unmerited, accumulation of riches;
3. By the silent operation of laws, which, without violating the rights of property, reduce extreme wealth towards a state of mediocrity, and raise extreme indigence towards a state of comfort;
4. By abstaining from measures which operate differently on different interests, and particularly such as favor one interest at the expense of another; and
5. By making one party a check on the other, so far as the existence of parties cannot be prevented, nor their views accommodated.[23]

This list of policies, meant to reconcile parties with republican government, was divided neatly into three categories. Policies one and four were aimed at treating citizens equally under the law and eschewing the temptation to redistribute power, wealth, or income. Policies two and three aimed to narrow the range of inequality by curbing unnecessary opportunities to acquire unmerited wealth without violating the rights of property. Policy five deployed among parties a familiar strategy from the Constitutional structure: checks and balances to limit excessive and oppressive partisan behavior.

Madison sagely recognized that parties could become engines of favoritism antagonistic to the public good; in addressing this problem, he offered a threefold division of the operative principles of government:

> *First.* A government operating by a permanent military force, which at once maintains the government, and is maintained by it; which is at once the cause of burdens on the people, and of submission in the people to their burdens.
>
> *Secondly.* A government operating by corrupt influence; substituting the motive of private interest in place of public duty; converting its pecuniary dispensations into bounties to favorites, or bribes to opponents; accommodating its measures to the avidity of part of the nation instead of the benefit of the whole; in a word, enlisting an army of interested partizans, whose tongues, whose pens, whose intrigues, and whose active combinations, by supplying the terror of the sword, may support a real domination of the few, under an apparent liberty of the many. Such a government, wherever to be found, is an imposter.
>
> *Thirdly.* A government, deriving its energy from the will of the society, and operating by the reason of its measures, on the understanding and interest of the society. Such is the government for which philosophy has been searching, and humanity been sighing, from the most remote ages.[24]

This essay together with the earlier two in the party press series showed the emergence of Madison's conception of a defensible role for a political party in a modern republic. The Republican Party that unseated the Federalist administration in the election of 1800 served to tutor public opinion about the choice it faced between continued dominance by a corrupt antirepublican Federalist Party and an emerging Republican opposition deriving its energy from the will of the society and appealing to the understanding and interest of the society by the reason of its proposed measures. For Madison, the future of the republican experiment he had labored so hard to launch was at stake.

Viewed from this perspective, the creation of party opposition, especially when that party was opposed to the empowerment of a false meritocracy based on access and favoritism rather than natural merit, was fully compatible with republican self-government. Indeed, it was indispensable to it. Party opposition played a crucial role in the preservation of republican government by sounding the alarm and tutoring public opinion about the dangers facing the country if the wrong path forward were chosen. Parties were the one—and the only—political institution in whose interest it was to mobilize widespread participation in elections and the only one that had effectively linked that participation to responsible government.

## The Constitution, the will of the people, and public opinion

Shortly before leaving Virginia for Philadelphia to attend the Constitutional Convention, James Madison penned a short piece entitled, "Vices of the Political System of the United States." Written in April 1787, it is a numerical list, with explanatory paragraphs, of faults he discerned in both state and federal governments. The eighth vice or fault is of particular interest: "Want of ratification by the people of the articles of Confederation."[25] Madison noted that, in some of the states, the Confederation was recognized by and formed a part of the state constitution, while in others, the Articles of Confederation were adopted only by normal legislative action. For him, this raised two distinct problems. First, if a state law were contrary to an act subsequently passed by Congress, it would be unclear which statute took precedence—the more ancient or the more recent. Since the decision would be made in a state court (there being no federal courts), it was likely that state laws would be found superior. Second, if the Confederation of states were understood as no more than a compact among the several states, then the breach of any article by any state would absolve all of the other members to the compact of their respective obligation to abide by it in each of its particulars. Avoiding these difficulties required that the federal Constitution be ratified by the American people, not just by the governments of the several states. It had to be interpreted as their will, superior to that of their state governments.

The link between the will of the American people and their Constitution, however, was not that simple. Madison's concern for learning from historical experience and his commitment to achieving stability in republican government shaped his understanding of the relationship of the people's will to their Constitution. In *Federalist* number forty-nine, he addressed an argument put forth by Thomas Jefferson in his *Notes on the State of Virginia* that would permit any two branches of the government to call a convention for altering the constitution upon a vote of two-thirds of their members.[26]

Madison conceded that there was great force to the reasoning behind Jefferson's recommendation but quickly noted that there were also insuperable objections to it:

> It may be considered as an objection inherent in the principle, that as every appeal to the people would carry an implication of some defect in the government, frequent appeals would, in a great measure, deprive the government of that veneration which time bestows on every thing, and without which perhaps the wisest and freest governments would not possess the requisite stability.[27]

Madison argued that were we a nation of dispassionate philosophers, veneration for the Constitution would be unnecessary because enlightened reason would be sufficient. But, we were not such a nation, and so we, like other nations, would find it advantageous to have the prejudices of the community on the side of our Constitution. Those prejudices were strengthened when they were both widely held and of long duration.

The requisite veneration for the fundamental charter was especially undermined, and its stability threatened, when partisan passions were aroused and engaged "by frequent reference of constitutional questions to the decisions of the whole society." Madison urged that consideration be given to the historical context or experience within which the state constitutions were formed:

> We are to recollect that all the existing constitutions were formed in the midst of a danger which repressed the passions most unfriendly to order and concord; of an enthusiastic confidence of the people in their patriotic leaders, which stifled the ordinary diversity of opinions on great national questions; of a universal ardor for new and opposite forms, produced by a universal resentment and indignation against the ancient government; and whilst no spirit of party connected with the changes to be made, or the abuses to be reformed, could mingle its leaven in the operation.[28]

He then asked whether we could assume that similar conditions would occur in the future and with regularity. He thought it unlikely. Frequent resort to conventions of the people to settle constitutional questions would almost certainly engage partisan passions and interests in the outcome. Reason could not be expected to prevail as it had in the fortuitous circumstances of the Revolution.

Madison concluded his argument against Jefferson's proposal with the objection that frequent reference of constitutional questions to the whole society would likely benefit the legislative branch, it being closest to the people. Consequently, continual augmentation of legislative power was the likely result of periodic conventions, accompanied by a gradual weakening of the executive and judicial branches. The consequences for a steady administration of the law and the rule of law would be dire. Surely, no matter who benefitted, the decision could never turn on the true merits of the question; the passions, not the reason, of the people would sit in judgment.[29]

Madison and Jefferson continued this debate over the proper relationship of the Constitution and public opinion (or popular will) for several years. Indeed, in February 1790, Madison responded to Jefferson's proposal that:

> As the earth belongs to the living, not to the dead, a living generation can bind itself only: In every society the will of the majority binds the whole; According to the laws of mortality, a majority of those ripe at any moment for the exercise of their will do not live beyond nineteen years: To that term then is limited the validity of *every* act of the Society: nor with that limitation, can any declaration of the public will be valid which not *express*.[30]

Madison replied that, while in theory the proposal may be applicable to the Constitution, it is in practice subject to powerful objections. He asked, "Would not a Government so often revised become too mutable to retain those prejudices in its favor which antiquity inspires, and which are perhaps a salutary aid to the most rational Government in the most enlightened age?" Again, he invoked the fear that such periodic revision would "engender pernicious factions that might not otherwise come into existence."

Madison then challenged the core of Jefferson's argument—the proposition that generations owe nothing to one another—asking,

> If the earth be the gift of nature to the living their title can extend to the earth in its natural State only. The *improvements* made by the dead form a charge against the living who take the benefit of them. This charge can no otherwise be satisfied than by executing the will of the dead accompanying the improvements...
>
> There seems then to be a foundation in the nature of things, in the relation which one generation bears to another, for the *descent* of obligations from one to another. Equity requires it. Mutual good is promoted by it. All that is indispensable in adjusting the account between the dead & the living is to see

that the debits against the latter do not exceed the advances made by the former. Few of the incumbrances entailed on Nations would bear a liquidation even on this principle.[31]

Madison thus rejected the radical individualism that was at the heart of Jefferson's argument that we owe nothing to one another across time, that we hold no debt to our ancestors for their bequest, and that each generation should care only for itself with no obligation to the past or future.

Madison's rejection of radical individualism in favor of intergenerational linkages extended beyond his debate with Jefferson about the role of public opinion in revising the Constitution to his understanding of the proper mode of Constitutional interpretation. As one of the last surviving Founding Fathers, his opinion on the Constitution and its proper interpretation had been frequently sought, especially in events leading up to the Nullification crisis of 1832. In an 1824 letter to Henry Lee, he observed that the Constitution itself had been caught up in partisan rancor and that he thought it important to give the document a "just construction" that might remove it from partisan squabbling. Such construction, he argued, emanated from "the sense in which the Constitution was accepted and ratified by the nation," for it was in this sense alone that "it is the legitimate Constitution," and that, "if that be not the guide in expounding it, there can be no security for a consistent and stable, more than for a faithful exercise of its powers."[32] Every succeeding generation thus owes a debt to the generation that accepted and ratified the Constitution to base its interpretation not on current partisan passion or whim, not on abstract textual or linguistic analysis, but on *history* and particularly the history of the state ratifying conventions where the will of the American people gave form and substance to the Constitution by their ratification.[33]

## Conclusion

James Madison was the principal architect of the modern republic. He arrived in Philadelphia in the early summer of 1787 with a plan of government that largely set the terms of debate for the Constitutional Convention and the Constitution it crafted. With Alexander Hamilton, he authored the collection of essays that turned New York from rejecting the proposed Constitution to ratifying it. By his speeches at the Virginia ratifying convention, he bested

Patrick Henry and delivered the Old Commonwealth to the ranks of the ratifying States. By his leadership of the House of Representatives, he secured ratification of the first ten amendments of the Constitution—the Bill of Rights. And by his partisan collaboration with Thomas Jefferson, he created the opposition party that successfully and peacefully transferred political power in 1800 from the Federalist administration to the Republican opposition by popular vote.

Throughout his long career, Madison held firm to a set of republican commitments outlined in the preceding pages: a belief in the superiority of scientific observation to speculative theory; a belief in the fallibility of human nature; a belief in the capacity of proper institutional arrangements to secure stability in a popular government; and a belief in the Constitution of the United States as the embodiment of the will of the American people that stretches over the ages and transcends the momentary whims of public opinion. Together, these commitments comprise the first Founding of the American Republic. It is this which the early twentieth-century reformers sought to alter or sweep aside in the name of "progress."

## Notes

1  James Madison, "The Federalist No. 10," in *Writings*, ed. Jack N. Rakove (New York: Library of America, 1999), 160.
2  Madison, "The Federalist No. 10," 164.
3  Madison, "The Federalist No. 10," 164.
4  James Madison, "Spirit of Governments," in *Writings*, ed. Jack N. Rakove (New York: Library of America, 1999), 510.
5  Progressive reformers ridiculed this Newtonian foundation of the first founding. Of it, Woodrow Wilson commented, "The Constitution of the United States had been made under the domination of the Newtonian theory. You have only to read the papers of the Federalist to see it written on every page. They speak of the 'checks and balances' of the Constitution and use to express their ideas the simile of the organization of the universe, and particularly of the solar system—how by the attraction of gravitation the various parts are held in their orbits and represent Congress, the judiciary, and the President as a sort of imitation of the solar system. No Government, of course, is a mechanism ... Society is an

organism, and every Government must develop according to its organic forces and instincts." Woodrow Wilson, "Government in Relation to Business," in *College and State: Educational, Literary and Political Papers: 1875–1913*, eds. Ray Stannard Baker and William E. Dodd (New York: Harper & Brothers), ii, 434.

6    Madison, "The Federalist No. 10," 161.

7    Madison, "The Federalist No. 10," 161.

8    Madison, "The Federalist No. 10," 161.

9    Madison, "The Federalist No. 10," 163.

10   Madison, "The Federalist No. 10," 162.

11   Madison, "The Federalist No. 10," 162.

12   For an examination of the origin of Madison's thinking on this issue in David Hume, see Douglass Adair, "That Politics May be Reduced to a Science: David Hume, James Madison and the Tenth Federalist," *Huntington Library Quarterly*, XX (1957), 343–360.

13   James Madison, "The Federalist No. 51," in *Writings*, ed. Jack N. Rakove (New York: Library of America, 1999), 295.

14   "Whilst all authority in it will be derived from and dependent on the society, the society itself will be broken into so many parts, interests, and classes of citizens, that the rights of individuals, or of the minority, will be in little danger from interested combinations of the majority," Madison, "The Federalist No. 51," 297.

15   Madison, "The Federalist No. 51," 295.

16   Madison, "The Federalist No. 10," 165.

17   Notice that the impetus for this debate, should it occur, was not a disinterested search for truth or wisdom, but rather the ambitious desire of each representative to win for the sake of reelection, self-esteem, or fame. This was yet again an example of Madison's policy in *Federalist* number fifty-one "of supplying, by opposite and rival interests, the defect of better motives."

18   James Madison, "The Federalist No. 63," in *Writings*, ed. Jack N. Rakove (New York: Library of America, 1999), 347.

19   Madison, "The Federalist No. 63," 348.

20   Madison, "The Federalist No. 63," 350.

21   James Madison, "Public Opinion," in *Writings*, ed. Jack N. Rakove (New York: Library of America, 1999), 500.

22   Madison, "Public Opinion," 501.

23  James Madison, "Parties," in *Writings*, ed. Jack N. Rakove (New York: Library of America, 1999), 504.

24  Madison, "Spirit of Government," 510.

25  James Madison, "Vices of the Political System of the United States," in *Writings*, ed. Jack N. Rakove (New York: Library of America, 1999), 73.

26  James Madison, "The Federalist No. 49," in *Writings*, ed. Jack N. Rakove (New York: Library of America, 1999), 286.

27  Madison, "The Federalist No. 49," 287.

28  Madison, "The Federalist No. 49," 288.

29  Madison, "The Federalist No. 49," 289.

30  James Madison, "To Thomas Jefferson, 4 February 1790," in *Writings*, ed. Jack N. Rakove (New York: Library of America, 1999), 474.

31  Madison, "To Thomas Jefferson, 4 February 1790," 475.

32  James Madison, "To Henry Lee, 25 June 1824," in *Writings*, ed. Jack N. Rakove (New York: Library of America, 1999), 803. For an insightful discussion of Madison's reliance on history to interpret the Constitution, see Drew R. McCoy, *The Last of the Fathers: James Madison & the Republican Legacy.* (New York: Cambridge University Press, 1989), especially chapter 2.

33  Madison made exactly this same point in his Congressional speech of April 6, 1796 on the Jay Treaty. See James Madison, "Speech in Congress on the Jay Treaty," in *Writings*, ed. Jack N. Rakove (New York: Library of America, 1999), 574.

# 3

# Nicholas Murray Butler: Universal Truths and the Foundations of Republican Institutions

Lonce H. Bailey
*Shippensburg University*

Robert La Follette, the great Progressive from Wisconsin, once denounced Nicholas Murray Butler on the floor of the US Senate as a sycophant, the "bootlicker of men of fortune" and "the handyman of privilege."[1] La Follette, of course, did not have the last word on Butler, an immensely influential educator, university president, and statesman, who left a mixed legacy that typifies the wide-ranging success and failures of many opposed progressive reforms. An overly egoistic personality with a legalistic, "neo-Kantian" approach to social analysis, Butler was a curious blend of reformer and staunch Hamiltonian, who argued for a republican form of government led by enlightened elites. A champion of educational reform and of administrative professionalism and efficiency, Butler was nonetheless adamantly opposed to virtually all of the progressive political reforms of his time, including the direct election of US Senators, direct primaries, and the initiative, referendum, and recall. The author of a short biographical essay concludes that Butler was an "elitist by temperament with a Hamilton-like fear of demagogues."[2] By almost every account, Butler did not believe in broad-based democracy and maintained a conviction, rooted in a sense of natural rights and biological determinism, that the proper evolution of the federal system required the best sensibilities of those with superior "natural talents."

Butler's inclinations and personality were influenced by his childhood and astonishing academic and professional success at a young age. He was born in 1862 in Patterson, New Jersey, into a comfortable middle-class, Republican family of English descent. He attended public school and graduated from high school at the age of thirteen, spent three years studying Latin, Greek, and mathematics, and began his collegiate studies in 1878 at Columbia College at the age of sixteen, the only university from which he would receive a degree. He earned a B.A. with a host of honors, at the age of twenty, an M.A. a year later, and a Ph.D. at the age of twenty-two. He paid almost all his college expenses by working while in school. In his memoirs, he devotes a chapter to his graduate studies and entitles it, somewhat oddly considering its brevity, "The *Years* of Graduate Study." (emphasis added) A one-year postdoctoral fellowship in Germany gave Butler ideas about pedagogy and philosophy and influenced his opinions on a host of social and political issues. His Masters thesis had been on Kant, and during this time in Germany he studied German philosophers such as Schopenhauer, Schelling, and Hegel. Butler clearly saw his life's work as an academic with "the philosophic study of education as its cornerstone and university building as its foundation."[3]

With graduate work completed, he returned to Columbia in 1885 as an assistant professor in the philosophy department at the age of twenty-three. Five years later, Butler became a full professor and dean of the Philosophy faculty. In 1901, at the age of thirty-nine, he became president of Columbia. He remained president for more than forty years. During this tenure, Butler was involved in a variety of activities including the founding of the Teachers College, membership on the New Jersey State Board of Education, leadership in the battle to rid New York of decentralized schools, president of the National Education Association, founder of the College Entrance Examination Board (CEEB), and founder and editor of the *Educational Review*.[4] Butler was also involved in Republican Party politics and "viewed himself as a Tory reformer who stood for an enlightened gradualist approach that avoided the extremes of standpatism and radicalism."[5] By most standards, he was much more of an old Republican with Tory sensibilities than he was a reformer. His reform activities were limited almost entirely to education and occasionally administration, promoting expertise and professionalism as president of Columbia. His pride in attending fourteen Republican National Conventions is evident in his memoirs, where he explains how unusual it is for someone to attend so many. He describes the conventions and his involvement in considerable detail and concludes that conventions "most clearly and most fully reveal the nation's political habits and the forces … at work in shaping our public policies."[6]

He was a close friend of Theodore Roosevelt until the two parted over TR's support of business regulations and his handling of union disputes. Butler's close personal association with and support of William Howard Taft led to his being nominated as Taft's vice-presidential running mate in 1912 following the death of the original candidate, James Sherman. He considered a run for the presidency in 1920 and then ran in earnest in 1928 as an anti-prohibition candidate. Later in life, he was much less influential with presidents but did have some cordial but insignificant contacts with both Franklin Delano Roosevelt and Harry Truman. He supported FDR's plans initially, especially when they included members of the Columbia faculty joining the administration, but wholeheartedly rejected Roosevelt's National Recovery Administration and his attempt to change the Supreme Court.[7] Earlier Butler had sharp words for Woodrow Wilson's administration, which he viewed with disdain and, at a dinner party, asserted that "the new tyranny, sometimes known as 'the new freedom', [had] at least proved a beneficent instrument of government in that it has prevented the Democratic legislative majorities… from wreaking the full fruits of its incompetence and folly upon the American people."[8]

Beyond the university and his role as a political activist and advisor, Butler was involved with international affairs and was a champion of peace. With Jane Addams, he won the Nobel Peace Prize in 1931 for his work with "Peace Societies" overseas and his advocacy of peace issues through his leadership in the Carnegie Endowment for International Peace. As in other areas of his life, Butler found ways to embrace diverse opinions and bring them together in an apparently coherent form. One biographer writes that Butler "was a remarkably symptomatic figure; his talent lay in gathering and harmonizing, embodying and reflecting, diverse tendencies, giving them wide and incessant publicity."[9] An example of this is the juxtaposition of his work in world peace and support for the World Wars and his visits and relationships with Kaiser Wilhelm in 1905 as well as Benito Mussolini in 1924.

But laced throughout all his activities—university president, politician, and international statesman—was a commitment to "public service in the sphere of liberty—not working against others as a rival, but working with others as a comrade."[10] Butler was an active, familiar, and influential public intellectual whose opinion and approval was often sought. He was a prolific author and speaker, and he weighed in on a variety of topics pertinent to social and political life in the United States and the world. Considering the breadth and length of activity, Butler produced a surprisingly consistent record in his opinions and views on a variety of topics. In this, he was a consistent and vigorous opponent of progressive attempts at democratic reform, an opposition that was grounded in a consistent critique of the progressive concept of democratic institutions. He offers perhaps the strongest case against Progressivism made in the early decades of the twentieth century. His antiprogressivism on government and politics may be explained by examining three themes in his writings and speeches: (1) a belief in universal truths and natural rights; (2) a strong belief in the primacy of liberty as the defining quality of the individual and society; and (3) an unquestioning dedication to a republican form of government and the centrality of representation as the protector of freedom and liberty.

## Universal truths and natural rights

Virtually all of Butler's views on the individual, society, and government derive from his belief in the existence of universal truths, divine laws, or biological determinism. This belief in a set of immutable truths was ingrained in Butler from an early age and underlies the consistency of his arguments for over the five decades of his public life. From enrollment at Columbia to his postgraduate work in Berlin, Butler was exposed to Hegelian and Kantian metaphysics that argues for immutable truths. In addition, he was familiar with the social and intellectual wave touched off by Herbert Spencer and Charles Darwin and had an extensive knowledge of the writings of the founding period and the natural rights arguments upon which they rest. Butler's understanding of society grew from this intellectual grounding.

Butler rarely incorporated specific reference to either Hegel or Kant, but his attachment to their thought and similar metaphysical philosophers is clear. Kant was the subject of his master's thesis, which has been lost, and biographers have detailed his attachment to faculty from whom he learned about the German philosophers. Of the three professors who had the greatest influence on Butler, John William Burgess of Columbia College was preeminent. He "furnished a metaphysical theory of the state, defining the terms in which [Butler] would view American political institutions."[11] One of the founders of political science, Burgess was among the first Americans to train in Germany and had a thorough schooling in German philosophy. He passed this on to his star pupil, laying the groundwork for Butler's understanding of the state. According to Charles and Mary Beard, Burgess trained a large number of political scientists and many in the legal profession to the point that his ideas and teachings "became the generally prevailing scheme and cast of thought in legal education, legal ideology, and juristic speculation by the close of the nineteenth century."[12]

Butler's attachment to Burgess's thought was more important than any of his other college experiences. After over forty years of university service, Butler still claimed that "if any more remarkable instruction than [that of Burgess] was ever offered in an American college, I do not know of it."[13] He gave Burgess credit, in particular, for shaping his understanding of government—based on the immutable existence of a "sphere of liberty" and a "sphere of government"— where government must be a servant to the purposes of free men.[14] This dichotomy, Butler claimed, "has controlled my thinking and my public activity during my entire life.... It offers a sure foundation for a true philosophy of democracy,"[15] adding, "if I were to put my finger on any one person or any one series of ideas that has most profoundly influenced my thinking, that person would be Professor Burgess and that series of ideas would be those which he expounded in his lectures."[16]

The intellectual climate in which Butler came to accept a metaphysics based on natural truths was dominated by the ideas of Charles Darwin as adapted to social theory by Herbert Spencer. Their theories of natural selection and evolution underscored his ideas about republican democracy as a superior form of government. As Albert Marrin observes:

> Butler eagerly grasped the Spencerian view that the existence of a dominant idea, institution, or political process was self-evident proof of its right to survive.... Thus evolution and the history of mankind confirm that certain things, after trial and error, are "settled once and for all."... similarly, any attempt to alter the principles upon which the Constitution rests is atavistic— is, indeed, in a favorite Butler term, "reactionary" and foredoomed to failure.[17]

Butler also drew on Spencer's ideas of specialization of function to support his view of complex political organizations. The development of a federal system, the institutionalization of separated powers, and the rise of a representative form of government all illustrated the progress of constitutional development in the United States to its advanced stage.[18] To suggest, as the Progressives did, that we should move toward a more direct democracy, or "backwards" toward a more simplified form of government as Butler saw it, would be not only dangerous but against the laws of nature.[19]

Butler's commitment to the ideas of Hegel and Kant also led to his appreciation for of a constitution as the main protection of liberty. Much like Aristotle, Hegel and Kant rejected democracy as dangerous, fleeting, and a threat to liberty. Butler too worried about the power of the masses and argued for a limited or "negative" government, with a written constitution and a bill of rights that would "protect the individual against the worst, the most cruel and the most selfish of despotisms, which is that of the majority."[20] This understanding of democracy and of majority rule has "permanent significance for Butler." It is a law of nature and cannot be challenged by even the most well-meaning progressive or by advances in society. He writes:

> Human history and human experience have taught and are teaching lessons of permanent significance and value [among which] ... that the civil liberty of the individual is at all hazards to be protected by fundamental law against the attacks and invasions of temporary majorities, whatever may be the speciousness or the power of the cause which they advocate; that the representative republic erected on the American continent under the Constitution of the United States is a more advanced, a more just, and a wiser form of government than the socialistic and direct democracy which it is now proposed to substitute for it. [21]

References to the "permanence" of laws, the "progress" of nature, and the "advance" of the constitution run throughout his writings. In this light, his reverence for and reliance on the founding fathers and arguments in the *Federalist Papers* is no surprise. Indeed, one virtue of the founders was their ability to learn from history and from what came before in order to establish the new. To Butler, these "giants" produced a "stupendous achievement" by developing a representative republic through their historical knowledge of what happened "in Greece, in Rome, in Venice, and in Florence."[22] Quoting Madison, he repeatedly cites their concept of representation and the distinction between "ultimate authority" and "administrative authority." The former resides with the people and later with those selected by them. This distinction between the "people" and the "government" is central to Butler's understanding of society.

Butler does not fault the progressives for abandoning a slower or more deliberate process of constitutional development or reform, but rather seeks to reconnect and re-entrench the natural foundations of government with the natural law that has emerged from thousands of years of social development. Where others criticized progressivism on developmental grounds (i.e. the process is wrong), Butler lays the grounds for his case by asking: "Need we destroy fundamental principles in order to correct temporary infelicities? Need we pull up our institutions by the roots because they do not grow quite fast enough to please us?"[23]

His evolutionary beliefs seem to draw also on ideas of race and ancestry. Butler traces the heritage and virtue of the American constitutional system and sees Progressives as assaulting the foundation upon which it rests. Democracy, he asserts, "strikes at the very root of the institutions that we call Anglo-Saxon, and it proclaims a failure that great movement for the establishment of liberty under law, controlled and carried on through the institutions of representative government, a movement which had its origin more than two thousand years ago in the forests of Germany, and which has persisted with constantly growing force and power throughout the history of English-speaking peoples down to our own day."[24] Indeed, he claims that it is the foundation of "everything which we call western civilization." From these ancient Anglo-Saxon origins, we have evolved to our current level of constitutional government. These foundations are "the product of the settled habits of thinking of the Anglo-Saxon race. It took many hundreds of years and countless struggles to discover and to establish them."[25]

The confluence of Kantian truths, natural laws, genetic inheritance, and the teleology of history are fitted by Butler into a framework provided originally by his mentor Burgess. The principle idea, which rests on his reverence for the universal truths of our constitutional republic, is the separation of society into two "spheres"—the sphere of government and the sphere of liberty. It is this distinction which informs virtually all of his arguments and drives much of his disdain for reform. He has a thinly veiled contempt for the arrogance of reformers trying to change a system that is right because, in a Kantian sense, it had survived the dialectic of history. Reforms against nature will fail. He also faulted reformers for violating the proper roles held by these spheres of government and liberty. In the contemporary sense, Butler was not only a constitutional literalist, he was a staunch libertarian.

The idea of universal truth drawn from Burgess not only influences Butler's views but, according to Marrin's biography, Butler takes Burgess one step farther in his understanding of spheres of government and liberty. This helps to clarify and solidify Butler's critique of progressivism. Beyond the distinction between the sphere of government and the sphere of liberty, Butler also differs from Burgess in his understanding of the "state." Burgess's definition of the "state," Marrin argues, is "the society, the sovereign people as a whole, as opposed to the government, [which is] merely an administrative instrumentality.... The state is anterior to government, its servant."[26] The state in their conception is a "sovereign" power above individual liberty and above government and defines these two spheres. This idea of the "state" may be seen as a type of "common will" and the ultimate authority. In advancing this concept of society, where neither government nor the individual is ultimately sovereign, Burgess clearly runs counter to most interpretations of natural rights, which place ultimate sovereignty within the individual via some conception of God or nature. For Burgess, the expression of the state's will took the form of the Constitution in the case of the United States. He sees it as a common agreed upon document that precedes and is superior to both government and individual liberty.

Butler argues that, while the common will or "state" does define the spheres of liberty and government, it must also obey a higher authority which displaces the ultimate sovereignty that Burgess assigns to the "state." The "higher" power of which Butler speaks is the immutable laws of nature or the universal truths that have come to us through experience. These truths are beyond the common will of the state, the sphere of government, or the sphere of individual liberty, and it is they which must be obeyed. Butler argues that, beyond all the various levels of politics, representation, and individual will, there is the realm of natural law.[27] It is a source of ultimate authority for Butler and provides clear distinction between right and wrong and supersedes the will of the majority. As Butler sees it, majorities might have sovereignty but majority decisions in violation of natural law are still wrong.[28]

This understanding underlies Butler's views on the various political reforms of his time. He sees the "will of the people," in its establishment of the spheres of government and individual liberty, as bound by universal truths and natural law. "The people" may define this relationship but, if this definition violates the history of observable truths, it runs the risk of failure. Elected officials and judges are "primarily the servants not of the people, but of the law," Butler argues, and therefore the recall of elected officials and judges violates these historical truths as does the initiative and referendum, the long ballot, the direct primary, and the attack on parties.[29]

Butler's defense of political parties rests on these ideological foundations. A champion of parties, even when his own Republican Party was extremely weak, Butler saw them not only as key to advanced systems of government but also believed the two-party system was a natural reflection of innately human propensities and therefore an inevitable and expected outgrowth of the type of representative republic we had devised. Again, he draws on the experiences of history as evidence of this truth: "The history of Government both in Great Britain and in the United States makes it pretty plain that free government functions best—and perhaps can only function at all—under the two-party system."[30] Beyond history, Butler draws on the "natural order" of things and biological determinism by claiming that parties conform to two "types" of the human psychology that determine the nature and different characters of the two existing parties. One party, he argues, "wishes to go ahead and make changes, the other wishes to keep things substantially as they are and to combat changes when proposed. Therefore the one party is Liberal or Progressive and the other is Conservative. These two parties and the two types of mind which they represent fit themselves to the framework of almost any form of free government."[31] The consequence for violating this necessary, historically proven, biologically determined arrangement is the loss of "one of the most powerful instruments of political effectiveness" the American people have.[32]

The "natural order" argument regarding parties illustrates Butler's use of biological determinism to rebut progressive reforms. The natural birth of parties, shortly after the founding of the republic, was essential in organizing human activity within a constitution that was also born of and was the result of a historical dialectic and natural law. Without parties, the natural divisions between men could not be properly organized and an imbalance would arise. Much as Spencer argued against government tampering with the natural order of the human condition, Butler sees the overregulation of parties by the state and the possible destruction of parties through the implementation of direct primaries as disturbing nature in unproductive ways.[33] Without the ability to organize human disagreement through a natural line that runs "through all classes alike," the nation will end up with a politics devoid of principles overrun by "demagogues" and by "the professional politicians and the men who can provide or secure the great sums of money needed to carry on a campaign for several weeks or months before a large and widely distributed body of electors."[34]

Indeed, Butler sees the antagonisms between parties as an inherently valuable force that drives men toward principles and creates the agitation necessary to produce responsible and honest government. This is true even during periods when one party is substantially weaker than another, such as the Republican Party was after 1912. He addressed this very issue following the 1912 election, by challenging his fellow party members to take on the role of the party in opposition, because "the Republican Party never had a greater obligation resting upon it than at this moment, and it never had a greater opportunity."[35] This role, Butler argues, is an "honorable and important one, and the public duty that it has to perform is hardly less significant than that which rests upon the party in control."[36] In addition to promulgating the existence of principles among the party and those who lead it, opposition, especially in the legislative process, provides an educative role that helps broaden the views of the electorate. This is the key for Butler, who sees the lack of principles and principled men as a sign of a dysfunctional political system that demands order. In a 1935 speech entitled, "Is Jefferson the Forgotten Man?," he laments:

> The Republican Party went on the rocks in 1912 and while there are still many millions of Republicans throughout the country, they are without any common body of political principle and without any definite political program. The historic Democratic Party was practically destroyed by Bryan and has never been rehabilitated and reunited. We must not be misled by appearances; there are parties but only in name. Many of those who call themselves Republicans and many of those who call themselves Democrats are in flat contradiction as to many fundamental principles and policies with others who claim the same party name. This illogical and, indeed, ludicrous situation has contributed mightily to bring our government to its present unhappy pass. We can no longer trust the promises and pledges of a political platform, because when elected, those who bear the party name may, and often do, treat that platform with entire unconcern and sometimes with flat contradiction.[37]

Butler attributes the sad state of the parties to the Progressive reforms. These dire consequences followed from tampering with institutions that were born form natural conditions and proven as a "truth" through historical experience.

## Liberty and society

At the core of Butler's understanding of liberty and society is the relationship of the individual to natural law. For him, the proper understanding of the human condition locates the individual between government, society, God, and other spheres of power. It is within this frame that he sees the progressive political reforms that empower majorities above all else as a threat to individual liberty. He shared the Federalist view that the greatest threat to individuals is majority rule and direct democracy. These reforms are a "return to tyranny," which substitute "a many-headed majority in the place of power once held by the single despot."[38]

Butler believes that liberty is expanded or limited by the arrangement of society and government. The social structure and the limitations that result define the kind and extent of liberty individuals enjoy. Most of modern political theory, he believes, is about liberty as defined by of the relationship between the individual, the state, and society. Virtually all of his critique of Progressivism focuses on this relationship. At bottom, it is about how individuals are to be trusted to participate in society. Confronting the progressives directly, in an attempt to turn their arguments on their head, he rejects the claim that their reforms would once again "trust the people with governing," arguing that "nothing could be further from the fact." Indeed, Butler differentiates between those who truly understand liberty and trust the people and those who only think they do, and he sees Progressives as the latter:

> Those who trust the people are the ones who believe in individual liberty, who have confidence that a man can work out his own fortune and build his own character better than any one else can work it out or build it for him. Those who distrust the people are the ones who wish to regulate their every act, to limit their gains and their accomplishments, and to force by the strong arm of government an artificial and superficial equality as a substitute for that equal opportunity which is liberty.... To trust the people is to leave them in fullest possible possession of their liberty and to call upon them to use that liberty and its fruits for the public good.[39]

A strong Spencerian influence is evident in the primacy Butler assigns to liberty in society. To tamper with human endeavor and human struggle is to tamper with nature itself and all that we have learned from history. Much like the good that comes from the conflict between political parties, the conflict and inequalities in individual human capacity drives the human race in a natural progression. His rejection of Progressivism rests on his understanding of the need for equality in society. Both the Progressives and their critics argue for maximizing liberty, but where the Progressives contend that equality requires expanding the opportunities for liberty, Butler argues that equality is impossible and that to seek equality you have to jeopardize liberty. It is impossible to have both, Butler insists, for while "equality is very easy to gain,... the penalty of equality is social, political, and economic death. Liberty is life."[40]

Curiously enough, the primacy of individual liberty does seem to be trumped by a "natural order," for it does not allow full sovereignty for the individual. To

Butler, liberty is dictated and superseded by both natural law and the general will. The general will or "the state" (as he was taught by Burgess) defines the sphere of liberty for individuals and therefore controls the amount that is given. But, the real check on this general will lies primarily in nature and not individual sovereignty or the state. The Progressives, on the other hand, view the individual as sovereign whose will is not restricted. They agree that individual rights are a primary component of the individual/state relationship, but look to further expand the individual's role and rights through the regulation of politics and parties and through expansion of the ballot. Butler, who sees individual rights as emanating from universal truths and historical experience, takes a more staunchly libertarian position.

For Butler, the insistence on maximizing individual liberty is clearly tied to the ends of society, which in turn, come from "two thousand five hundred years" of progress and a path that "leads every individual to exert himself to the utmost, not alone that he may profit, but that he may be the better able to serve."[41] With this natural path established, Butler insists that, in determining the soundness of reform, we must always ask:

> Does it tend to exalt the individual at the expense of the community in a way that makes for privilege, monopoly, anarchy? If so, reject it. Does it tend to exalt the community at the expense of the individual in the way that makes for artificial equality, denial of initiative, stagnation? If so, reject it. Does it tend to call out the individual constantly to improve himself for wider and more effective service and good citizenship? If so, adopt it. It makes for progress.[42]

Butler then clearly calls for responsible citizenship and rejects all that tamper with nature in the name of equality. Equality is the nemesis of liberty and a hindrance to progress, asserting that, "There is no progress in abandoning liberty."[43] Butler claims that the progressives do not want progress but instead want only "change," which is a "restless and ill-considered disturbance of condition with little or no regard for the teachings of experience."[44] True progress can be found on the "sunlit heights of individual opportunity, where a fair chance is given to every man to stand erect and to do a man's work in the world, knowing that thereby he is serving the state and helping to build civilization on a yet securer basis."[45]

To preserve liberty and therefore the natural order of humanity, one must rely on institutions to organize conflict and to regulate human and institutional activity. It is the Progressive assault on these very institutions that draws the ire of Butler. A primary example of this is the judiciary. Butler's love for the judiciary and his disdain for the idea of judicial recall brings out his harshest attacks on any of the political reforms, because he sees the judiciary's loyalty to law and the constitution as the ultimate safeguard of the individual. As an institution, the judiciary is dedicated to the protection of individual liberty. For Butler, the creation of the independent judiciary is one of the most important and original contributions to the understanding of government because an independent judiciary provides "the protection of fundamental law [to] the humblest individual and [holds] both legislature and administrative officers to the strict observance of their constitutional limitations," which "is the chief glory of our American system of government."[46] In a speech to the Commercial Club of St. Louis in 1911, he denounces the idea of judicial recall as "much more than a piece of stupid folly. It is an outrage of the first magnitude!"[47] The result of such a reform, both in the judiciary and for other elected officials, will be diminution of "the consistency, the intelligence, and the disinterestedness of government."[48]

In the specific case of judges, Butler clearly takes the Federalist approach claiming the judiciary's primary role is to serve the Constitution and not the whims and wishes of the people. Like the *Federalists Papers*, he points to the fact that the nature of the bench stems from the method of judicial selection, the courts designated constituency, and the institutional character of judicial office. Responding directly to the Progressive claim that the judiciary is the servant of the people and therefore responsible to them, Butler exclaims, "No! The judges stand in a wholly different relation to the people from executive and legislative officials. The judges remain primarily the servants not of the people, but of the law."[49] As an institution, it is their judicial responsibility to "hold law-making bodies to their constitutional limitations, not to express their own personal opinions on matters of public policy."[50]

Turning again to history to defend the institution, Butler warns that tyranny and injustice will result if we create a judiciary reliant on the will of the masses. "The History of England," he claims, "tells a plain story of the tyranny and injustice which grow out of a judiciary that is made representative not of the law, but of the crown."[51] He adds that it would not be long before we suffered a similar fate if we made the judiciary "immediately dependent upon a voting population."[52] Without an independent judiciary, the sphere of individual liberty is threatened as well as is the natural progress of society. "A fearless and independent judiciary," for Butler, is needed to protect a system of government that was designed by the will of the people from the flippancy of public opinion. To clarify his point, he uses an easier target than the socially acceptable Progressives, namely Eugene Debs. Quoting a Debs speech in which he advocates for the recall of elected officials and judges: "Don't you see what it means, comrades, to have in the hands of an intelligent, militant working class the political power to recall the present capitalist judges and put on the bench our own men?," Butler takes him to task, questioning his sanity, and asking "Can anyone outside of Bedlam support a public policy such as this?"[53] He concludes with the strongest possible language:

> To make the actions or the words of a judge the subject matter of popular revision at the polls with a view to displacing a judicial officer because some act or word is not at the moment popular, is the most monstrous perversion of republican institutions and of the principles of true democracy that has yet been proposed anywhere or by anybody.[54]

The basic way in which institutions can protect liberty is by upholding the laws that define the actual sphere of liberty and the limits of government. "It is law," insists Butler, "which imposes the limitations that are characteristic of liberty. Law is nothing more nor less than the system or collection of principles and rules of human government in their application to property and conduct."[55] His strong objections to this reform only point to the centrality of liberty and limited government in his thought. He sees the particular combination of separated powers in the American governmental system to be uniquely equipped to protect the laws that secure liberty because "the principles underlying our civil and political liberty are indelibly written into the Constitution of the United States, and the nation's courts are instituted for their protection. We Americans are thus in possession of an apparatus unlike anything which exists elsewhere in the world to protect the principles of liberty."[56]

One reason liberty is critical for Butler is what it does for individual activity and, therefore, for the overall good of society. Individual liberty is not something that is good in and of itself. It is simply the best condition for the individual and, by the unleashing an individual's potential, the best for society as well. Again, with a nod toward Spencer's ideas of biological determinism, Butler holds that you must allow natural leaders to emerge and act. The imposition of reforms that provide for equality goes against his understanding of the society. Equality of talent does not exist for Butler; there is only equality before the law. Equality among individuals cannot exist due to "the deepest law of nature."[57] Because inequality of talent and economic condition is part of nature, there is little you can do about it that would not violate the natural order and impede real societal progress. Liberty has its value, in this regard, as the fuel of progress; to limit liberty for the sake of creating artificial conditions of equality would undermine the onward march of history. "All progress," Butler explains, "is the result of inequality, or difference:"

> Set a thousand men free at this moment and make them all absolutely equal, and to-morrow at sundown not two of them would be alike. Nature forbids. In America and in other nations we are face to face with the question "do you prefer liberty, or will you seek equality at the expense of liberty?" That is the ruling political problem in the world to-day and in every part of the world.[58]

In a 1919 speech before the commercial club of Cincinnati, he drives the point home more directly: "where there is individual opportunity there will always be inequality.... the only way in which this inequality can be prevented is to substitute tyranny for liberty and to hold all men down to that level of accomplishment which is within the reach of the weakest and the least well-endowed."[59]

In explicating his view of liberty as the fire of progress, he describes a society in which individuals are allowed to exercise their talents and responsibilities and where the stronger leaders, the more responsible individuals, and the more ingenious capitalists at once survive and lift society as a whole. But, this requires conditions in which the individual can "exercise his own capacities."[60] Laws exist to guarantee this realm of liberty both for each individual and to protect against other individuals and the government from encroaching on an individual's liberty. His understanding of liberty and society is that the latter will also be improved by unleashing individual talent, which with some control and a good moral sense will enhance the individual's "usefulness as a citizen." For Butler, liberty means that an individual should "be permitted to hold opinion[s] of one's own choosing, to pursue the calling of one's own preference, to move about as inclination and opportunity may lead, to retain as one's own possession the rewards of one's labor and skill."[61] This type of liberty, within the proper governmental system, will enable the individual to grow "in power and in grace as he lives and works with others who have the same privileges and opportunities as himself."[62] It is a relationship between liberty and law, between individual action and rightly ordered institutions that will lead to progress as Butler sees it. The reforms of the Progressive, on the other hand, will sacrifice responsibility and diminish liberty through their backward march toward direct democracy.

Butler also sees the initiative and referendum as a threat to law, liberty, and responsibility. Taking away legislative responsibility from elected officials, he argues, will undermine their role in the constitutional framework and limit their "liberty" in making decisions for the public. It will undermine the very nature of legislative bodies as we have devised them and remove much of the motivation to serve. Butler asks a rhetorical question, "should we get a better class of representatives, or worse, if we took away their sense of responsibility, took away their dignity and authority, and set ourselves up on every side to duplicate or possibly to overturn their every act?"[63] The result of undermining legislative liberty would be to "reduce them to intellectual, oral and political impotence."[64] By undermining representative liberty you also undermine the legislative process that allows these "men of intelligence" to debate in committee, take time to reason through legislation, and consider, on the whole, what is best for the nation. In his final judgment, the initiative will not "bring support to the fundamental guarantees of civil and political liberty upon which our national government rests."[65] Taking the critique straight to progressive claims, he concludes, "This is not a policy which makes for stable and consistent government. This is not a Progressive policy. This is not a policy which will develop and strengthen the institutions that we have inherited and that we are seeking to apply to new conditions."[66]

With respect to political parties and the legislature, Butler clearly relies on a biological determinism in arguing that these institutions are organic, designed by the immutable truths garnered from nature and historical development. He attacks the Progressives on their own grounds, critiquing their understanding of how societies progress and how individual liberty, and not equality, is the key to this progress. Indeed, he turns their arguments against them, contending that maximizing liberty treats humans with more respect than does the undermining of effective and efficient governmental institutions grounded in a biological and historical order that enables the best and the brightest to rise to serve government and society. This understanding of republican government and society underlies his criticisms of all Progressive reforms from the direct primary, through the short ballot to the initiative and the role of parties.

## Republicanism and representation

Butler's love for the republican form of government is evident throughout his writings on virtually every topic from economics through education to politics. The philosophical understanding he had, as detailed above, did not intrude upon most of his public speeches and writings which, for the most part, focused on defending the institutions that were devised by the Founders and then completed by the vision and statesmanship of Lincoln.[67] Underlying his support for these institutions is his strong belief in representative government.

Butler embraces an essentially Burkean view of representation and administration, much like the American Founders, echoing on the Englishman's understanding of the responsibilities of elected representatives to parliament. For Edmund Burke, elected representatives were statesmen, free agents who should act according to their own insights, moral compasses, and understanding of the greater issues facing the state. They were not delegates bound to consult their constituencies on issues and act as a mere reflection of the opinions of their districts. A true and effective representative, Burke argues, brings his judgment to public matters, not the directives of his constituents, and indeed, Butler argues, "when we [reduce] the representative from the high, splendid, and dignified status of a real representative chosen by his constituency to give it his experience, his brains, his conscience and his best service, [we make him] a mere registering machine for the opinion of the moment."[68] He quotes Burke at length, drawing from him a famous passage that defines Butler's views of representation, as well as Burke's: "Your representative owes you not his industry only, but his judgment; and he betrays instead of serving you, if he sacrifices it to your opinion .... You choose a member indeed, but when you have chosen him, he is not a member of Bristol, but he is a member of Parliament."[69]

With this understanding of representation, it is clear why Butler's views are at odds with the Progressive push toward direct democracy. The Progressive attack on representative democracy in favor of the power of public opinion and instruments that remove the monopoly that elected leaders have is anathema to Butler who invokes the *Federalist* explanation of the Constitution and wonders why Progressives could so easily reject the Founders who carefully considered and then disavowed a direct form of democracy. The consequences of the Progressive plan to move away from representative institutions are truly revolutionary in Butler's mind and a dangerous step backward toward more simplified, less complex, and less evolved forms of governance. "It is not difficult," he writes, "to prove that the substitution of direct democracy for representative institutions is and must necessarily be a long step backward." It is a rejection of evolution and history. "When it is proposed to strike down those [constitutional] safeguards," he asserts, "when it is proposed to modify those provisions, believe me, my friends, it is a programme of reaction, not of progress." It is instead a "return to the shackles and chains out of which, through long generations and through centuries, our ancestors had to come with toil and tribulation and suffering, and even at pain of death."[70]

Butler sees this shift in the idea of representation as one from the protection of minority interests by means of Madisonian principles to one of majority rule that permits the mob, through public opinion, to trample others and threaten the liberty of individuals. Giving power directly to the people and eliminating effective legislative safeguards will mean, in Butler's eyes, that "any majority, however small, however fleeting, however unreasonable, or however incoherent, would then have at its immediate disposal the life, liberty, and property of each individual citizen of the United States." "This may be a good form of government," he concludes, "but it is certainly not the American form."[71] It is a rejection of the republican form of government that was agreed upon by the states and their people at the founding, and for this reason, it is to his eyes not a simple reform but instead closer to a revolutionary turn that threatens tyranny.

The initiative in particular shifts institutions away from representative forms toward more direct reforms. Using quintessential Butler language, he refers to the initiative as "the most preposterous and the most vicious" of the progressive reforms.[72] One of its primary difficulties, beyond the question of representation, is that a "very small number of persons" can instigate these proposals and then move on "without any opportunity to perfect it, even phraseology; without any chance to receive and act upon suggestions for its extension, its narrowing, or its betterment."[73] For Butler, it is more than a matter of bypassing the benefits of legislative process: it is minority rule. In support of his assertions, he frequently cites the small number of people who vote on initiative and referendum questions and the absence of debate that accompanies these proposals. "Under the action of the initiative," Butler argues, "a community is called upon to say yes or no to a proposal framed by five per cent of anybody .... some preconceived scheme for which there is a sentiment among a small portion of the community [that] must be accepted or rejected in toto."[74] Overall, it strikes at the heart of representative government and dismisses all the benefits that associated with deliberation.

Beyond the initiative, Butler sees the direct primary as but another Progressive attack on representation. To him, parties are natural outgrowths of the human condition, needed to manage conflict in a complicated system of politics. They are private associations, in many ways like churches and other social groups, and therefore, the state should not be involved in regulating them or in writing legislation restricting their functions. To do so was "not a step forward, but rather, backward." "The attention of state government," Butler argues, "should be fixed on the election, and on the election alone." The result of state interference in party activity, Butler predicts, will be that "we shall find ourselves confronting problems arising out of this legal relation … that will rival in complexity and difficulty those that have already arisen in European countries between the state and legally recognized churches. The result will not be progress, but reaction."[75]

Butler's predictions about the effects of the direct primary are prescient. Conceding that direct participation might work in small homogenous settings, such as the New England town meeting, he finds it "highly disadvantaged" when used on a scale such as a state or the country as a whole. The result of substituting direct primaries for party conventions is that they will, among other things, "exalt the professional politician and the man who can provide or secure the great sums of money needed to carry on a campaign for several weeks or months before a large and widely distributed body of electors."[76] The solution lies in "freeing the convention system from abuses, not in abolishing it."[77] Butler is not naïve about problems associated with the party convention in selecting the party slate. Even the convention can produce elected officials who are not Burkean representatives but delegates of the party. Butler, who had considerable convention experience, knew well the dark side of closed-door politics and the reality that many party leaders (and even the parties themselves) lacked principles that would move the nation forward. Nonetheless, he insists that

> in its practical working [the direct primary] has brought to pass evils that are still more serious than those which it was instituted to cure. No such system was ever heard of in the democracies of Great Britain, France, Holland, Switzerland, or Canada. It is our own invention, and it has become one of the chief obstacles to making our government truly representative of the people and truly responsive to the public will.[78]

Again, like the initiative, Butler is concerned that small minorities can use the system to exert their will over the majority. He deplores the possibility of a ruling majority that can crush the liberty of minorities, yet also warns that the rule of a small minority could result from progressive reforms. Like the *Federalist*, Butler is concerned about the suppression of minority opinions by the majority within representative institutions. With direct democracy, however, the concern runs in the opposite direction: minorities can overwhelm a majority through the workings of initiatives and direct primaries. Butler is especially concerned that direct primaries present the real possibility that the minorities will be able to manipulate the technical process in these elections to their narrow advantage. In such a system, he writes, "a very small fraction of the qualified electorate regularly name candidates for public office," with the result that "conflict over personalities takes the place of conflict over principles, and the attention of the electorate is increasingly distracted from issues to individuals."[79] He is of course describing a politics of demagogues rather than a politics of organization. Despite admonishing parties for their own loss of principles, Butler still believes that, as organizations which grew out of the nature of mankind, they are better than turning such an important political process into one that will produce a "cult-of-personality."

For Butler, parties are institutions that foster a better quality of social and civic life and protect citizens through the maximizing individual liberty. Speaking in 1924 to the Republican State Editorial Association in Indianapolis, he bemoans the experience with direct primary systems:

> The Conditions that result [from direct primaries] have certainly lowered the tone of our public life and have made new openings for the demagogue, for the persistent office-seeker, and for the man who can command large financial resources in support of his candidacy. Public office is now beyond the taste, as well as beyond the reach, of many of those who, in earlier days, were the most distinguished and most effective servants of the people.[80]

The remedy he offers is the political party:

> It is important to discard formulas and phrases, to think straight and clear, and to bring into existence a less elaborate, a less costly, and a more democratic electoral machinery .... if organized political parties were left free to name their candidates for office in whatever way they might choose, if other groups were given precisely the same privilege, and if all candidates so named were placed on an equality [sic] on the ballot, the annual election in November would, in effect, be both a primary and an election, and upon it the whole attention and interest of the electorate might be centered.[81]

As this solution suggests, Butler was interested in simplifying the system of elections, and especially in reducing the number of offices filled by election. The effect of a more simple system would be to separate further the activity of selecting elected representatives from that of administration. Butler's strong belief in a republic with Burkean representatives led him to conclude that voters should not be administrating government from the ballot box, but rather should be giving elected officials the opportunity to lead and defend their work at each election. This, of course, is not the goal of Progressive reforms which was that individuals, through a broader use of the ballot and through public opinion, could be more influential in a system of direct democracy. To Butler's eyes, these reforms only encouraged discontent with democracy and subsequent low election turnouts. He was convinced that, without parties and with long complicated ballots, the efficacy of democracy would at least appear diminished and serve only to frustrate voters who were told they could administer from the box but found that they could not.

Simplifying the ballot would also improve peoples' views of democracy. Railing against the Progressive tendency toward diversifying the number and types of elected officials, Butler calls for the short ballot as a way to centralize responsibility and allow for a more efficient administration of the state. For the most part, the long ballot reforms appeared at the local and state level, and Butler calls upon these governments to look to the success of the federal ballot (and his home state of New Jersey) as successful examples of using a short ballot. "It will be a step in advance," he asserts, "when we extend this principle to all the states."[82] The result of adopting the short ballot in Butler's opinion is that "public interest and attention are centered upon the most important executive and legislative officers, and they are chosen and held responsible for the selection of their associates in the minor offices of government."[83] In this way, he is similar to progressive critics like Henry Jones Ford, who was also concerned about the problems of the long ballot and, in particular, its negative effects on the administration of government agencies.[84] Like Ford, Butler believed that the long ballot only diffused accountability and hindered a common direction for government. "A large part of the extravagance and maladministration in county government throughout the United States," Butler laments, "is due to the election by the people of a long list of minor officials who have no common sense of responsibility and no common purpose."[85]

## Conclusion

Butler was a stern man of great intellectual capacity. He sought to hold to strict philosophical grounds when thinking about everyday politics. Albert Marrin relates a joke that was popular at the time to describe Butler:

> Having arrived at the pearly gates, … Sigmund Freud was surrounded by angels. "Come with us quickly," they implored. "We want you to see God … professionally. He has been acting strangely. He has hallucinations. He thinks he is Nicholas Murray Butler."

But, beyond his ego, Butler was a public intellectual in the truest sense. Devoted to a public life "in the sphere of liberty" in a role that was played by very few. He spoke on a national stage but through local audiences, was involved in politics on all levels of government, and took seriously the treat posed by the Progressives' reforms to American government. He was, Albert Marrin recognizes, a man constantly battling against the prevailing political current of his time. That is exactly where we would expect the "poster boy" of the antiprogressives to be.

## Notes

1   "La Follette Assails Butler in Senate," *New York Times*, 22 June 1922, 14.
2   Nicholas Murray Butler, *Dictionary of World Biography, Vol. 7, The 20th Century* (Chicago: Fitzroy Dearborn Publisher, 1999), 525.
3   Nicholas Murray Butler. *Across the Busy Years* (New York: Charles Scribner's Sons, 1939), 92.
4   "Nicholas Murray Butler," entry in *American Decades* (New York: Gale Research, 1998).
5   Butler, *Dictionary of World Biography*, 524.
6   Butler, *Across the Busy Years*, 207.
7   Albert Marrin, *Nicholas Murray Butler* (Boston: Twayne Publishers, 1976), 50.
8   "1,000 Republicans Dine with Whitman," *New York Times*, 18 December 1914, 9.
9   Marrin, *Nicholas Murray Butler*, 141.
10  P.W. Wilson, "Dr. Butler Contrasts Two Eras," *The New York Times*, 17 October 1926, SM1.

11 Marrin, *Nicholas Murray Butler*, 101.

12 Charles A. Beard. *Public Policy and the General Welfare.* (New York: Farrar & Rinehart, 1941) 143. See also, Marrin, *Nicholas Murray Butler*, 101.

13 Butler, *Across the Busy Years*, 68.

14 Butler, *Across the Busy Years*, 68.

15 Butler, *Across the Busy Years*, 68.

16 Butler, *Across the Busy Years*, 69.

17 Marrin, *Nicholas Murray Butler*, 104–105.

18 Marrin, *Nicholas Murray Butler*, 105.

19 Marrin claims that Butler was greatly influenced by Spencer: "Butler was more familiar with Spencer's works than most of his contemporaries, having been raised in a household where they were openly discussed and readily accessible." 104.

20 Nicholas Murray Butler, *Liberty, Equality, Fraternity.* (New York: Charles Scribner's Sons, 1942), 30.

21 Nicholas Murray Butler, *Why Should We Change Our Form of Government?* (New York: Charles Scribner's Sons, 1912), xii–xiii.

22 Butler, *Why Should We Change*, 7.

23 Butler, *Why Should We Change*, 21.

24 Butler, *Why Should We Change*, 5.

25 Butler, *Why Should We Change*, 60.

26 Marrin, *Nicholas Murray Butler*, 103.

27 Marrin, *Nicholas Murray Butler*, 111.

28 Marrin, *Nicholas Murray Butler*, 111.

29 Butler, *Why Should We Change*, 40.

30 Butler, *Liberty, Equality, Fraternity*, 34.

31 Butler, *Liberty, Equality, Fraternity*, 34.

32 Butler, *Liberty, Equality, Fraternity*, 34.

33 Nicholas Murray Butler, *Is America Worth Saving?: Addresses on National Problems and Party Policies* (Freeport: Books for Libraries Press, 1972), reprint of 1920 edition, 171–172.

34 Butler, *Is America Worth Saving?*, 173.

35 Nicholas Murray Butler, *The Republican Party in Opposition* (Boston: n.p., 1913), 2.

36 Butler, *The Republican Party in Opposition*, 2.

37 Butler, *Liberty, Equality, Fraternity*, 35.

38  Butler, *Is America Worth Saving?*, 163.

39  Butler, *Is America Worth Saving?*, 163.

40  Nicholas Murray Butler, *Faith of a Liberal: Essays and Addresses on Political Principles and Public Policies.* (New York: Charles Scribner's Sons, 1924), 53.

41  Butler, *Is America Worth Saving?*, 166.

42  Butler, *Is America Worth Saving?*, 166–167.

43  Butler, *Faith of a Liberal*, 132.

44  Butler, *Is America Worth Saving?*, 155.

45  Butler, *Is America Worth Saving?*, 181.

46  Butler, *Why Should We Change*, xiii.

47  Butler, *Why Should We Change*, 40.

48  Butler, *Why Should We Change*, 39.

49  Butler, *Why Should We Change*, 40.

50  Butler, *Why Should We Change*, 40.

51  Butler, *Why Should We Change*, 41. Butler also uses Athens as a historical example of the foolishness of the recall, 45–46.

52  Butler, *Why Should We Change*,

53  Butler, *Why Should We Change*, 42–43. Parenthetical Debs quotation is quoted from Butler.

54  Butler, *Why Should We Change*, 42.

55  Butler, *Why Should We Change*, 105.

56  Butler, *Why Should We Change*, 106.

57  Butler, *Faith of a Liberal*, 53.

58  Butler, *Faith of a Liberal*, 53.

59  Butler, *Is America Worth Saving?*, 8.

60  Butler, *Why Should We Change*, 104.

61  Butler, *Why Should We Change*, 104.

62  Butler, *Why Should We Change*, 105.

63  Butler, *Why Should We Change*, 25.

64  Butler, *Why Should We Change*.

65  Butler, *Why Should We Change*, 27.

66  Butler, *Why Should We Change*, 27.

67  Butler, *Why Should We Change*, 127–128.

68  Butler, *Why Should We Change*, 19.

69  Butler, *Why Should We Change*, 20.

70  Butler, *Faith of a Liberal*, 132.

71  Butler, *Is America Worth Saving?*, 162–163.

72  Butler, *Why Should We Change*, 25.

73  Butler, *Why Should We Change*, 25.

74  Butler, *Why Should We Change*, 26–27.

75  Butler, *Is America Worth Saving?*, 173.

76  Butler, *Is America Worth Saving?*, 173.

77  Butler, *Is America Worth Saving?*, 173–174.

78  Butler, *Faith of a Liberal*, 96.

79  Butler, *Faith of a Liberal*, 97.

80  Butler, *Faith of a Liberal*, 97.

81  Butler, *Faith of a Liberal*, 98.

82  Butler, *Is America Worth Saving?*, 177.

83  Butler, *Is America Worth Saving?*, 177.

84  Ford was particularly concerned with issues of responsibility. He felt that by diversifying the number of offices in municipalities, no one elected official could be held responsible for the success or failures of the government. In this way, citizens could easily become disenchanted with their officials and distrustful of their municipality. Henry Jones Ford, "Politics and Administration", *The Annals of the American Academy of Political and Social Science* 16 (September 1900), 187.

85  Butler, *Is America Worth Saving?*, 177.

# 4

# Henry Jones Ford: The President and Responsible Democracy

Lonce H. Bailey
*Shippensburg University*

Jerome M. Mileur
*University of Massachusetts Amherst*

Henry Jones Ford was a public figure in American life for over fifty years, beginning his career as a newspaperman in the final decades of the nineteenth century but earning his greatest prominence as a scholar and public intellectual in the first quarter of the twentieth century. Born in 1851 in Baltimore, Ford graduated from Baltimore City College in 1868 at the age of seventeen. He worked at various jobs over the next few years before joining the *Baltimore American* in 1872 as an editorial writer and spent the next three decades in the newspaper business. In six years, Ford rose to become managing editor of the *American*, then in 1879 accepted a position on the editorial staff of the *New York Sun* whose editor Charles Dana was perhaps the most well-known newspaper executive in the country. The son of immigrant working class parents, Ford shared Dana's belief in social diversity and his toleration of cultural differences. Dana regularly denounced those who discriminated socially and economically against the foreign-born and in particular against attempts to impose pietistic religious views on them through legislation. A nominal Democrat, Dana focused his sharpest criticism on "highbrow" politician reformers and their pretense as custodians of public virtue and embraced Tammany Hall as the "only trustworthy conservator of real Democracy in New York City," although he did dissent regularly in matters of municipal governance, Dana attacked the Mugwumps in the 1880s (his career preceded the Progressives) and was especially hostile to civil-service reform which he saw as driven primarily by issues of ethnicity and class.[1]

Ford absorbed the political and intellectual excitement of working for the *Sun*, especially the importance given to ethnicity and party, but he never embraced the "outsider" role in which Dana seemed to revel. In an age of growing professionalism in many areas of American life—law, medicine, and education, as well as journalism—Ford was part of the new "educational" press that aspired to greater objectivity in informing public opinion, being focused more on researching news stories and less on taking sides in partisan and intra-party fights. In 1883, he left the *New York Sun* to become city editor of the *Baltimore Sun*. He remained for three years before moving west to Pittsburgh to work as an editorial writer for the *Commercial Gazette*, rising quickly to be its managing editor. In 1895, he accepted the same position with the *Pittsburgh Chronicle Telegraph*, leaving it in 1901 to become editor of the *Pittsburgh Gazette*, a position he held until 1905.

During his years in Pittsburgh, Ford launched his career as a scholar with the 1898 publication of *The Growth of American Politics*, a work that one scholar called a pioneering study in the history of American party politics. Ford argued that parties had grown up naturally outside the formal constitutional framework because representative government required some mechanism for the pursuit and administration of power and by which those in office could be held responsible for their actions. Parties performed these political functions more effectively than any other organization, the more so as government offices multiplied in an expanding nation greatly increasing the burdens of democracy impossible for the individual citizen. He also saw parties as important in drawing the growing number of immigrants into the political life of the nation, a process in which party machines transformed a narrow politics of varied allegiances into a broad-based national one that transcended ethnic identities. It was, however, the president who played the preeminent role in a responsible democracy, the office having been transformed by Andrew Jackson from a narrowly executive one into being a representative of all the people that drove political debates to which Congress could only respond.

Ford did not ignore the problems in the political system that arose from the self-serving character of immigrant groups and party bosses, but he was primarily concerned with describing what he saw as a natural development of political parties as institutions in the constitution of the nation's governance. Ford was at most an incidental reformer, more in the tradition of Herbert Croly than that of the passionate Progressives. His analysis was more broadly institutional and, in many of his numerous scholarly articles, he was harshly critical of direct-democracy reforms and reformers, recalling his mentor Richard Dana's disdain for Mugwumps. Ford differed as well from most scholars at the time whose primary focus was on the House of Representatives with its tradition of strong Speakers, whereas Ford's concern with responsible democracy centered on the role of the president as leader of both his party and Congress.

In 1906, Ford left the newspaper business to accept an appointment as a lecturer in political science at Johns Hopkins University. In 1907, he joined the faculty at the University of Pennsylvania, and a year later, on the invitation of the school's president Woodrow Wilson, he moved to Princeton University as a professor of politics and government. Over the next twenty years, Ford proved to be a prolific scholar, writing biographies of George Washington, Alexander Hamilton, Grover Cleveland, and Woodrow Wilson, the latter for his presidential campaign in 1912. For the most part, these were descriptive works focused on politics and administration and on the virtue of strong executive leadership. He also authored three works on government: *The Natural History of the State*, *The Cost of Our National Government*, and *Representative Government*, all of them historical in their approach and dealing generally with the importance of executive management of administration and of its importance to popular control of government. All were consistent with calls for a shorter ballot that would reduce the number of executive offices filled by election, but Ford while sympathetic does not appear to have been associated with that movement. Indeed, he was no reformer, though often, especially in his numerous scholarly articles, he was harshly critical of reforms and reformers, especially those that eroded representative democracy through the introduction of direct-democracy forms.

At Princeton, Ford became closely associated with Woodrow Wilson. When the latter became governor of New Jersey, Ford joined his administration as commissioner of banking and insurance. When Wilson moved to the White House, he once more called upon Ford to serve on a special mission to the Philippines and again in the final year of his presidency when Wilson appointed him as an interim member of the Interstate Commerce Commission. Ford's academic career was crowned in 1918 by his election as president of the American Political Science Association. He remained a member of the Princeton faculty into the 1920s and continued to be a productive scholar until his death in 1925.

## The constitution of responsible government

Henry Jones Ford was a constitutionalist who revered the work of the nation's founders. He was an institutionalist who shared their belief in a system of checks upon the excesses of ambition and power and in a representative system of democracy as the best form of popular rule in an expanded republic. His overriding concern was that citizens have effective control over the operation of government, which required that voters know whom to hold responsible for the actions of government. Nothing was more important in a democracy. He thought the direct-democracy reforms of the progressives would not only fail to achieve this, but would indeed undermine responsible government by fragmenting the electoral process. He also saw their proposals as mainly the product of theory, of abstract thought, whereas he believed that history and experience should guide change. Moreover, he thought the Progressives were overly concerned with how power is *gained* rather than with how it was *exercised.*

The ideas of power and authority are at the center of Ford's critique of the progressives. He saw their reforms as having the effect of separating responsibility and control from the locus of power and authority. "Power will rest somewhere," he writes, but with the progressive reforms "few will know where," which will in turn release officeholders from "any responsibility for the results" of governmental actions. He shared the progressive passion for democracy and good government, but unlike them did not believe that either would result from simply "devolving" power directly to the voters. Both democracy and good government required a proper arrangement of institutions through which power would be exercised and, in turn, be held accountable. Ford rejected the idea that power resided in the moral consciousness of the people and dismissed the reformers claim that, "if there were no organized control, the people would select their wisest and best for public office," as "mere sentimental cant."[2]

Responsible government, Ford argued, is undermined by the multiplicity of executive offices in state and municipal governments filled by popular election. The national government in which the president was elected while all other executive offices were filled through appointment was for him the model that every other level of government should emulate. The multiplication of elected offices was a tenet of Jacksonian democracy and had been embraced by Progressive reformers who claimed that filling these many offices through election made officials directly accountable and responsive to the will of the people.[3] Ford, however, maintained that this argument was bogus and that experience taught precisely the opposite lesson. The national government is least reformed, yet it, he argued, "works with superior vigor and efficiency," while state governments are periodically reformed but were "a long way behind in quality of administration," and municipal governments which were always being reformed are "the perpetual subject of malediction and despair."[4] Logic and deduction aside, the evidence was that those political institutions which worked most poorly were those that had been reformed the most, and he saw no reason to think Progressive reforms would be different:

> If direct popular supervision of the conduct of government had the importance which the dominant school of reformers attach to it, municipal government should be best administered, since it comes closer to the people than state or national government, and the consequences of mal-administration are more direct and immediate in their effect. By like inference, state government should be superior to the national government in quality of administration; but as a matter of fact, the graduation of satisfactoriness is just the other way.[5]

The Progressives confused administration with control by failing to recognize that the people should "control" the government, not "administer" it. At the national level, the people "can do the one because they do not have to do the other."[6]

Citing John Stuart Mill, he argued that "it is not possible to fill administrative office by popular election and at the same time have representative government" because this violated "the essential nature of representative government, namely that it is a control over the government by the people, who, while not present at the seat of government in person, are nevertheless present by their representatives." But, he continued, "if the people choose any officer of government other than representatives, they themselves are answerable for his character and conduct and the representative system is correspondingly abridged."[7] The constitutional design of the executive branch at the national level of government conformed to this model of representative government. Only the president was chosen through election and all lesser executive offices were filled by appointment. One office is thus responsible for the administration of government, and voters can easily pass judgment on the activities of that executive and his party. Ford regarded the institutional structure of the national executive as a "higher form" of government, one that had evolved from "lower forms" such as direct democracy. The people would acquire real control over government at the other levels, he insisted, only "when state and municipal elections become simply a consultation of the people upon administrative policy, as in the presidential election." Instead, the Progressive reforms asked that the people be given the capacity to direct the management of public affairs. Indeed, Ford saw the number of executive offices in state and local government filled by election to be the "great hindrance to constitutional growth" in responsible administration at those levels.[8]

Ford's admiration for the design of the federal executive did not extend to the division of powers between the president and Congress, which he believed was too wide. It limited power and authority, but also blurred lines of responsibility. The party system, which "supplies administrative connections between the executive and legislative branches of the government," had come into existence to overcome this problem and was a "necessary phase of political development" that "furnishes public opinion with an organ of control which, although imperfect, is certainly better than none at all."[9] The Progressive reforms that aimed at weakening parties would only make problems arising from the separation of powers worse. Their alternative solution for bridging the constitutional gap between the branches of government was to strengthen the position of the executive. Through civil-service reform and a greater use of experts in administration, a popularly elected chief executive, they argued, would give the people greater control over both direction and management of government. But, for the most part, Ford argued, this solution wrote the legislature out of the equation, and this he believed would put constitutional government at risk. The good character and sincere patriotism of a president did not afford the sufficient security for the public, yet Progressive reformers apparently did not see this because they held "false but plausible theories of civic virtue" that ignored the critical role that politics played as a guardian against government corruption.[10]

To Ford, the Progressive solution presented two interrelated problems in the arrangement of power and authority. On the one hand, it would further estrange Congress from the president, thereby widening the separation between legislative and executive power, and on the other, it would reduce the role of political parties as a legitimating force in both communicating the wishes of voters to elected officials and framing negotiations within and between the branches. Ford insisted that parties and politics were essential to good governance and fretted that civil-service reform would diminish their role as a guide to public action, as would the use of experts. They would remove an important level of protection for the public by enabling a president to pursue his own policies regardless of popular sentiment.[11] Public opinion, even in the expanded role envisioned by Progressives, could not provide an effective check upon executive action because it was easily ignored. Ultimately, the Progressive model of governance gave greater power to the president as the head of a bureaucracy of nonpartisan experts with little effective guidance from public opinion and little or no regard for the concurrence of the legislature. The reformers argued that the president would be guided by a sense of duty in the administration of government and that, if Congress did not concur, then "it was not the fault of the president, but of politics" if public affairs were mismanaged. The president would have "done his duty and was not to be blamed if Congress did not do its duty."[12] Ford argued that this placed entirely too much reliance upon the character and patriotism of the president and failed to provide adequate protection for the public. Erroneous theories of civic virtue had led the Progressives to disregard this consequence.[13]

The indifference of the reformers to institutions especially rankled Ford who saw this as a major difference between them and the nation's founders. Progressives, he believed, had abandoned institutional relationships because they thought them corrupted by business and commercial interests. They saw a new and more virtuous citizenship, together with experts and public opinion, as the way to erase the influence of these self-serving private interests in governance. Ford was mindful of the spoils system, party corruption, inefficient government, and unresponsive officials, but he thought the solution advanced by the reformers was "preposterous." Their mode of reasoning, he observed, was "continually presented with perfect gravity and in all seriousness" throughout the reformist literature. Yet, the "popular character which is found inadequate by the reformers underlies the national government, all social institutions and all business activities, as completely as it does state and municipal government, and if that character can accomplish satisfactory results in national administration or in private enterprise it is quite as able to do so in state or municipal government under proper conditions." Only in politics, he concluded, do educated people accept reform of government "based simply upon good intention and a desire to do something."[14]

Ford saw the Progressive proposals as "theories" lacking in genuine substance and thus unlikely to make government more democratic or efficient. If anything, they were more likely to have the opposite effect. He condemned the imposition of reform upon the political system, arguing that change should be a "gradual outgrowth" of that system guided by reason and born of experience. Influenced by the ideas of Walter Bagehot and Edmund Burke, as well as Charles Darwin, he understood the state to be an organism that was continually evolving as it adapted to its ever-changing environment. In this process, "there is an adaptation between every part and the whole and hence reform anywhere must disturb the balance of all the functions of the organism." Natural change may be slower but was preferable to that which was imposed because the latter can affect other organs in ways that could be dangerous to the whole. But, for the reformers, it was Rousseau, not Burke, who was the "architectonic influence" on their thought. They did not see the state as an organism, Ford argued, but as "an organization effected through the operation of opinion and consent, and subject to rearrangement at will in accordance with the dictates of opinion."[15] He believed that the vibrancy of politics and the health of institutional and electoral relationships were the best guarantees of good government, and that it was through them that effective changes in governance were most likely to be achieved. But, reformers saw the problem as being corrupt officeholders, and they held that a change in the electoral relationship of voters to them was necessary to achieve good government. Ford heartily disagreed. Citing the observations of Edmund Burke, he insisted that, where there is a regular scheme of operations carried on, it is the system, not any individual person who acts in it, that is truly dangerous. Ford added that "the notion that the general vileness of municipal politics is due to a fortuitous concourse of bad man in the business of municipal government was so puerile that its prevalence was difficult to reconcile with the practical common sense of the American people in other respects."[16]

Power and authority resided in institutions, not in individual will, and it was the formation of institutions that shaped the outcomes of government. Man may be a social animal, but unlike the Progressives who saw society as made by man, Ford saw it the other way around: it is society that makes the man.[17] Where the Progressives thought civic virtue would reform government, Ford, like the founders, saw civic virtue as the outcome and not the cause of good government. It was only through responsible institutions and healthy politics— or what Ford called "hygienic processes"—that sound and stable reform could be achieved. The relationship between institutions and the activity of politics evolved within the body politic, and it was change through this process, grounded in history and experience, that would prove best. Quick reforms imposed with an overreliance on the methods of direct democracy could only harm these relationships. Indeed, Ford concluded that relying on suffrage as the defining institution was a mistake because it undermined authority and power:

While the suffrage is incapable of serving as an organ of administration, it is capable of serving as an agency of control; but to be an efficient instrument of control, it must act upon some organ of government possessing administrative authority so complete that it may be held to full accountability for results.[18]

His counsel was simple: for representation, elect; for administrative service, appoint.[19]

## The inevitability of politics

Inherent in Ford's constitutionalism and his ideas of power and authority is a belief in the virtue of politics. Progressives saw only the base and corrupting influence of politics, which they thought could be mitigated through the morally cleansing effects of direct democracy, as well as by civil-service reform, a reliance on experts in administration, and executive leadership guided by public opinion. In contrast, Ford saw politics as central to the framers constitutional design, inevitable in a free society, and essential to popular government. Where reformers deplored rule by "politicians," Ford saw it as both inevitable and essential in a democratic polity, arguing what he thought should be obvious: "Politics has been, is, and always will be carried on by politicians." The desire to take power away from politicians was a fruitless endeavor because "the only thing that is open to control is the sort of politicians we shall have." He dismissed the Progressive desire to remove power from politicians as "pure nonsense." His disdain apparent, he added, "we can never put the politicians out of business, although we can put the reformers out of business."[20]

Of all the Progressive reforms, the direct primary evoked Ford's most spirited response. He saw it as an example of how mistaken the reformers were in their understanding of both politics and human nature. They failed to appreciate the primacy of politics in the behavior of humans, as well as its centrality to free government. Their antagonism toward politics, he argued, derived more from theory than experience and ignored the historical truth that institutional arrangements produced both a distinctive type of politics and a certain kind of politician. When any reform was proposed, Ford argued, we should form our judgment of its merits not by the pretenses accompanying it, but by the scrutiny of the conditions it will establish and by consideration of the sort of men it will tend to bring into power—that is to say, the kind of politicians it will breed.[21]

It was therefore not a question of whether the direct primary was more democratic, but rather a question of how it affected the conditions that governed political activity. It could not eliminate politics or politicians because that was impossible, and it was a "mockery" to pretend that it gave power to the people. "All that the direct primary or any other political reform can do," Ford insisted, "is to influence the character of the politicians by altering the conditions that govern political activity."[22] Nominations to office, he argued, "will always be made by the few no matter how many may seem to participate."[23] "The reality," he added, "is that [the direct primary] scrambles power among faction chiefs and their bands, while the people are despoiled and oppressed," and in doing so, it would almost surely have a negative impact on the responsible administration of government by complicating and confusing the institutional link between elections and governance. It was foolish to believe that the Progressive reforms would remove politics from governance or that they would shift power away from those who organize politics and serve in public office. It could do nothing more than change the conditions.

Since politics is inevitable in a free government, the question for Ford was how to organize it to facilitate proper representation and responsibility. The Progressive reforms would weaken institutions such as parties that mediate differences within the electorate and, at the same time, double the burden on voters by establishing "a series of elections in advance of the present series."[24] Indeed, Ford believed that the number of elections should be sharply reduced by making all administrative positions appointive except for that of the chief executive.[25] The larger number of elections, he argued, would increase the importance of both money and ambition in politics. Primaries would also encourage a system of personal politics in which skills at electioneering would trump those of governing and appeals to voters would be made on the basis of individual issues rather than on that of a broadly framed party platform. Elections that diminished the role of the political party were also most likely to replace "existing boss rule [with] a far more corrupt, degraded and impervious sort of boss rule" which would replace the efficiency of party responsibility with the fragmentation of factional favor.[26]

Ford feared that the direct primary would lead ultimately to a breakdown of the party system. Acknowledging that it was "gross and imperfect," "unconstitutional," and a "poor substitute for representative government," he nonetheless saw the party system as "an integrating force [that] makes towards responsible government."[27] Like Winston Churchill's quip that democracy was the worst form of government except for all the others, Ford argued that, for all their shortcomings, political parties had proven to be the most effective way to overcome the difficulties of governance created by a constitutional system of separated powers. Whatever their defects, parties were "a necessary phase of political development" because "party mediation supplies administrative connection between the executive and legislative branches of the government, and furnishes public opinion with an organ of control which although imperfect is certainly better than none at all."[28] The strength of the "genuine" organizing principles of the parties, moreover, encouraged participation, brought voters into their orbits, and led to a kind of party government that set a barrier against rule by faction. The reformers offered no institution to replace the political party and appeared to believe, naively in Ford's opinion, that public opinion was an adequate and preferable substitute.

With power divided within and between levels of government, the Constitution created an unusually complicated system with an inordinate number of governmental units. The centrifugal force resulting from these multiple institutions encouraged factionalism bordering on anarchy. That a manageable order had been achieved was due primarily to the role played by the political parties and the system of regular elections based on republican principles. Parties were not only an effective check on the ambition of politicians, but also facilitated a two-way communication between voters and officeholders. By weakening parties, the direct primary undermined both of these functions. Ford rejected the Progressive claim that primaries would make the system more democratic. "Nothing is further from the truth," he asserted, "than to describe the direct primary as a democratic institution. It is the negation of democratic rule, and nothing of the sort is found where democratic government really exists," adding that "the rule of bosses and party machines, while a poor substitute for democratic government, is better than any other substitute available in the conditions to which American politics has been subjected."[29]

The "master force" behind the direct primary was its promise to give political power to the people, but Ford rejected this claim. Defining the term "power" as Alexander Hamilton had in *Federalist* 33, as "the ability or faculty of doing a thing," Ford argued that the direct primary would only empower that "portion of the community so circumstanced as to have the time, means and opportunity of attending to the business" of politics and would diminish the power of the rest. Because "the issues in the direct primary [are] purely personal" and do "not directly involve any issue of public policy, [they] do not appeal to the general mass of citizenship." The result was that voter turnout would always be much lower in primaries than in general elections and always biased in favor of those interests having time and money. This would produce "class rule of a singularly degraded and irresponsible character" which would not increase but instead reduce the power of the people.[30] All that changing the electoral system could accomplish, Ford insists, was to "take advantage and opportunity from one set of politicians and confer them upon another set," and primaries would shift advantage to those with more money and take it away from those with less. Continued rule by party bosses was preferable:

> Since boss rule represents power founded on organized personal connection, it may admit poor men to its sphere and may select poor men for its candidates. ... but when power is conditioned upon the ability to finance costly electioneering campaigns, plutocratic rule is established.[31]

Ford was dedicated to the development of a constitutional democracy capable of achieving the goals to which the founders aspired: a moderate and deliberative politics with balanced power, clear lines of responsibility, and representative institutions in a republican form of government. He thought the activity of politics was critical to the "functional development" of the constitutional order over time and credited the rise of political parties with having democratized the national government by making the Electoral College insignificant and thereby shifting control of the presidency to a popular base. Parties were able to do this because they bridged the gap between president and Congress and "brought the political activities of the various states into subordination to centralized party authority."[32] It was imperative, Ford argued, that politics and parties be a controlling influence at all levels of government, and he faulted the Progressives for wanting to convert elections into a management mechanism. The function of parties and elections in a democracy should be to secure the power of citizens to control the actions of government, not to direct the actions of government as the Progressives would have it. Only in this way can there be clear lines of responsibility in which the officeholders have a reasonable amount of freedom and power and the voters can effectively endorse or reject their actions. As for primaries, Ford concludes:

> I have yet to find an instance in which the direct primary has actually tended to promote good government, and it is only by some dire confusion of thought that good men can advocate such a pernicious nostrum.[33]

## The importance of political parties

Ford's overriding concern about the Progressive reforms was their impact on the structure of government and political system created by the Constitution. The Progressive insistence on quick reform, with its disregard for institutional arrangements, posed in his opinion a serious threat to orderly constitutional and political change. Most objectionable to Ford was "the disposition of the reformers to force conditions to suit their institutions instead of following nature's method of suiting institutions to conditions."[34] Echoing the views of the British statesman Edmund Burke, he argued that rightly ordered institutions evolved slowly in response to changing conditions, which led in turn to orderly adjustments in the arrangements of power, authority, and responsibility within both the constitutional frame and the political system.

At the same time, Ford recognized that the American understanding of "reform" makes it especially difficult to challenge proposals advanced in its name. In Britain, the word "reform" had no normative connotation: it meant to "re-form," i.e., to form again or make anew, whereas in the United States reform had "become synonymous with improvement."[35] Thus, in England, reforms could be debated as would any other proposal, and the foes of reform would continue to be seen as statesmen. But, in America, opposition to reform left politicians in the uncomfortable position of being perceived as enemies of good government.[36] This left little room for debate and made it easy to cast aside other possibilities for change, including that for slower-paced constitutional development. "That reform may be pernicious sounds to the average American reader like a contradiction in terms," Ford wrote in evident frustration, "and any argument to that effect has to combat a settled tendency of thought."[37]

This linguistic curiosity stifled debate about reform in the United States which handicapped the critics of Progressive reforms. In the first place, Ford observed, any idea that won the *label* "reform" enjoyed support even though it ignored any consequences a change might have for the balance between the institutions of governance. In addition, a "reform" was commonly urged as the *only* solution to a problem, thereby casting any who questioned it as being allied with the forces of corruption. But, direct-democracy and civil-service reform, Ford argued, required serious deliberation on the most fundamental of levels because both rejected an organic understanding of government and subscribed instead to an organizational model that assumed quick reform would correct a defective component of the system without affecting anything else. Where the critics of reform looked beyond symptoms and sought organic balance by treating the disease, the reformers were concerned only with the symptoms and called for "excising the organ" without regard for the effects of the surgery on the body politic as a whole. Organisms adjust slowly to new conditions and, while constitutional development may be imperfect at times, the result, Ford insisted, was more stable and satisfactory change because it grew from the needs of the citizens and was not imposed upon them.

Ford used political parties to illustrate the difference between organic and managerial approaches to change. Parties were a natural organic response to the difficulties of communicating across the divisions of government and those of the electorate in conveying political preferences to elected officials. They may not be ideal agencies for these purposes, but they were consistent with and sustained both republican principles of governance and representative institutions. They were also accepted by voters as a legitimate part of the constitutional system. There was no popular outcry to change them. But, the Progressives saw parties as an impediment to democratic rule, thought the direct primary was the way to remove or circumvent them, and sought to impose their solution on the political system with little regard for the preferences of the electorate or for the effects this change might have on any other parts of the government. Ford explained:

> The predilection of the people in favor of casting a group vote for a party ticket has inspired a strong desire [among reformers] to abolish party organization so far as possible by providing for the nominations by direct vote. This effort to grind citizenship into what Burke described as "the dust and powder of individuality" will, so far as it can succeed, set up dire processes of political degeneracy. Human nature is so constituted that to reduce citizenship to an inorganic mass acting by units instead or corporately is impossible, but what may be done is to substitute for the agency and control of responsible party management the *casual incitements of demagoguery* and the *transient cohesions of mob impulse.*[38]

To further illustrate the difference between organic and managerial change, Ford cited the experience with reform in the national government as opposed to that at the state and local levels. The federal Constitution, he noted, was structured to resist quick changes so as to avoid reforms endorsed by fluctuations in public opinion. Federalism and the process of constitutional amendment created a complicated system that resisted quick change, whereas state and municipal constitutions rarely offered a similar resistance.[39] The "immobility" of the federal

Constitution, Ford observed, had successfully resisted reforms for the popular election of the president. Yet, "the same end has been so completely accomplished by processes of constitutional development that the mass of the people now do not even know that there was a time when they had no vote as to who should be president. The whole character of the government," he continued, "has been popularized and the presidency has been converted into a representative institution, without any reform whatever in political structure." This "immunity from reform has permitted the gradual adaptation of institutions to the needs of the community" while at the same time maintaining the legitimacy and stability of the national government.[40]

At the same time, reforms that failed at the national level have succeeded at the state and local levels with the result, Ford lamented, that responsibility had been muddled, parties and politics weakened as mediating institutions, and institutional capacity reduced and rendered less stable. He wrote:

> The waves of impulse which beat in vain upon the impregnable constitutional barriers of the federal union went roaring over the state constitutions. Then began the multiplication of elective offices which dissipate public responsibility and destroy popular control in state and municipal politics. The people can control the national government because every administrative office is comprehended in a system of responsible appointment at the head of which stands the president whom the people elect.

It was only through a "gradual adaptation to the needs and responsibilities of public service," Ford concluded, that a stable and responsible governmental system can be maintained.[41]

Ford's argument was akin to that of the founders, though his scientific analog for change was Darwinian evolution rather than the Newtonian mechanics of the Enlightenment. Biological models might replace those grounded in physics but both were committed to a constitutional framework in which humans were seen through the lens of Madisonian realism. Moderate outcomes avoided "extravagant expectations from the every-day human nature which forms the stuff of politics," and while change may be slower, the result was greater stability and more consistent responsibility. In itself, a slower pace was not a bad thing, Ford asserted, adding it avoided a "national hypochondria" which was "a worse evil than national corruption." Echoing Tocqueville, he argued that the American people were vulnerable to but still free from hypochondria: "they are disgusted but not dismayed by the [political] situation [and] have deep conviction that they will eventually find ways and means of dealing with it."[42] The Constitution, republican government, and the people all pointed toward evolutionary political development as preferable to the sudden and abrupt managerial approach to reform advocated by Progressives.

## The presidency and democratic governance

Henry Jones Ford has often been cast as a Progressive. This stems in part from his close association with Woodrow Wilson, both academic and political. He was recruited to the Princeton faculty by Wilson, wrote a biography about him for the 1912 election, and was appointed to both state and national offices by him. Many have also associated Ford's earliest and best known scholarly work, *The Rise and Growth of American Politics*, with progressivism because it describes the democratic development of the political system and shares the reformers' view of the presidency as the preeminent institution in the nation's constitutional frame.[43] In addition, he was in general agreement with the Progressive desire for a more expansive and energetic role for government, but he was sharply critical of their views about politics and political parties and, as has been shown here, mounted a strong practical and philosophical case against their direct-democracy reforms. He challenged their direct-government reforms as well, which he believed would further confuse responsibility and reduce the capacity of the people to control their government.

Indeed, the similarity between the Progressive and Ford's views of the presidency is superficial, limited largely to regarding the office as the centerpiece in the American constitutional arrangement. For Ford, the President was a national "boss" at the head of a party government, a view held more or less in common with Wilson. Most Progressives idealized the office, as they had idealized Lincoln. They saw the president as standing alone, an individual above politics and independent of party, representative of all the people, and answerable only to them, whose duty was to provide moral leadership, guided by public opinion and good government principles, assisted by experts and a nonpartisan civil service. Ford believed this Progressive view was ahistorical. It flew into the face of the natural political development of the presidency which had democratized the office and transformed it into a representative institution. Rather than a moral leader standing above politics, he saw the president as Politician-in-Chief, immersed in the nation's politics, the most powerful figure in the battle for the country's future. The presidency of Jackson had established the idea that democratic government was party government in which "presidential duty was subject to party obligation, so that the power and patronage of the president were to be regarded as a party trust, to be exercised for public ends, as seen and approved by party sentiment, under his instruction and advice."[44] Ford saw Abraham Lincoln as the embodiment of the Jacksonian model who showed in his presidency that, being a great politician and great party leader, made for being a great statesman.[45]

The Jackson/Lincoln example of the president governing in the public interest through the institution of party, Ford continued, was "quite acceptable to the mass of the people," but it was not acceptable to "impatient reformers." Patronage, the glue of Jackson/Lincoln party system, was the primary target of civil-service reformers, while displacing the power of party bosses and party organization was the principal goal of direct primary advocates. The Progressives turned against the idea of party government, arguing that the highest duty of a president was "to assert and maintain his independence of party connection when that conflicted with his individual convictions of duty."[46] They assumed that Congress would follow the lead of the Chief Executive unless its members fell under the corrupting influence of party politics and politicians. They too saw Lincoln as the model president but celebrated the Great Emancipator for his moral leadership of the nation, who they saw as acting directly in the interests of the people as a whole and not through the malign influence of a political party. Ford ridiculed this view, arguing that it was "contradicted by all the facts of our constitutional history," and he deplored what he saw as the conversion of the presidency into "the headship of a bureaucracy, with only a hortative relation to Congress," a role that gave only "an irregular operation to the play of political force" and in effect "subverted the constitutional basis of the government."[47]

In the end, it was the Progressive disdain for politics that was most distressing to Ford, who reserved some of the sharpest arrows in his quiver for the advocates of nonpartisanship. He had no illusion about political corruption and party bosses, but insisted that, as an institution, the political party was essential to the effective operation of responsible government. New nostrums may come and old ones go, but the aim of reform remained the same: it was "to take away the 'fuel' of combat." The claims of reformers notwithstanding, he argued that "there is abundant evidence to confirm the opinion that party organization continues to be the sole efficient means of administrative union between the executive and legislative branches of the government, and that whatever tends to maintain and perfect that union makes for orderly politics and constitutional progress."[48] To Ford, the party system, despite all its shortcomings, rightly enjoyed a commanding influence in the nation's governance. He agreed with Frank Goodnow, professor of public administration at Columbia University, that but for the office of party in connecting a divided political structure "we should have anarchy instead of government."[49]

Ford saw responsibility at the heart of popular government, agreeing with Thomas Jefferson that it is "a tremendous engine of free government."[50] But, responsibility, like popular control of government, meant being able to hold those in elective office accountable for their actions. It did not mean directing them in what they do. Yet, the direct-government reforms of the Progressives promise the latter, and in doing so compromise the former. Responsibility required clarity. But, through multiple executive offices filled by election, the double set of elections produced by the direct primary, the creation of a professionalized public service by civil-service reform, and the abandonment of party government, Progressive reforms only clouded and confused responsibility and thereby undermined popular control of government. The evolution of constitutional democracy in America, Ford argued, had produced representative institutions, but the nation had yet to attain responsible government and the Progressive reforms only moved it farther from that goal. The reformers, he lamented, were simply focused on the wrong question, being more concerned with how power was attained than with how it was exercised.

## Notes

1   Janet E. Steele, *The Sun Shines for All: Journalism and Ideology in the Life of Charles A. Dana* (Syracuse: Syracuse University, 1993), Ch. 8.
2   Henry Jones Ford, "The Direct Primary," *North American Review*, 190 (July 1909), 12.
3   Ford traced the "disintegration of executive authority" to the Puritans and town meeting government in New England. It worked well enough, although crudely for secular purposes while still under clerical control, but it deteriorated quickly as a form of secular rule after church membership was no longer a qualification for membership. There remained, he lamented, "idyllic" views about its "character and value," and though impractical for large centers of population, it continued to be regarded as

an "ideal" to which "actual governmental arrangements should conform so far as possible." Henry Jones Ford, *Representative Government* (New York: Henry Holt, 1924), 266–267.

4   Henry Jones Ford, "The Results of reform," *The Annals of the American Academy of Political and Social Science*, 21 (January–June 1903), 224.

5   Ford, "Politics and Administration," 182.

6   Ford, "Politics and Administration," 187.

7   Ford, *Representative Government*, 256.

8   Ford, *Representative Government*, 188.

9   Henry Jones Ford, "Political Evolution and Civil Service Reform," *The Annals of the American Academy of Political and Social Science*, 15 (March 1900), 155.

10  Ford, "Political Evolution," 155.

11  Ford was a sharp critic of civil-service reform. Noting that, at the time of its passage, improvement in the quality of the civil service was "the lesser part of the benefits expected" from it. The primary argument was that the law would improve our politics, the benefits of which would be felt throughout the whole government. The result, however, had been a bitter disappointment. "Instead of an increase of moderation, order, judgment and control in the management of public affairs," he argued, "there was an increase of passion and recklessness" and the politics that followed has been "distinctly retrogressive" on both the institutions of governance and the state of public opinion. Ford seemed also to agree with critics of civil-service reform who believed that its real objective was to exclude the flood of new immigrants entering the country from government service. Ford, "Political Evolution," 145–146.

12  Ford, "Political Evolution," 153 and 156.

13  Henry Jones Ford, "Municipal Corruption," *Political Science Quarterly*, 19: 4 (December 1904), 681.

14  Ford, "Results of Reform," 225–226.

15  Ford, "Results of Reform," 224.

16  Henry Jones Ford, "Principles of Municipal Organization," *Annals of the American Academy of Political and Social Science*, 23 (March 1904), 199.

17  Henry Jones Ford, *The Natural History of the State* (Princeton: Princeton University Press, 1915), 45.

18  Ford, "Municipal Corruption," 681.

19  Ford, *Representative Government*, 256.

20  Ford, "Direct Primary," 2.

21  Ford, "Direct Primary," 3.

22  Ford, "Direct Primary," 3.

23  Ford, "Politics and Administration," 186.

24  Ford, "Direct Primary," 9.

25  Though clearly sympathetic with the movement for a short ballot, Ford seems never to have been actively associated with it. On the short ballot, see Charles Beard, "The Ballot's Burden," *Political Science Quarterly*, 24 (December 1909), 589–614.

26  Ford, "Direct Primary," 9.

27  Ford, "Direct Primary," 9.

28  Ford, "Political Evolution," 155.

29  Ford, "Direct Primary," 11.

30  Ford, *Representative Government*, 270–271.

31  Ford, *Representative Government*, 270–271.

32  Ford, "Politics and Administration," 187–188.

33  Ford, "Direct Primary," 14.

34  Ford, "Politics and Administration," 187–188.

35  Ford, "Politics and Administration," 223.

36  Ford, "Results of Reform," 221.

37  Ford, "Results of Reform," 221.

38  Ford, "Results of Reform," 231 (emphasis added).

39  Ford noted that the difficulty of change in the structure of the national government had meant that political change had taken the form of "functional development," whereas in the more flexible constitutions of state and municipal governments, it had taken the form of "structural partition." Ford, "Politics and Administration," 182.

40  Ford, "Results of Reform," 227, 231. It was soon apparent, however, that, as in the case of presidential primaries, the federal government was not immune from the effects of political reform at the state level.

41  Ford, "Results of Reform," 227–228.

42  Ford, "Municipal Corruption," 676.

43  Henry Jones Ford, *The Rise and Growth of American Politics: A Sketch of Constitutional Development* (New York: Macmillan, 1898). See too the symposium on Ford in *PS* (Washington: American Political Science Association, 1999), 227–236.

44  Ford, "Political Evolution," 154–155.

45  In his analysis of Woodrow Wilson, Daniel Stid argued that Ford's view of
the president as head of a party government "bolstered Wilson's willingness
to let go of long-held views on the basic dynamics of American politics." He
quotes Wilson's praise for Ford's *Rise and Growth* as "lucid and convincing,"
and noted that he recommended it to students as a useful counterpoise
to his *Congressional Government*. Daniel Stid, *The President as Statesman:
Woodrow Wilson and the Constitution* (Lawrence: University of Kansas,
1998), 43–44.

46  Ford, "Political Evolution," 155.

47  Ford, "Political Evolution," 156.

48  Ford, *Rise and Growth*, 356.

49  Quoted in Ford, "Politics and Administration," 184.

50  Quoted in Ford, *Rise and Growth*, 349.

# 5

# William Howard Taft: The Constitutionalist as Critic of Progressivism

## Paul M. Rego
### *Messiah College*

William Howard Taft was dedicated to the law and devoted his life to it. He was, in fact, more cut out to be a lawyer, a judge, and an administrator than a politician.[1] By nearly all accounts, the political side of the presidency—the cultivation of public opinion and the press, as well as legislative leadership—did not seem to interest him, and he was not particularly good at any of it.[2] As president, Theodore Olson observes, Taft lacked "charisma, innovator's impulse, fighter's mentality, concern for his public reputation, and political savvy to function as an effective leader in the greatest of political arenas." In light of these political deficiencies, it is not surprising that Taft wrote to his wife, Nellie: "Politics, when I am in it, makes me sick."[3]

The law had consumed most of Taft's prepresidential life. After graduating from Yale, he went to law school and opened a private practice in Ohio. By the time he was thirty-two, Taft had been an assistant prosecutor and a superior court judge in Ohio. In 1890, President Benjamin Harrison appointed Taft to be the Solicitor General of the United States. Two years later, he became a federal appellate judge but resigned this position when asked by President William McKinley to head a commission to establish civil government in the Philippines. He ultimately served as the first civil governor of the Philippines. In 1904, President Theodore Roosevelt made Taft Secretary of War, and by 1908, TR had decided that Taft should succeed him as president. Over the previous four years, Roosevelt and Taft had become friends, and Taft had been a staunch defender of Roosevelt and his policies. But, if Taft tended to sympathize with the aims of Progressives like Roosevelt, he was increasingly concerned about their approach. In the end, a majority of Progressives, including Roosevelt, abandoned him and his presidency.[4]

As this chapter will attempt to show, Taft believed that, while government had a role to play in improving economic and social conditions, reform should not come at the expense of individual rights or the constitutional framework that the founders erected to protect those rights. Specifically, he was troubled by what he perceived to be Progressivism's disregard for personal liberty, especially private property rights, a concern that is most prevalent in (but not exclusive to) his criticisms of direct democracy. He insisted that direct-democracy reforms (especially attacks on an independent judiciary) would allow tyrannical majorities to ignore and to violate the rights of unpopular minorities and individuals. Thus, resisting direct-democracy reforms, protecting the independence of the judiciary, and preserving individual rights were, for Taft, one and the same; and they were vital to upholding the Constitution as the true will of the American people.

## Economic reform, property rights, and the power of the president

Taft regretted that support for direct-democracy reforms was, in the minds of many, the mark of true Progressivism. He understood that many problems accompanied the economic and social changes of the late nineteenth and early twentieth centuries and applauded the strong feeling of community that inspired many Americans to help one another. Moreover, he was pleased to see that the "fraternity of feeling among members of society toward each other" had enhanced the responsibilities of government. Taft dissociated himself from the doctrine of laissez-faire, as he believed that "the Government can wisely do much more than that school [laissez-faire] would have favored to relieve the oppressed, to create greater equality of opportunity, to make reasonable terms for labor in employment, and to furnish vocational education [for] the children of the poor." Still, he wanted his fellow citizens to remember that "there is a line beyond which Government cannot go with any good practical results in seeking to make men and society better." These attempts, he added, were destined to "result in failure and a waste of public effort and funds." Taft charged that many Progressives had forgotten this and persisted in pushing naive and unrealistic reforms.[5]

This appreciation of the limits of reform is typical of conservative thought. The "philosophical" conservatism of Edmund Burke, for example, reminds us that there is so much about the world and the human experience that we do not understand; and even when the way to improvement seems evident, reformers cannot anticipate every consequence of change. In other words, while human reason has its place, it has its limits.[6] Of course, conservatives do not reject all change, but they warn that reform should not be undertaken lightly. More specifically, they fear excessive and hasty alterations of social and political arrangements. As we shall see, this was Taft's view. He accepted change but urged Progressives to proceed slowly and cautiously. This deliberate approach to reform, which Taft shared with other critics of Progressivism, seemed to reflect the Burkean belief that society was the culmination of time-tested experience and learning. For this reason, society should not be modified to indulge every impulsive demand for change; and when change was necessary, reformers needed to "build on the existing structure rather than renovate its foundations." This has been difficult for many political reformers to accept, however. "Disregarding the lessons of centuries and the proved worth of ancient institutions," Andrew Hacker explains, "they see all political problems as contemporary and their solutions as the work of an hour." They assume, moreover, "that political institutions are the creations of rational men, and that those men may arrange them howsoever is necessary to achieve their political ends." But, Taft and the other critics of Progressivism had their doubts, because they recognized the distinction between society and government. Society comprises government; therefore, "[p]atterns of social behavior, which are unplanned and often accidental, must modify and limit governmental power." Stated simply, government is constrained by society. As Hacker concludes, "Society is the master . . . and government is its servant."[7]

Throughout the presidency of Theodore Roosevelt, Taft defended all of the Rough Rider's major policies. He echoed Roosevelt's belief in "the absolute necessity" for workers to unionize and to bargain collectively with their employers over wages.[8] In addition, he believed that government had a legitimate role to play in relations between employees and employers. Taft, for example, supported Roosevelt's decision to investigate charges that various contractors with the federal government were working their employees more than eight hours a day without compensation and in violation of the law. He also celebrated TR's success in persuading Congress to pass a law that made interstate railroads liable for their injured workers.[9] In accepting his party's presidential nomination in 1908, he urged his fellow Republicans to continue their effort "to do justice to the wage-earner" by supporting "a more comprehensive measure for compensation of [injured] government employees." Taft also defended the right of unions to strike. "They have a right to use such persuasion as they may," he observed, "provided it does not reach the point of duress, to lead their reluctant co-laborers to join them in their union against their employer, and they have a right, if they choose, to accumulate funds to support those engaged in a strike, to delegate to officers the power to direct the action of the union, and to withdraw themselves and their associates from dealings with, or giving custom to, those with whom they are in controversy." From Taft's perspective, labor did not have cause to use violence, or to destroy property, which was the same position that TR took throughout his public career.[10]

During the 1908 presidential campaign, Taft praised Roosevelt's "vigorous action" as president. He noted approvingly that Roosevelt used the Sherman Anti-Trust Act, as well as the Interstate Commerce Act, to take on many illegal monopolies. Roosevelt also had worked with Congress to enact various regulations, compiling a list of achievements that, in Taft's opinion, "has never been equaled in our time." For his part, Taft claimed to have supported every one of these reforms (the Hepburn Act, the Pure Food and Drug Act, and the Meat Inspection Act), which he saw as "framed for the purpose of stamping out the abuses which had grown up in the conduct of business by some corporations that were flouting the law and the interests of the public."[11]

At the same time, Taft cautioned that the national government had to respect the principle of individualism. He understood that some corporations were engaging in practices that undermined the public good (which is why he supported "a limitation upon the use of property and capital" in order to guard against various "evils"), but he also stressed that reforms should "interfere with the institution of private property and the maintenance of a motive for individualism and thrift as little as possible."[12] In Taft's view, private property was "indispensable to individualism and [was] one of the two chief means [along with 'civil liberty'] by which man raised himself from a low estate near to that of the beasts of the field to his present condition." He was, therefore, opposed to socialism as a way of dealing with the problem of concentrated economic power. It was fortunate, Taft believed, that Roosevelt had shown how the government could use its regulatory authority to prevent economic abuses without eliminating private property and thereby threatening individual liberty.[13] Taft's reverence for the right to property placed him squarely in the

Lockean tradition of America's founding fathers. Like Locke, they had believed that the right to property was essential to both liberty and the right to pursue happiness.[14] Taft regularly celebrated the connection between property and individual freedom. As A.E. Campbell explains, he believed that property was "intimately linked" to liberty, and "the single truth to which he held most firmly, other than the necessary supremacy of the law, was that property rights were sacred."[15]

But, Taft's goal of reconciling individual rights, especially private property rights, with the public good was not widely shared by Progressives. These reformers objected to the conflation of property rights with the Social Darwinian principle of "survival of the fittest," which justified poverty and the miseries associated with it. In addition, Ronald Pestritto explains that they dismissed the concept of natural rights, especially a natural right to property, because they understood that this idea undermined their efforts to regulate the acquisition and use of property. Pestritto, for example, points to Frank Goodnow, an administrative reformer and the first president of the American Political Science Association, who declared: "The rights which [an individual] possesses are … conferred upon him, not by his Creator, but rather by the society to which he belongs. What they are is to be determined by the legislative authority in view of the needs of that society. Social expediency, rather than natural right, is thus to determine the sphere of individual freedom of action."[16] Similarly, Woodrow Wilson, as Jean Yarbrough explains, "rejected social contract theory as too abstract." He also rejected "the idea that the so-called state of nature reflects an insight about the moral primacy of the individual or the legitimate purposes of government." He believed that "it was not the rights-bearing individual who matters but the society as a whole." For Progressives like Wilson, individual liberty and private property rights were secondary to "the common good."[17]

Notwithstanding his uneasiness with Progressives, Taft supported many of their reforms during his presidency. The most famous of these was, perhaps, the Mann-Elkins Act, which gave the Interstate Commerce Commission (ICC) power to regulate telecommunications companies. The ICC already possessed authority to prohibit interstate railroads from charging discriminatory rates. The Mann-Elkins Act gave it the added authority to review and to modify any rate changes "on its own initiative" and to halt rate increases until they were approved. This power was subject to judicial review, however. To that end, Mann-Elkins established a United States Court of Commerce to review ICC decisions regarding the maximum rates that railroads could charge.[18] Taft believed that a judicial agency, such as the commerce court, would give much-needed consistency to regulation and, by establishing legal precedents regarding rates, help to clarify the rules to which railroads would be held liable.[19] His desire to provide businesses with a way of knowing precisely what they could and could not do under the law also led Taft to use the Sherman Anti-Trust Act to break up more trusts than Roosevelt had destroyed. Paolo Coletta notes that, because of Supreme Court decision-making and the failure of Congress to clarify the rules of the game, big business was even more confused by the end of Taft's term. Moreover, Roosevelt had always preferred the regulation approach to the anti-trust approach.[20] Nevertheless, Taft regarded his efforts as cementing and building upon the achievements of the Roosevelt administration, which he believed to be his major responsibility, something that was "distinct from [but] a progressive development of" all that Roosevelt had done.[21]

Yet, Taft's strong devotion to the Constitution led to his disagreement with Roosevelt about the source and use of presidential power.[22] Unlike TR, he did not believe that presidential authority derived from "an undefined residuum of power" that allowed the Chief Executive to take "responsibility for the welfare of all the people in a general way," unless explicitly prohibited by the Constitution. Instead, Taft pointed to the law—to the Constitution and to ordinary statutes—as the sole source of presidential authority. Specifically, Roosevelt claimed that the president was "a steward of the people bound actively and affirmatively to do all he could for the people," and that "the executive power was limited only by specific restrictions and prohibitions appearing in the Constitution or imposed by Congress under its constitutional powers." But, Taft retorted that "The true view of the Executive functions is, as I conceive it, that the president can exercise no power which cannot be fairly and reasonably traced to some specific grant of power or justly implied and included within such express grant as proper and necessary to its exercise. Such specific grant must be either in the Federal Constitution or in an act of Congress passed in pursuance thereof."[23]

At the same time, Taft recognized that the Constitution gave the president broad powers, indeed. He did *not* take a narrow interpretation of the president's constitutional responsibilities over appointments and removals, enforcement of the law, war and peace, or foreign relations.[24] "The Constitution," he acknowledged, "does give the President wide discretion and great power, and it ought to do so. It calls from him activity and energy to see that within his proper sphere he does what his great responsibilities and opportunities require."[25] In addition, Taft would surely have agreed with Wilson Carey McWilliams that, when executive power is rooted in laws based on the will of the people, the president is more, not less, powerful. McWilliams insists that Taft's executive model makes for a stronger office, "since it encourages a president who is psychologically more autonomous, less dependent on public sentiment, and more able to set his or her own course."[26] Responding to Roosevelt's claim that there were two kinds of presidents (strong "Lincoln Presidents" like Roosevelt and weak "Buchanan Presidents" like Taft), Taft was quick to observe that Lincoln's acts, unlike TR's, were rooted in the Constitution and/or the laws of Congress. When taking aggressive action against the rebellious states, as when he suspended *habeas corpus* or issued his Emancipation Proclamation, "Mr. Lincoln always pointed out the [constitutional or statutory] source of the authority which in his opinion justified his acts, and there was always a strong ground for maintaining the view which he took."[27] Like Taft, Lincoln located his authority in the law, and not simply in some nebulous claim of responsibility for "the welfare of all the people." This challenge to the Progressive understanding of Lincoln and his presidency was yet another aspect of Taft's disagreement with Progressives, one shared generally by Progressivism's critics.

## Democratic reform

Whereas Taft sympathized with many Progressive aims, he rejected any legal or institutional changes that undermined the constitutional order established by the founders.[28] This was especially true of Progressivism's challenge to republican values and institutional arrangements. In the election of 1912, when TR ran for the presidency as a third-party candidate, Taft opposed his calls for various direct-democracy reforms such as the initiative, the referendum, the direct primary, and *especially* the recall of both judges and judicial decisions, declaring, "If I were nominated, even though I were to go down to defeat, I should be on a conservative platform and rally the conservative forces in this country and keep them in a nucleus of party strength, so that after four years the party could gather itself together and probably reestablish itself in control."[29] "In other words," David Potash explains, "Republicans viewed the possibility of defeat in 1912 as little more than a setback, provided Roosevelt was thwarted." Taft won only Vermont and Utah, yet he remained convinced that winning was less important than his effort to defend the American constitutional system from the Progressives.[30]

Taft articulated a rather nuanced understanding of the term, "popular government." According to him, the Constitution's invocation of "We the people" proved that the framers created "a popular government" in which the people were the fountain of all legitimate authority. Popular government also meant that "every class" was guaranteed "a voice," and only when all classes were represented were the rights and the well-being of "each class" assured. For Taft, however, "popular government [was] not an end." It merely provided the "means" by which people could achieve happiness. Indeed, Taft thought that "all our civil institutions are nothing but means for the promotion of the happiness of the individual and his progress."[31] Like the authors of the *Federalist Papers*, then, he argued that the happiness of individuals and the promotion of their prosperity were the great goals of government. For that reason, responsible government required guarding against those who were willing to jeopardize the common good and individual liberty in the pursuit of their selfish economic agendas.[32]

Echoing James Madison, Taft worried about the tyranny of the majority, specifically broad populist movements that favored the interests of one economic class (the poor) at the expense of another class (the rich).[33] In fact, Taft saw elements of socialism in direct-democracy reforms such as the initiative, referendum, and recall.[34] In his eyes, these Progressive reforms were more radical than they appeared at first glance: "This movement back of the referendum, initiative, and recall does not find its only promptings in a desire to stamp out corruption. There is another basis for the movement today which gives strength to the proposal to put unrestrained and immediate control in the hands of a majority or minority of the electorate. It is in the idea that the unrestrained rule of the majority of the electors voting will prevent the right of property from proving an obstacle to achieving equality in condition so that the rich may be made poorer and the poor richer. In other words, a spur, conscious or unconscious, to this movement is socialistic."[35]

For Taft, then, popular government was simply a way "of enabling people to live together in communities, municipal, state, and national, and under these conditions to secure to each individual and each class of individuals the greatest measure of happiness." Those who adopted and ratified the Constitution, he emphasized, understood that majorities would not always respect the right of minorities or unpopular individuals to live in freedom and to pursue happiness. So, in ratifying the Constitution, the people accepted limitations on their power, such as definite "guaranties of individual rights."[36]

Taft stressed the dilemma peculiar to popular government. "The problem in a popular government is so to arrange its organization that, with due protection to individual and minority rights, which experience has shown to be useful to society and its progress, the expressed will of a majority of an electorate may be truly interpreted and executed in effective action by the government."[37] Taft here described two attributes of legitimate government. First, it had to secure individual rights. Second, it had to rest on the consent of the governed. Taft also recognized that these two values often conflicted with one another. The majority tended to infringe upon individual rights, especially those of the minority. This was the dilemma that confronted the founders, who devised and defended a constitutional framework that relied upon republican institutions to ease the tension between liberty and majority rule.[38]

Beyond the dilemma of popular government, the "business" of government itself was complicated. This was why Taft stressed the importance of having experienced public servants at the helm. When people needed legal advice, they hired a lawyer. When people got sick, they went to a doctor. Nobody crossed a bridge that had not been constructed by engineers, nor wanted to live in a house that had not been erected by skilled builders. But, Taft noted, when it came to policymaking, many people did not think twice about refusing the services of men who possessed the legislative expertise to write laws that would solve problems and survive judicial scrutiny. Besides, a representative system was the best form of government precisely because the interests, the needs, and the wishes of the greatest number of people were more likely to be considered than in a pure democracy, where millions of voters could not gather to make policy themselves.[39]

Taft repeated that he understood and shared the "social consciousness" of Progressives, but that he opposed their antirepublican reforms. He lamented especially that conservatives like him were dismissed as "reactionaries." Yet, despite being "unjustly classed," Taft was determined to persist in his defense of republican values. In his opinion, there was no reason for "the so-called Progressives" to believe that their proposed social and economic reforms could not be achieved in a republic. Change would come more slowly, he acknowledged, but that was not necessarily a bad thing. Progress was not achieved at once; it evolved as the result of "careful consideration." Here was that Burkean recognition that change had its place, but that it needed to be slow, incremental, thoughtful, and cautious. Taft admitted that republican government had allowed certain economic and social problems to develop, but he cautioned that politicians would adapt themselves as well to the "weaknesses" of a direct democracy. More importantly, Taft saw social and economic injustice as the result of more than the "mere machinery" of government; it was a consequence of "the sluggishness of the people and a sort of tacit sympathy of the people with those who were promoting the expansion and the material progress of the country in which the people expected to share." In other words, the people had supported and even subsidized the development of big business, ignoring many troubling excesses, when they expected to benefit from that development. And, in their condemnation of representative government, reformers failed to recognize that it was this same system that had enabled the people, after "awakening" to the problems around them, to achieve various reforms, including the direct-democracy reforms. When reformers replied that, without further change, "the people will be lulled to inertia again," Taft asked how this logic explained the many people who were angered by economic and social conditions. How did it explain efforts to make the representatives of the people more mindful of the public interest?[40]

Of the Progressive political reforms, Taft arguably had least objection to the referendum, which enabled voters to approve or to reject a bill passed by their legislature. He acknowledged that it had "long been known in the political machinery of this Government," noting that constitutional amendments were ratified by the people, after they had been adopted by legislatures or constitutional conventions. He also observed that the referendum was "used for years as a condition upon which local legislation enacted by a state legislature [went] into effect." When passing prohibition laws, for example, many state legislatures allowed local voters to decide whether those laws would apply to them. Some argued that this amounted to an unconstitutional delegation of legislative authority, but Taft agreed with those courts that upheld the prohibition laws "on the theory that the legislation was the act of the legislature, and that the legislature had the authority to impose such conditions … as [it] might choose."[41]

Yet, Taft had a problem with those who wanted to use the referendum in a very different way. Specifically, Progressives wanted to mandate its use. The advocates of direct democracy, Taft explained, believed that the only way to prevent reforms from being blocked or undermined by corrupt politicians was to give all of the voters a direct voice in the adoption of laws. The premise of the Progressive argument was a belief that the people as a "whole" were incorruptible.[42] But, Taft shared Madison's understanding that men were not angels and thought that the Progressives were too optimistic.[43] It was entirely possible, he argued, that corrupt political bosses and special interests would figure out how to make the direct-democracy reforms work for them, and their ability to do so would stem from the *un*willingness of most people "to perform their heavier political duty under the new system." Taft asked whether the people would be willing and able to study dozens of detailed bills during every election. In places where the referendum had been instituted, it took hundreds of pages to explain the purposes of the bills that had been submitted to the voters. Taft asserted that, "if the reader does not lay down the [pamphlets] containing [these explanations of bills] with fatigue, confused mind, tired eyes and a disgusted feeling, I am mistaken." According to him, most people simply did not have the time, the motivation, or the expertise to study proposed legislation.[44]

To support this view, Taft pointed to data which proved that, although voters were willing to choose candidates for office, they were often unwilling to decide policy themselves. In various elections across the country, the majority of voters voted for individual candidates but left questions about particular issues unanswered. "Examine the record in referendum states," Taft advised, "and you will find that the total vote on legislative referendums varies from 75 percent to 25 percent of the votes cast for candidates at the same election." Progressives insisted that they would educate voters about "the problems of government" and thereby stimulate "interest" in public policy, but Taft observed that this had not happened so far. Besides, he concluded, if the success of democratic participation depended on teaching the people, it was more reasonable "to retain the old system in which the lesson to be learned is so much simpler and so much more easily taught."[45]

While Taft agreed that excessive corporate influence in politics was a problem, he cautioned reformers to be aware of the dangers associated with "slavish subordination" to the passions of the people. He understood that elected officials were tempted "to coddle the people, to flatter them into thinking that they cannot make a mistake, and to fail to tell them the truth as to their own errors and tendencies to error."[46] But, it was disingenuous to suggest that all of the nation's problems stemmed from "the machinations of wicked men," and that the people did not shoulder any of the blame. Taft also recalled that the framers of the Constitution understood the defects of direct democracy, not the least of which was the tendency of majorities to violate the rights of minorities and individuals.

Most Progressives, however, denied that individual rights were absolute. "The contention," Taft explained, "is that a man has no rights, independent of the will of the people with whom he lives, that he does not inherently possess personal liberty, the right to property, the right to freedom of religion, the right to free speech or that protection secured to him under the title of 'due process of law,' and that these can be taken from him by legislative or executive action, if sanctioned by a popular vote, with the same ease and dispatch that the repeal of any ordinary law could be effected." This notion, Taft concluded, stood in stark opposition to the principles articulated in the Declaration of Independence and institutionalized in the Constitution. The founders "saw a possible tyranny in a majority in popular government quite as dangerous as the despotism of kings and they prepared a written constitution intended to preserve individual rights against its exercise."[47]

Despite the founders' warnings about the dangers of direct democracy, the Progressives were determined to establish a direct link between citizens and their leaders in government, and one way of doing this was by weakening the influence of political bosses and machines. Reformers promoted the direct primary system in which voters chose the candidates for their party in the general election. Direct primaries, in the words of James Ceaser, were intended "to enhance the status of individual candidates during the electoral process, freeing them from the constraints of traditional parties and allowing them to create a popular constituency of their own making." Primary elections, in other words, would connect the people directly to the candidates; the latter could "appeal" to the former without having to work through dishonest and narrow-minded "party intermediaries." In this way, candidates would be free to engage in "moral leadership" that not only articulated the real needs and aspirations of the people but also taught and motivated the country.[48]

Taft agreed that there was a need to reform the candidate selection system; however, as David Potash points out, he articulated three concerns about the direct primary. First, he worried that Democrats and Republicans would vote in each other's primaries. If so, this would undermine the intent behind the direct primary, which was to gauge the true "voice of the party."[49] Taft also contended that conventions were more likely to choose moderate candidates. The professionals who served as delegates to the party conventions were primarily interested in winning the general election; therefore, they preferred to nominate candidates who would appeal to the general electorate. As Taft predicted, "One tendency in a direct election of candidates in a national party will be to select a popular partisan, while that of a convention system will be to take the more moderate man whose name will appeal to the independent voter."[50] Taft's final objection to the direct primary was the benefit that it gave to "the men with wealth and of activity and of little modesty, but of great ambition to be candidates, without real qualification for office," as opposed to "the men who, having qualifications for office, are either without means or refuse to spend money for such a purpose, and are indisposed to press their own fitness upon the voters." In other words, Taft noted that direct primaries mainly benefitted wealthy people, who had the resources and the gall to create their own organizations outside of the party system.[51]

Still, Taft conceded that "the boss system" enabled corporate interests to corrupt the parties (and thus the government), and that something needed to be done. In exchange for financial contributions, party bosses (who were concerned with nothing more than acquiring and maintaining political power) allowed corporate bosses to shape important economic legislation. When they became aware of "corrupt corporate control in the government," the people "directed their energies toward legislation which would take away the means of support upon which bosses and machines had thrived." The problem was with the local nominating conventions—for local offices, the state legislatures, Congress, and the state nominating conventions. They offered little opportunity for "the real rank and file of the party" to choose candidates and to determine the direction of their party. Taft agreed that these local conventions were essentially the tools of bosses and of special interests, and that the only solution (at least for the time being) was to replace them with direct primaries. Thus, Taft accepted direct primaries in lieu of local nominating conventions; however, he remained opposed to Progressive efforts to eliminate state and national nominating conventions.[52]

## An independent judiciary

Taft was serious in his opposition to most direct primaries, but nothing concerned him so much as Progressive challenges to the authority of the judiciary.[53] Believing that many judges, in their "legalistic" defense of private property rights, paid no attention to the real-world implications of their decisions, Roosevelt and his Progressive supporters advocated for the right of the people to recall both judges and judicial decisions. TR conceded that judges, like other public servants in the executive and legislative branches, needed to listen to their consciences, especially when the people were determined to "do wrong." But, he added, the people also had the right to "follow their conscience, and when they have definitely decided on a given policy they must have public servants [including judges] who will carry out that policy."[54] While he recognized the possibility that his proposed reforms could result in a "tyranny of the majority," TR maintained that the current problem was "the tyranny of the bosses and of the special interests." Moreover, he charged that opponents of judicial reform seemed to believe that judges possessed absolute wisdom and virtue. Conservatives talked "as if the judges were somehow imposed on us by Heaven, and were responsible only to Heaven," but Roosevelt reminded the American people that judges were as corruptible as other mortals.[55] While Roosevelt intended for his judicial reforms to apply only to state courts, Taft feared that the Rough Rider and his supporters would eventually demand their application to the federal courts, including the Supreme Court.[56]

Regardless, Taft stressed, the US Constitution was "the fundamental law," and if the legislative and executive branches clearly overstepped their rightful powers under the Constitution, such actions should not be recognized or sanctioned by the judicial branch, which had the responsibility to interpret the law (including the Constitution) when deciding cases. This was the upshot of *Marbury v. Madison* in which Chief Justice John Marshall declared, "The Constitution is either a superior, paramount law, unchangeable by ordinary means, or it is on a level with ordinary legislative acts, and like other acts, is alterable when the legislature shall please to alter it." Taft agreed wholeheartedly with Marshall's reasoning, adding that it "has been accepted as sound in practice for 125 years." The opposing view was that the elected branches should judge the constitutionality of their own acts. The problem with this, Taft insisted, was that the elected branches (especially Congress and the state legislatures) often ignored definite constitutional restrictions in order to placate popular passions.[57]

As president, Taft had rejected a congressional resolution for admitting Arizona into the Union, because its proposed constitution allowed the people to recall judges. Taft used this episode as an opportunity to teach the country, and he even quoted extensively from his veto message in his 1914 book, *Popular Government*.[58] "In a proper sense," Taft explained, "judges are servants of the people; that is, they are doing work which must be done for the government, and in the interest of all the people, but it is not work in the doing of which they are to follow the will of the majority, except as that is embodied in statutes lawfully enacted according to constitutional limitations." Of course, legislators and executive officers were also expected to respect the restraints imposed by the Constitution and to govern for the benefit of both the majority and the minority. Because this did not always happen, however, judges with sufficient autonomy were needed to hold the people and their elected officials accountable to both "law and justice." In any legal dispute, he explained, a judge should be bound by statutory law or, if there was no relevant statute, "the unwritten law." (Such "unwritten law" was rooted in precedent.) But, if a statute contradicted the Constitution, which was "the fundamental law," a judge needed to set aside that statute in favor of the Constitution. Again, all of this required judicial independence. In Taft's view, the security of fundamental freedoms, as well as the continuance of "our constitutional balance," depended upon judges having the power and the "courage" to override the will of the majority "when justice and law require."[59]

Taft conceded that many judicial decisions were extremely unpopular, but that did not justify the recall of judges. Decisions involving controversial matters such as organized labor, religion, race, criminal rights, and prohibition certainly provoked outrage and resentment. Yet, he wanted his fellow citizens to remember the difference between ordinary criticism of a particular decision and the "hasty" cry to replace "a conscientious judge" who made an unpopular ruling. "The recall is devised to encourage quick action, and to lead the people to strike while the iron is hot." It assumed that a judge was "the instrument and servant" of the masses. Before the end of his term (at which time his temperament and ability could be considered more dispassionately in light of many decisions), a judge was recalled "because he has failed, in a single decision, [perhaps], to satisfy the popular demand." To those reformers like Roosevelt who justified the recall as the best means of eliminating judges who had been corrupted by special interests, Taft countered that the ability of the people to adopt such "radical" reform as the recall proved that the special interests were no match for an angry public. In such an atmosphere, Taft asked, why not resort to impeachment? Through the centuries, he maintained, the impeachment process had handled allegations of malfeasance effectively and fairly.[60]

The recall of judges was championed by those who assumed that it could "bring the judges more into sympathy with the popular will," but Taft contended that most judges were not really that "out of touch." In most instances, the language of the law was clear, and judges did not have an opportunity to inject their political or economic ideologies into decisions. But, even when they were tempted to allow their personal views to predetermine their decision-making, they were never completely free from the sway of public opinion. "Surround the judiciary with all the safeguards possible," Taft suggested, "create judges by appointment, make their tenure for life, forbid diminution of salary during their term, and still it is impossible to prevent the influence of popular opinion from coloring judgments in the long run." In other words, judges did not live in a vacuum. Taft assured his fellow Americans that because most judges were smart and empathetic, they were capable of considering, and even responding to, the needs of the time in which they lived.[61]

Taft next turned to the separate but related issue of recalling judicial *decisions*. He understood that the recall of judicial decisions, such as the recall of judges, grew out of frustration with rulings that struck down economic regulations on the grounds that they violated liberty of contract. Progressives believed that such regulations were permissible uses of the government's "police power" (its power to protect the health, safety, welfare, and morals of the people). Tired of working through intermediary republican institutions, they argued that those who "establish a constitution" should be permitted "to interpret it."[62] To Taft, however, this reasoning overlooked the difference between approving fundamental constitutional values and interpreting specific laws in light of those fundamental values. The first was much easier. He observed as well that "a popular majority does not generally ratify a constitution, or any principle of it, or amend its terms until after it has been adopted by a constitutional convention or a legislature, and the final approval is, and ought to be, surrounded with such checks and delays as to secure full information and deliberation." Finally, Taft concluded, the recall of judicial decisions subjected inalienable rights (especially property rights) to the whims of popular opinion, opening the door to socialism.[63] The recall of judicial decisions, in short, "lays the ax at the foot of the tree of well-ordered freedom and subjects the guaranties of life, liberty, and property without remedy to the fitful impulse of a temporary majority of an electorate."[64] Many of these arguments against the recall of judges and judicial decisions echoed Alexander Hamilton's defense of an independent judiciary.[65] And, like James Madison, who criticized Thomas Jefferson's proposal for occasional conventions to decide constitutional matters, Taft believed that allowing the electorate to settle questions concerning constitutional law eroded the respect that people had for the Constitution.[66] "The strongest objection to these instruments of direct government," Taft explained, "is the effect of their constant use in eliminating all distinction between a constitution as fundamental law, and statutes enacted for the disposition of current matters."[67]

## Conclusion

A.E. Campbell accurately identifies Taft as one of the "conservative Progressives."[68] To be sure, Taft was conservative in his defense of the American constitutional order but was progressive in his advocacy of particular social and economic reforms. Throughout his presidency, he worked to build upon the achievements of Theodore Roosevelt.[69] At the same time, he believed that Roosevelt had a tendency to pursue reform so vigorously as to give short shrift to legal/constitutional considerations (especially with regard to the powers of the presidency).[70] As Alan Brinkley explains, Taft "was a man of cautious, legalistic temperament, who instinctively recoiled from doing what Roosevelt reveled in doing—bending the rules, and at times the law, to achieve his objectives."[71] And, when Roosevelt, along with other Progressive reformers, began to advocate direct democracy, and to attack the judiciary, Taft helped to lead the conservative resistance.[72] While agreeing that various economic, social, and even political reforms were needed, he maintained that they should not be purchased at the cost of fundamental rights or the carefully constructed constitutional system that was intended to secure those fundamental rights, especially the right to property. Taft believed that republican government could both protect individual liberty and promote the general welfare. This was, he insisted, the principal hope behind the Constitution, which represented the ultimate intent of "We the People" to perfect the Union.

## Notes

1     James Chace, *1912: Wilson, Roosevelt, Taft & Debs—the Election that Changed the Country* (New York: Simon and Schuster, 2004), 23; Alan Brinkley, "William Howard Taft," in *The American Presidency: The Authoritative Reference*, eds. Alan Brinkley and Davis Dyer (New York: Houghton Mifflin Company, 2004), 295; Theodore B. Olson, "William

Howard Taft," in *Presidential Leadership: Rating the Best and the Worst
in the White House*, eds. James Taranto and Leonard Leo (New York:
Wall Street Journal Books, 2004), 131, 133; Wilson Carey McWilliams,
commentary on *The President and His Powers*, ed. Wilson Carey
McWilliams, vol. 6 of *The Collected Works of William Howard Taft*, ed.
David H. Burton (Athens: Ohio University Press, 2003), 5; A.E. Campbell,
commentary on *Present Day Problems*, ed. A.E. Campbell, vol. 1 of *The
Collected Works of William Howard Taft*, ed. David H. Burton (Athens:
Ohio University Press, 2001), 71.

2   See, for example, Sidney M. Milkis and Michael Nelson, *The American
Presidency: Origins and Development, 1776–2011*, sixth edition
(Washington: CQ Press, 2012), 236–237; Brinkley, "William Howard Taft,"
286, 288–289.

3   Olson, "William Howard Taft," 132.

4   Olson, "William Howard Taft," 131; Brinkley, "William Howard Taft,"
285–286, 288; Milkis and Nelson, *The American Presidency*, 235; Paolo E.
Coletta, *The Presidency of William Howard Taft* (Lawrence: University Press
of Kansas, 1973), 11.

5   William Howard Taft, *Popular Government*, ed. David Potash, vol. 5 of *The
Collected Works of William Howard Taft*, ed. David H. Burton (Athens:
Ohio University Press, 2003), 35–36. See also Coletta, *Presidency of William
Howard Taft*, 17. This belief that there were limits to what government
could do to improve society is what distinguished Progressive reformers
from the more conservative, or "Old Guard," Republicans who united
behind Taft in 1912. See Norman M. Wilensky, *Conservatives in the
Progressive Era: The Taft Republicans of 1912* (Gainesville: University of
Florida Press, 1965), 43.

6   Andrew Hacker, *Political Theory: Philosophy, Ideology, Science* (New York:
The MacMillan Company, 1961), 358–359.

7   Hacker, *Political Theory*, 352–356.

8   William Howard Taft, "Speech at Boise City," November 3, 1906, in *Present
Day Problems*, ed. A.E. Campbell, vol. 1 of *The Collected Works of William
Howard Taft*, ed. David H. Burton (Athens: Ohio University Press, 2001),
181–182.

9   Taft, "Speech at Boise City," 182.

10  William Howard Taft, "Speech of Acceptance," July 28, 1908, in *Presidential
Addresses and State Papers*, ed. David H. Burton, vol. 3 of *The Collected*

*Works of William Howard Taft*, ed. David H. Burton (Athens: Ohio University Press, 2002), 18–19; Campbell, commentary on *Present Day Problems*, 70–71.

11  William Howard Taft, "The Present Issues of the Two Great Parties," August 21, 1908, in *Political Issues and Outlooks: Speeches Delivered Between August 1908 and February 1909*, ed. David H. Burton, vol. 2 of *The Collected Works of William Howard Taft*, ed. David H. Burton (Athens: Ohio University Press, 2001), 21.

12  Taft, "The Present Issues," 23.

13  William Howard Taft, "Address at Columbus, Ohio," August 19, 1907, in *Present Day Problems*, ed. A.E. Campbell, vol. 1 of *The Collected Works of William Howard Taft*, ed. David H. Burton (Athens: Ohio University Press, 2001), 216–217.

14  Robert H. Webking, *The American Revolution and the Politics of Liberty* (Baton Rouge: Louisiana State University Press, 1988), 103–104. A.E. Campbell offers a similar observation: "Unless a man had security in his property, he could hardly be said to have liberty in any sense." See Campbell, commentary on *Present Day Problems*, 70–71.

15  Campbell, commentary on *Present Day Problems*, 70. Campbell's essay provides a helpful lens for viewing Taft's attitude about the role of government in addressing economic challenges. Specifically, Campbell classifies Taft among the "conservative Progressives," noting his belief that acquisitiveness, while necessary to the advancement of society, could not be given free rein. A healthy awareness of "social responsibility" was needed as well. Thus, Campbell explains, "he thought it right to keep a very close eye both on the means by which a man acquired his property—hence, for example, his regard for workers' right to claim injury compensation against employers, which he was ready greatly to extend—and on what he did with his property once he had acquired it—hence his readiness to look closely into the behaviour of monopoly trusts." See Campbell, commentary on *Present Day Problems*, 71.

16  Quoted in Ronald J. Pestritto, "Leaving the Constitution," *The Claremont Review of Books*, June 8, 2006, http://www.claremont.org/writings/crb/spring2006/pestritto.html (accessed November 21, 2013).

17  Jean M. Yarbrough, "The New Freedom," *The Claremont Review of Books*, January 31, 2006, http://www.claremont.org/writings/crb/winter2005/

Yarbrough.html (accessed November 21, 2013). For more on the Progressive rejection of individualism, see Michael McGerr, *A Fierce Discontent: The Rise and Fall of the Progressive Movement in America, 1870–1920* (New York: Free Press, 2003).

18  Forrest McDonald, *The United States in the 20th Century: 1900–1920*, vol. 1 (Reading: Addison-Wesley Publishing, 1970), 177; George E. Mowry, *Theodore Roosevelt and the Progressive Movement* (New York: Hill and Wang, 1960), 102.

19  Coletta, *Presidency of William Howard Taft*, 126, 129.

20  Chace, *1912*, 95; Coletta, *Presidency of William Howard Taft*, 153–154, 156, 162–163, 165. Both before and during his presidency, Taft frequently referenced the Sherman Anti-Trust Act. In a 1908 campaign speech, for example, he talked quite extensively about it, arguing that a string of prosecutions under the law would allow a businessman to "find out quickly what the law is and how far he can go, how far legitimate business methods will go." See William Howard Taft, "Mr. Bryan's Claim to the Roosevelt Policies," September 8, 1908, in *Political Issues and Outlooks: Speeches Delivered Between August 1908 and February 1909*, ed. David H. Burton, vol. 2 of *The Collected Works of William Howard Taft*, ed. David H. Burton (Athens: Ohio University Press, 2001), 48–49.

21  David Potash, commentary on *Popular Government*, ed. David Potash, vol. 5 of *The Collected Works of William Howard Taft*, ed. David H. Burton (Athens: Ohio University Press, 2003), 5; Milkis and Nelson, *The American Presidency*, 235, 236; Coletta, *Presidency of William Howard Taft*, 13; Taft, "Speech of Acceptance," 7.

22  As Theodore Olson observes, "Taft agreed with much of Roosevelt's presidential agenda, especially in the areas of regulation of industry and natural resource conservation, but he questioned the constitutionality of Roosevelt's methods." See Olson, "William Howard Taft," 131.

23  William Howard Taft, *The President and His Powers*, ed. Wilson Carey McWilliams, vol. 6 of *The Collected Works of William Howard Taft*, ed. David H. Burton (Athens: Ohio University Press, 2003), 104, 107–108. See also McWilliams, commentary on *The President and His Powers*, 6; Milkis and Nelson, *The American Presidency*, 235; Coletta, *Presidency of William Howard Taft*, 11–12.

24  McWilliams, commentary on *The President and His Powers*, 6–7.

25  Taft, *The President and His Powers*, 116–117.

26  McWilliams, commentary on *The President and His Powers*, 6.

27  Taft, *The President and His Powers*, 107, 110.

28  As Norman Wilensky explains, this view was common among the more
conservative, or "Old Guard," Republican Party "regulars" who supported
Taft in 1912. Many of these men agreed with the majority of Progressives
that the government had a role to play in managing the economy. Thus,
they tended to support "federal regulation of tariffs, monopolies, natural
resources, taxes, and banking." But, they drew the line at "changes in law
and government." When it came to political reform, Wilensky stresses, Taft's
supporters shared his view that direct-democracy reforms undermined
"respect for the law," including the Constitution, and thus threatened to
destabilize the country. See Wilensky, *Conservatives in the Progressive
Era*, 44–45, 47. Similarly, David Potash stresses that both moderate and
conservative Republicans were not unified merely by their opposition to
Theodore Roosevelt. "Old Guard and moderate Republicans discovered
a surprising intensity of agreement on fundamental principles: the
Constitution, the status and prerogatives of the judiciary, liberty, order,
and the preservation of the rights of private property … The movement
toward direct democracy and constitutional reform quickly became the
focus of conservative Republican attacks. Initiative, referendum, and recall
undermined the American way of life, conservatives warned, and, if not
checked, could lead to revolution and anarchy." See Potash, commentary on
*Popular Government*, 6. The reader should note that, in addition to providing
background about Taft's 1914 book, *Popular Government*, Potash's invaluable
essay is a comprehensive yet succinct summary of Taft's main arguments in
that book, as well as the "conservative principles" behind those arguments.
See Potash, commentary on *Popular Government*, 8, 11–14.

29  Quoted in Potash, commentary on *Popular Government*, 8.

30  Potash, commentary on *Popular Government*, 8–9. As Potash explains,
throughout the 1912 campaign, Taft and other conservative Republicans
tried to teach the American people about the nature of republican
government. These campaign speeches formed the basis for several high-
profile academic lectures that Taft delivered at Yale in 1913. In 1914, the
lectures were published as *Popular Government*. See Potash, commentary
on *Popular Government*, 3–4, 8, 11.

31  Taft, *Popular Government*, 21. See also Potash, commentary on *Popular
Government*, 12.

32  See *The Federalist Papers*, ed. Clinton Rossiter, with a new introduction and notes by Charles R. Kesler (New York: Signet Classic, 2003), nos. 30, 43, and 10, pp. 73–74, 187, 276.

33  In *Popular Government*, Taft even quoted extensively from *Federalist* #10 to support his contention that direct democracy threatened the rights of unpopular factions and individuals. See Taft, *Popular Government*, 57–59.

34  Potash, commentary on *Popular Government*, 12.

35  Taft, *Popular Government*, 65.

36  Taft, *Popular Government*, 21.

37  Taft, *Popular Government*, 30–31.

38  Marc Landy and Sidney M. Milkis, *American Government: Balancing Democracy and Rights*, second edition (New York: Cambridge University Press, 2008), 7–11.

39  Taft, *Popular Government*, 31.

40  Taft, *Popular Government*, 37–39.

41  Taft, *Popular Government*, 40, 42–43.

42  Taft, *Popular Government*, 43–44.

43  In fact, as Norman Wilensky asserts in his study of the conservative "Taft Republicans," Taft's supporters in 1912 "accepted as fact the idea that the sin and selfishness of mankind were nearly ineradicable." This radically different conception of human nature is what separated the more pessimistic "Old Guard" Republicans from the more optimistic Progressives. See Wilensky, *Conservatives in the Progressive Era*, 39.

44  Taft, *Popular Government*, 44–45.

45  Potash, commentary on *Popular Government*, 13; Taft, *Popular Government*, 46–47, 49. By the twenty-first century, Taft's remarks have proved prophetic. As Jerome Mileur explains, direct-democracy reforms have made the political system even more complicated, and this has deterred participation. Specifically, direct-democracy reforms place greater "intellectual demands" on supposedly "educated" and "fully informed" voters, in addition to which the system is made more confusing and challenging by "the temporal separation of elections for national, state, and local offices," as well as by nonpartisan elections that eliminate the party designations which most voters rely on as cues. Finally, the elimination of most political patronage positions, through civil-service reform, has destroyed a once powerful motivation for voting. Put simply, the sacrifices of political engagement are greater than the perceived rewards, especially

for traditionally underrepresented and politically powerless groups. "In many ways," Mileur observes, "the measure of Progressive 'success' is to be found in the declining levels of voter turnout throughout the twentieth century and the changed pattern of turnout in which poorer, less educated, working class, minority, and immigrant populations are disproportionately missing from the voting booth." Of course, Progressives like TR saw democratic reform as helpful to their effort to strengthen the power of government. Mileur notes the irony that, for over forty years, in various states such as California, initiatives and referenda have been used especially by antitax groups to starve the government of revenue that would otherwise allow it to take on more responsibilities. See Jerome M. Mileur, "The Legacy of Reform: Progressive Government, Regressive Politics," in *Progressivism and the New Democracy*, eds. Sidney M. Milkis and Jerome M. Mileur (Amherst: University of Massachusetts Press, 1999), 279–280, 269.

46  Taft, *Popular Government*, 51. Like many opponents of Progressive *political* reform, Taft wanted representatives to remain free from excessive popular influence. "The men who are really the great men of any legislative body," Taft declared, "are those who, having views of their own, defend them and support them, even at the risk of rousing a popular clamor against themselves." Quoted in Wilensky, *Conservatives in the Progressive Era*, 42. This notion that all public servants—judges, executives, and even legislators—should avoid succumbing to every momentary shift in the popular mood united Taft with other "Old Guard" conservatives, most of whom "considered themselves to be republicans rather than democrats." See Wilensky, *Conservatives in the Progressive Era*, 42, 50. In addition, Taft's views echoed the writings of both Madison and Hamilton in *The Federalist Papers*. See, for example, *Federalist Papers*, nos. 10, 62, 71, and 78.

47  Taft, *Popular Government*, 51–53.

48  James W. Ceaser, *Presidential Selection: Theory and Development* (Princeton: Princeton University Press, 1979), 31, 33, 35, 205, 190–192.

49  Potash, commentary on *Popular Government*, 13; Taft, *Popular Government*, 73–75.

50  Potash, commentary on *Popular Government*, 13; Taft, *Popular Government*, 77.

51  Taft, *Popular Government*, 77–78; Potash, commentary on *Popular Government*, 13.

52  Taft, *Popular Government*, 70–71, 79, 81; Potash, commentary on *Popular Government*, 13.

53  As Norman Wilsenky observes, efforts to undermine the independence of the judiciary "alienated" Taft, as well as nearly every "Old Guard" Republican opponent of direct-democracy reforms. See Wilensky, *Conservatives in the Progressive Era*, 49. David Potash agrees, writing that "the very notion of a recall of judicial decisions galvanized conservative Republicans." See Potash, commentary on *Popular Government*, 7.

54  Theodore Roosevelt, "Address before the Ohio Constitutional Convention," February 21, 1912, in *Social Justice and Popular Rule*, vol. 17 of *The Works of Theodore Roosevelt*, national edition (New York: Charles Scribner's Sons, 1926), 137.

55  Theodore Roosevelt, "Address at Philadelphia," April 10, 1912, in *Social Justice and Popular Rule*, vol. 17 of *The Works of Theodore Roosevelt*, national dition (New York: Charles Scribner's Sons, 1926), 202–203.

56  Taft, *Popular Government*, 113. With regard to the recall of judicial decisions, Roosevelt conceded, "What the Supreme Court of the nation decides to be law binds both the national and the state courts and all the people within the boundaries of the nation. But the decision of a state court on a constitutional question should be subject to revision by the people of the state." That ruling of the people would be final, unless overridden by the Supreme Court of the United States. See Roosevelt, "Address before the Ohio Constitutional Convention," 139–140. James Chace also stresses that, when calling for the recall of judicial decisions, TR "was referring to state judges." In addition, he did *not* mean that the people had a right to override decisions in criminal and civil trials; the recall would be confined to those "cases involving a juridical interpretation of the Constitution." See Chace, *1912*, 105.

57  Taft, *Popular Government*, 105–106.

58  Taft's veto of Arizona's application for statehood was due entirely to the fact that Arizona's constitution included a judicial recall. After the judicial recall was dropped from the constitution, Arizona was admitted into the Union. Once admitted, Arizona reestablished the recall. See David H. Burton, commentary on *Presidential Messages to Congress*, ed. David H. Burton, vol. 4 of *The Collected Works of William Howard Taft*, ed. David H. Burton (Athens: Ohio University Press, 2002), 2; Taft, *Popular Government*, 107–108.

59  Taft, *Popular Government*, 108–109.

60  Taft, *Popular Government*, 109–110.

61  Taft, *Popular Government*, 110–111.

62  Taft, *Popular Government*, 111–112.

63  Taft, *Popular Government*, 112–114.

64  Quoted in Potash, commentary on *Popular Government*, 7–8. See also Coletta, *Presidency of William Howard Taft*, 228.

65  See *Federalist Papers*, no. 78.

66  See *Federalist Papers*, no. 49.

67  Taft, *Popular Government*, 52. This was Taft's main objection to the recall of judicial decisions; he feared that, through constant revision, the Constitution would take on the character of a regular, run-of-the-mill statute. Wilensky notes that the opponents of direct-democracy reforms venerated the Constitution, "because it embodied for them the conclusions of some of the wisest, purest, and best men of history as to what was necessary for the preservation of liberty, justice, and order." See Wilensky, *Conservatives in the Progressive Era*, 49–50, 48.

68  Campbell, commentary on *Present Day Problems*, 71. See also McWilliams, commentary on *The President and His Powers*, 4.

69  Potash, commentary on *Popular Government*, 8, 5.

70  Olson, "William Howard Taft," 131.

71  Brinkley, "William Howard Taft," 286.

72  Potash, commentary on *Popular Government*, 6–8.

# 6

# Joseph G. Cannon: Partisan Majorities and Responsible Democracy

Douglas B. Harris
*Loyola University Maryland*

Congress was the center of power in national politics as the nineteenth century ended, and no office was more powerful than that of Speaker of the House of Representatives. The prerogative powers of the Speakership had grown through rules and precedent since the adoption of Reed's Rules in 1889. Upon becoming Speaker in 1903, Joseph G. Cannon used those accumulated powers to make the office the determinative influence in the House legislative process, earning him the nickname "czar."[1] Moreover, Cannon used his influence to oppose Progressive reforms.[2] A traditional conservative in his skepticism toward change, the Illinois Republican said, "I will not help change existing law unless you put something better in its place." Progressive policy and political reforms did not meet this test and were frequently derided by Cannon.[3] Nowhere was Cannon's standpat attitude more evident than on business issues, especially the protective tariff. Conservative to the core, he dubbed the recession and ensuing financial panic of 1907 a mere "flurry" and argued strenuously against "tinkering with the tariff" in any way that would "inevitably disturb business conditions" even more.[4] To Cannon, the market would correct itself so long as Congress did no harm. Cannon repeatedly rejected the need for reform, responding to reformers that America was "a hell of a success."[5]

Both Cannon's power in the House and his conservative politics raised the ire of progressive reformers. Often called the "tyrant from Illinois," Cannon was also seen as the "archfoe" (even the "black beast") of insurgency and the "brakeman of the House."[6] By blocking, slowing, or amending reform proposals, he provoked a progressive reaction against "Cannonism" that erupted within the House in 1909 and 1910 and spilled over into the media with the Speaker becoming a political issue in and of himself. Campaigning against Cannon in his Illinois district, Samuel Gompers, president of the American Federation of Labor, called him "the worst enemy of economic, social, and political reform that the people have."[7]

To be sure, progressive portraits of Cannon as interested only in personal power and as an entrenched foe of the progressive agenda are compelling stories easily told. But, it is too often forgotten that Cannon, though antiprogressive, was also *for* something. He was a proponent of the traditional or orthodox conception of American society and governance that valued the role of political parties in organizing the nation's politics. As for many in his time, partisanship defined both who Cannon was and what responsible democracy was. "Every man who is practical, who is of substantial value to civilization," Cannon once asserted, "is a partisan."[8] In this, the "czar" did not stand alone in the House but rather stood with a phalanx of Republican "regulars" who shared his views and his power. Within the House, the "tyrant from Illinois" was also "Uncle Joe" who enjoyed the affection of many members for working to free the House from Senate dominance and restore its independent and equal place in the constitutional balance of power. Outside the House in the broader Republican party, he was the champion of conservatives and a national party leader throughout the McKinley-Roosevelt-Taft era. "Boomed" for the vice presidency in 1904 (the press often had fun with cannon puns) and considered a presidential contender in 1908, he was recognized as a major influence in the selection of James Sherman as vice president. Indeed, William Allen White, covering the convention, noted "how little enthusiasm those delegates had for Mr. Taft. They cheered the reactionary leaders. Joe Cannon was their idol—not Taft."[9]

Despite Cannon's importance to the intra-party and policy battles of his time, scant attention has been given to his political thought and its place in debates during the Progressive era. Yet, his arguments about party, policy, and representative government found in House debates and two major speeches delivered to business leaders on "Abraham Lincoln" and "Protection and Prosperity" set forth the stakes in the party struggle between GOP regulars and "insurgents."[10] The three long days of House debate in the 1910 revolt against Cannon's strong legislative leadership dramatize the partisan–progressive struggles within the broader party system, as well as Congress.

## Cannon, the party of Lincoln, and the progressive era

Animosities arising from the Civil War and the legacy of Abraham Lincoln persisted in both inter- and intraparty political debates throughout the latter half of the nineteenth century.[11] The Civil War, fresh in the minds of Democrats and Republicans alike, fueled suspicions that limited interparty cooperation. By the same token, within the dominant Republican Party coalition, both regulars and insurgents seized upon Lincoln's image to justify their different visions of national purpose. An Illinoisan, Joseph Cannon had an especially deep commitment to the "party of Lincoln;" he considered the Democrats the "party of rebellion." As a young Republican in the 1850s and 1860s, he had met and known Lincoln. He claimed to have attended two of the Lincoln–Douglas debates and to have been a delegate to the Illinois state Republican Convention that proposed Lincoln for the presidency.

Familiar with the martyred president, Cannon claimed to know and defend the true Lincoln, his policies, and his party. Annoyed by Progressive efforts to appropriate Lincoln's legacy, Cannon liberally dropped the martyred president's name in all manner of intra-party policy battles. To conservationists lining up against the timber industry, Cannon reminded them that Lincoln had made fenceposts out of walnut trees. To the temperance ministers, Cannon recalled that a young Lincoln had sold whisky as "a clerk in a little country store."[12] To those who sought tariff reform, Cannon cited Lincoln's early espousal of the protective tariff. Rather than merely following Roosevelt and the Progressive wave, Cannon stood for orthodox Republicanism as represented in the party platform. Indeed, a half century after the War, the Republican Party, Cannon insisted, was still the "party of Lincoln." "If you want to know what was the platform adopted at Chicago [in 1860]," Cannon told a business group, "read the last Republican platform [in 1908]; and you have everything in that platform that was in the platform adopted in 1860, touching economic questions, and which platform the pen of Abraham Lincoln drew."[13] As Cannon saw it, progressive reformers only pretended to understand Lincoln; the true Lincoln had built the Republican Party, articulated its core philosophy and key policies, and secured that philosophy and those policies (especially "Lincoln's protective tariff") by building a strong and perpetual party organization which was, to Cannon, the "most fitting monument to Lincoln."[14]

Fierce rivalries characterized the "fourth party system" in which sectionalist issues and the legacy of the Civil War and Reconstruction played important roles in the partisan rhetoric of both Democrats and Republicans: the one suspicious and resentful about the growth of national government power, the other ever mindful of the treachery of the "party of rebellion."[15] Strong party organizations were grounded in elaborate patronage networks that delineated the party in power from the party out of power and thereby perpetuated these divisions. Moreover, the deep historical, coalitional, and organizational divisions between the two parties produced rhetorical and policy conflicts that were intensely ideological. Based on an extensive analysis of presidential campaign rhetoric, John Gerring argues that, from 1828 to 1924, "Nationalism" dominated Whig and Republican rhetoric with a heavy emphasis on order. Republicans regularly sought positive uses of the national state to promote order in commerce, society, and the law in the face of opposition commonly framed on anarchy and disorder.[16] Indeed, to a Republican Party that in the forty years after 1860 had lost three presidents (Lincoln, Garfield, and McKinley) to assassination at the hands of a secessionist, a lunatic, and an anarchist, "order versus anarchy" had a particular resonance.

Joseph Cannon's career and beliefs were shaped by these partisan battles. He became a true believer in this Republican orthodoxy and its policies, including those designed to promote commerce, such as the Homestead Act and railroad expansion in the West, and especially the tariff that provided revenue for these programs while protecting the entrepreneurs and industries that made them possible. "One of the greatest achievements of Lincoln," Cannon believed, "was that through his partisanship … he led in the formation of the Republican party, that party which has been longer in power than any other in the history of the Republic." His "policies … have dominated the Republic" and, thereby, his party has produced "the most marvelous history of human achievements ever recorded by any people in any time since the beginning."[17] Under half a century of Republican rule, Cannon argued, America was transformed: the population had tripled, the number of wage earners nearly quintupled, wages increased nearly eightfold, the value of manufactures tenfold, and total national wealth increased by 1910 to eight times what it had been in 1860. It was "Lincoln's policy of protection" that deserved credit for this "period of our greatest development in agriculture, manufacture, and commerce;" "What marvelous things have been wrought under those policies!"[18]

Cannon's critics were dubious about his story and the effects of these policies in the 1890s and early 1900s. Abuses of workers by corporations and protectionist policies that raised prices on consumers, especially farmers and rural communities, led many to question exactly what kind of "order" the Republican Party was providing and for whose benefit. Progressives from the Midwest, Plains, and West, affiliated with the Republican Party but with roots in populist protests, shared a world view which clashed with that of the party regulars, making the job of managing an already large GOP coalition all the more difficult for Cannon and his Old Guard allies. The insurgents shared the populist interest in direct-democracy reform and sometimes crossed party lines to court the support of Democrats, but the party divide was too great for them to abandon their birthrights as Republicans. Like the regulars, the insurgents, David Sarasohn writes, "still fought the Civil War" against Southern Democrats and were uncomfortable with "the other center of Democratic power, the city and its immigrants."[19] These progressives worked from within to reform the Republican Party and allied with Democrats only in "grudging cooperation" when necessary to accomplish those aims.[20]

Still, like many Democrats, Progressives saw the growth of corporate power and wealth due to monopoly and corrupt alliances with party bosses to be the greatest threat to liberty. Regular Republicans like Cannon rejected their efforts at reform as creating uncertainty that would interrupt the progress of the nation.[21] Challenging the Republicanism of the insurgents, Cannon declared them merely "Populists who call themselves Republicans."[22] Intra-party divisions were neither new to the GOP nor to Cannon. He had entered Congress in 1872 on the "regular" side of the intra-party split over "Grantism," which for reformers meant "corruption and spoilsmanship."[23] To a party builder like Cannon, patronage was a natural and essential part of politics. Like Lincoln, he had emerged from a political system in Illinois that rewarded party fidelity and advanced men who defended the party faith.[24] In the ensuing years, factionalism recurred in the Republican Party as divisions between "stalwarts" and "half-breeds" posed persistent challenges to party unity.[25] Roosevelt saw Cannon and the "ruling clique in the Senate, the House, and the National Committee" as a formidable and seemingly immovable impediment to progress and, in his first years in office, he relented often to its power.[26]

After his large reelection victory in 1904, Roosevelt shifted to a more aggressive agenda becoming a hero to Progressives and intensifying the threat of insurgency. Despite Roosevelt's claims to party leadership, Cannon believed that it was he and not the president who was holding true to Republican orthodoxy. Indeed, Cannon believed that neither he nor Roosevelt was more important than the Republican platform and, as Speaker, he was bound by party loyalty to support TR when that which the president proposed was consistent with the platform but not when a proposal violated Republican Party principles.[27]

Roosevelt's more progressive friends bristled at Cannon's intransigence, but the president did not want a straight-up fight and, indeed, often defended the Speaker and other congressional leaders as "not only essential to work with" but, given their power, talents, and effectiveness, "desirable to work with."[28] When the first rumblings of anti-Cannonism emerged in 1906, Roosevelt chose to defend the Speaker.[29] In a letter to Cannon loyalist James Watson, the president preached the Republican gospel of order over anarchy: "With Mr. Cannon as Speaker working hand in hand and in hearty fashion with the Senate, Congress has accomplished a literally phenomenal amount of good work... A change would substitute purposeless confusion for the present orderly progress along the lines of a carefully thought out policy."[30]

The Speaker, however, was increasingly the target of Progressives for whom "Cannonism" became the symbol of corruption in the nation's politics. With Democrats fanning the flames by denouncing the Republican Congressional leadership as an "oligarchy" in their 1908 platform,[31] insurgent Republicans, like Washingtonian Miles Poindexter, "decidedly opposed" Cannon's reelection because of "a certain air of dictatorship and intimidation" in his leadership.[32] The anti-Cannon onslaught in the Plains and Midwestern states continued in 1910 as most delegations had elected to vote against Cannon for Speaker.[33] These insurgents nonetheless considered themselves to be Republicans. Judge R.P. Rees, for example, a Kansas insurgent, vowed to "do everything he possibly can to defeat Cannon at the Republican caucus," but added that "if Cannon is the caucus nominee, and the caucus is run on the square," he would vote for Cannon over Champ Clark for Speaker.[34] For most Progressives, even the "black beast" was preferable to a Democrat.


## "The most fitting monument to Lincoln": Cannon's attachment to party

The grandest monument to the greatness of Lincoln, Cannon believed, was the political party he built. "For more than a generation," the Speaker told a business audience, "poets, orators, historians, artists, and architects have been trying to build enduring monuments to Lincoln ... but to me the most fitting monument to Lincoln is the party he helped organize and the achievements of the policies he helped develop for the lasting benefit of the whole country."[35] Cannon saw Progressivism as an assault on this party. It advanced an entirely new conception of American democracy that sought to weaken and, in many instances, displace party as an intermediary between the people and the government. Unlike Cannon, Progressives saw the political party as the lynchpin of a corrupt system whereby business interests and the well-connected benefited at the expense of the people.

Not only did Cannon discount progressive criticisms of party, but he insisted that party organization was essential to govern a democracy of ninety million people. In what other way, he asked, could "a government of the people, as contradistinguished from an absolute monarchy or a limited monarchy" be achieved and operated through majority rule?[36] The great party organizations made democracy possible and became even more important as the American population and society grew increasingly in size and complexity. "The Bryans, the LaFollettes, the fault-finders, the Populists," the Speaker chided, "would tear down, but they are unable to build up."[37] Their vision for organizing democracy looked to group associations, to an increasingly independent and reformist press, to individualistic politicians who, once freed from party control, might divine and pursue the "true" public interest, and, ultimately, to all manner of direct-democracy instruments including the initiative, referenda, and recall. A staunch believer in party organization, Cannon argued that all of these alternatives were inferior to a party-regulated democracy. Organization by groups was fine so far as it went, but group interests, Cannon argued, should be included in party organizations that would moderate their influence by balancing one group's interests against others in the party's coalition.[38]

Cannon was also a long-time critic of "the uplift magazines" and the "metropolitan papers."[39] He had seen the press move from party sponsorship to the market orientation of the penny press in the last decades of the nineteenth century and wondered what could make such "independent" newspapers responsible. He faulted "a sensational press" that "thunders for a purpose from false premises" to advance the "sale of its wares" and even blamed it for some of the most violent examples of anarchy in the past half century. Its writers and editors, he claimed, had "inspired those unbalanced egotists [Booth, Guiteau, and Czolgosz] to assassination."[40]

Cannon also saw too little democracy in the Progressive ideal of individual politicians working for the people in the name of a nebulously divined "national interest." Without the party organizing voter choice and facilitating collective responsibility, a leader could not be sure that he represented the majority. Without responsible leaders, the public would be unable to differentiate between enlightened statesmen and demagogues.[41] The potential for demagoguery was a regular talking point for Cannon who ridiculed the idea that an individual, a small interest group, or a newspaper could divine the public good better than a party organization. Cannon denounced "the demagogue, the short-sighted man, the crank," the "wild-eyed son of destiny," and "the self-constituted righteous of the Republic who criticize without judgment and without knowledge,"[42] believing that these and other "altruistic" men would "in the end do more harm than good."[43]

Cannon's critiques of progressivism were more than merely a party leader's self-interested defense of strong party organization. He believed that a functioning democracy required more than individual politicians' imagined sense of the public interest and that parties provided a kind of collective and perpetual democratic responsibility that other institutions (interest groups, the press, and the new breed of independent politicians) could not. In a speech to the Pittsburgh Chamber of Commerce, he argued,

> It is of the very essence of the perpetuity of the great Republic that majorities shall control. With real majorities there is full responsibility, and with our frequent elections, if the real majorities make mistakes, with full responsibility, the voting population ... will make the minority that [which] was a majority in fact. Therefore I am a partisan.[44]

Indeed, not only was a partisan definition of the public good more reliable than that of the press, the group, or the individual, but it checked the potential for demagoguery in the White House as well. Specifically, Cannon thought Theodore Roosevelt's view of presidential activism was an inferior form of democracy, and he claimed that Lincoln shared this view.

Theodore Roosevelt might invoke Lincoln as precedent for extraordinary presidential leadership in the broader interest, but Cannon countered by recalling Lincoln's belief in "constitutional checks and limitations." "There was nowhere in that [first] inaugural," Cannon insisted, "or in any state paper, or in any statement, or in the mind of Lincoln, that the Chief Executive could do anything except that which was authorized in a government of the people by law; and it remains for wild-eyed sons of destiny of a later day to say that the Executive can do anything that is not expressly prohibited by the letter of the law."[45] Cannon was clearly closer to Taft's more restrained view of presidential leadership and believed Lincoln to be as well. This was, moreover, consistent with his view of the legislative process: "it is the duty of Congress to deliberate and to act with caution when a great question is involved, and not to yield to any sudden hysterical demand."[46]

## Revolt and chaos in the sixty-first Congress

The revolt against Joseph G. Cannon culminated in a three-day marathon debate in March 1910 that is a signature moment in the history of the House of Representatives. Representative George Norris of Nebraska initiated it by introducing a resolution, which he claimed was privileged by the Constitution, to remove the Speaker of the House from his chairmanship of the House Committee on Rules and to strip him of the power to appoint other members of that Committee. These were key to the Speaker's (and, by extension, the majority party's) control over access to the floor, amending activity, and the legislative schedule. In the end, enough Republican insurgents (mostly progressives) were joined by minority party Democrats to depose the Speaker as Chairman of the Committee on Rules. Cannon's removal is generally seen as the conclusion (or at least the beginning of the end) of strong party dominance and as the origin of the "textbook Congress" of weak parties, stronger committees, and cross-party coalitions to enact legislation.[47] The revolt against Cannon's Speakership exemplifies the political and rhetorical struggles between progressives and "regular" Republicans that raged outside Congress in the broader party system. The Norris Resolution was a frontal challenge to the appropriateness of party control of legislative proceedings and to the legitimacy of American democracy grounded in party majorities as opposed to one of nonpartisan or cross-partisan majorities. The rhetorical battle between progressive insurgents and party regulars echoed with threats of "chaos" and charges of "tyranny." In laying open each side's conception of party governance, it mirrored the larger public debate over party reform as well as the ideological debate between the parties.[48]

The revolt against Cannon is commonly attributed to "overreach" by the Speaker and to his having lost touch with his "procedural majority," but it is also the case that Cannon's "procedural majority" and the very underpinnings of Republican Party control had been slipping from beneath him for some time.[49] In the elections of 1906 and 1908, the Republicans lost thirty-two seats, many of them held by Cannon supporters. The continued presence of progressive Republicans (whom he dubbed "Populists") meant that the Speaker no longer had effective control over the House. The potential for revolt was obvious to many and hung like the sword of Damacles over the lower House. Cannon himself fretted that neither he nor the country could "tell from day to day whether, with a Democratic minority, there are not enough of Populists who call themselves Republicans to flock with that Democratic-Populistic minority, plus a few cowards, to make a majority ... leaving us without an efficient Republican majority in either body."[50]

The opening of the sixty-first Congress was chaotic. On the first vote for Speaker, a dozen insurgent Republicans, many of whom had campaigned against "Cannonism," voted against Cannon.[51] Yet, more significant was that thirty insurgent Republicans voted against the leadership's rules package necessitating an alliance between regular Republicans and a handful of Tammany Hall Democrats to win adoption. For insurgents, the Republican–Tammany alliance was additional evidence of party tyranny and of a triumph of corrupt interests over the people.

It could not have comforted Cannon and other leaders, who treasured order based on party regularity, that they had to rely on Democratic votes simply to organize the House. This rocky start foretold more trouble. Cannon thought party organization and discipline to be essential to Congress which needed a strong majority party to deal with the more than 30,000 bills introduced, for which "there must be a sifting-out process, and preference must be given to the measures that are of vital importance."[52] With no "sifting-out," "every committee would work twenty-four hours every day from the beginning of the session to the end" and still "could not consider one-third of the bills." There was, moreover, no way the whole House could consider all of them should they come to the floor.[53] If not by the party leadership, how, he asked, would this "sifting-out" take place and who would judge which bills were of "vital importance" to the nation? It was through party control of committees, especially the Rules Committee, that responsible prioritizing of bills was achieved. The Rules Committee, he insisted, "simply provides the machinery by which the House can do its business," and ultimately, the "majority is responsible for accomplishment" of that work.[54] To Cannon, it was imperative that the party responsible for legislation should have full power to do its job. Thus, he ratcheted up party organizational control of the House to this end.[55]

Although some might question the wisdom of ratcheting up party leadership control of the House at precisely the time that intra-party divisions were so prominent, Cannon's actions are consistent with the Republican ideology of the day. It was a typical regular Republican response to the uncertainty and organizational "chaos" of the sixty-first House to seek institutional structures and processes necessary to restore "order."[56] To be sure, the insurgents claimed that these efforts were further evidence of "tyranny."

## Order or tyranny in the House?

The House debate, launched by the Norris Resolution, focused on the threats posed by strong party control of the legislative process. It reflected the broader ideological debates of Republican "order versus anarchy" and Democrat "liberty versus tyranny" which in turn traced to that between Hamilton and Jefferson in the nation's formative years.[57] Central to the debate was whether Cannon was a "tyrant" or the progressives were inviting "chaos." Regular Republicans objected to the Norris Resolution, arguing that reform of the rules should be worked out in party conference: "the question before us," Charles Townsend of New Jersey argued, "is one which we can settle in our own party." Regular Republicans saw the Norris Resolution as not merely a threat to Cannon but also a threat to order and representative government as they understood it. In the hands of the minority, Townsend claimed, the Norris Resolution would allow for "filibustering in its worst form."[58] Indeed, J. Warren Keifer of Ohio saw the progressive–insurgent proposal as revolutionary: "I want the country to understand that you are doing what has never been done here before, that you are doing that which leads inevitably to anarchy and the overthrow of the power of the House to do the business we are sent here to do."[59]

Insurgents, on the other hand, believed that they were sent to Congress not to represent party but to challenge the "tyrant from Illinois" and the corrupt interests he and the Republican Party regulars had come to represent. Whereas Keifer and other regulars pleaded for the "order" that only party could provide, the insurgents denied that maintaining the Speaker's power was a matter of party principle. John Nelson of Wisconsin, for example, saw the Speaker's power not as promoting "order over anarchy" but instead, as Democrats might see it, as "an autocracy against which we are in rebellion today."[60] Representative Henry Allen Cooper of Wisconsin dismissed party as a "shibboleth," contending that the idea that a party could bind its members presented the threat of tyranny. To Cooper, there was no democracy in the right of a party Caucus "to control my vote against my well-considered, honest judgment."[61] Other insurgents expanded on these themes throughout the debate.

The fundamental difference, then, between regulars and insurgents was what John Gerring identifies as "Nationalist" Republican orthodoxy versus the "Jeffersonian" Democratic faith: Was Cannon's rule through strong party government the bulwark against the threat of disorder and anarchy, or was it the "tyranny" of the "interests" over the "people"?

## "A majority" versus "the majority"

Insurgents also challenged the idea of what constituted a legitimate majority for the purposes of organizing the House. Reformers wanted to displace rule by the duly election *partisan majority*, arguing that any majority of 50 percent plus one was the most appropriate and legitimate means to secure *democratic* control of Congress. Regulars, led by Cannon, understood this to be a direct challenge to party government and, as such, an affront to the Constitution. Jacob Fassett of New York, with the assent of the Speaker, defended the fact of partisanship:

> We have developed inside of the Constitution, and outside of the Constitution … a government of a great people by great parties, parties that depend for their charters upon the votes of a free people from the various sections of the country, the highest source from which governmental charters have ever proceeded … In this House we are divided by one great line of separation, invisible, but recognizable as clearly as that center aisle is recognizable. On one side are men who have come from constituencies who believe … in the promises and platforms, in the principles, and in the purposes of the Democratic party. On the other side are men who come here as Republicans and govern themselves according to the purposes of the entire Republican party officially expressed. So every man who is a man, and not a jellyfish, is a partisan.[62]

Progressives and Democrats understood their alliance to make them a majority for specific purposes, not as a permanent organization, whereas regular Republicans thought cross-partisan alliances were counter to the principle not only of party government but of majority rule itself. Cannon Republicans believed a bipartisan alliance which sought to control the House had not been authorized by the people in elections. Progressive Republicans may have run against Cannonism, but they had not run promising to cross party lines to achieve that end, and regulars doubted that many of them, if any, would have won had they done so. The Cannonites denounced insurgent efforts to "take the power that the whole people have given to the entire Republican majority and hand it over to the Democratic minority" through "an unnatural and abhorrent alliance with our natural born enemies" who are "not for what your platform declares for."[63]

Regular Republican criticisms of the Progressive view of majoritarianism were twofold: first, Progressives were but a small minority of the majority party and had violated the principle that majorities should rule within parties; and, second, there could be no collective responsibility for the workings of Congress if *any majority* could displace *the majority* in controlling its operation. William Reeder of Kansas put the question squarely: "the question before us to-night is … will we support this effort of a small minority of the majority party to set aside the theory that the majority shall rule? … They insist that they will rule the majority or they will ruin it."[64] Cannon agreed wholeheartedly that parties which controlled the House should reform themselves only through internal democratic processes, which he saw as essential for linking the internal workings and legislative products of the House to choices of the broader public. The conceptual division between reformers and regulars was so deep that they were, for the most part, talking past one another. The Progressive view, which prized the individual over party, seemed to the regulars like an invitation to demagoguery. To Cannon and his allies, the political party was the core of Republican orthodoxy, and efforts to replace the duly-elected partisan majority in the House with any alternative combination was "to substitute disorganization for organization, … disorder for order … personal whim for party responsibility, [and] to substitute the desire of two minorities to become a majority for the legally elected majority, [and] to bereave the American people of its duly elected majority."[65] Differences within the party should be contested within the party, regulars believed, and all members should abide by the majority's decision. Otherwise, the people would not know whom to hold responsible for the actions of the House.

Cannon rarely spoke during the debate, leaving defense of the regular Republican position to subordinates. But, he did engage the House minority leader, Democrat Champ Clark, directly on the issue of this difference between *the majority* (the Speaker's majority) and *any majority*. Defending the coalition's right to change the House rules, Clark argued that he and the Speaker had "always agreed ... that it is competent for a majority of this House to do whatever it wants to do." But Cannon, stressing the importance of organization and responsibility, raised the stakes by responding that "a majority of the House ... could, if it desired, elect ... [Clark] Speaker of the House, and could do it to-day." When Clark replied, "I think it would be doing a very good thing if it did," Cannon responded, "If a majority agreed with the gentleman, then he would be Speaker" adding that he was "prepared" to allow for a vote on the Speakership "whenever any gentleman thinks that the minority has become the majority."[66] It was, however, anti-Cannonism that united Democrats and Republican insurgents and only the most ardent of the insurgents were willing to replace Cannon as Speaker with Champ Clark.

Indeed, during the debate, Clark asked Republican James Mann of Illinois: "Is not the sum and substance of your argument this, that if the majority is a Speaker's majority it has a right to do as it pleases, but if it is an anti-Speaker's majority there ought not to be any attention paid to it?"[67] Mann dismissed Clark's question as not serious, though it may well have been one of the more incisive questions posed in the debate. Regulars might recognize the right of nonpartisan majorities to rule on certain questions, but they nevertheless believed that partisan majorities were more responsible, and thus more legitimate, than any alternative coalitions when it came to control of the legislative process. Cannon articulated the commitment to party government and to the virtue of competition between Democrats and Republicans:

> Out of the two great organizations—the minority from time to time putting the majority on its good behavior, seeking to become the majority—will come correct legislation and correct appropriations for the greatest good to the people of the Republic. And if we lose sight of our own importance and of our own position for the time being there will come in our own places better and wiser men, who will not lose sight of the necessity to provide for an orderly procedure under which a majority can work its will. Where responsibility rests, there must be power with the majority to move on, being responsible.[68]

For the most part, insurgents agreed. They just did not want Cannon and "Cannonism."

Reserving his post-revolt bitterness for the insurgents, Cannon had "not one word of criticism" for Champ Clark and respected his efforts as a party leader. "It was his duty to his party to resort to any legitimate tactics to obstruct the majority. There were traitors in the ranks of his enemy [the Republicans], and he [Clark] made use of them for his own advantage."[69] Cannon later drew a military analogy in a speech to the National Association of Manufacturers:

> If there were two great armies facing each other in actual war, and in one army there were those who professed to be with that army, but so professing refused to charge when the order was given by the general in command and availed themselves of that condition to betray their army to the opposing forces, do you know what would be done with them? [A voice, "Shoot them!"] Shooting would be an honorable death under such circumstances. [Laughter and applause.] In actual war they would be hanged.[70]

In their unwillingness to be "regular," the insurgents were, in Cannon's view, traitors not only to the Republican Party but to democracy as well. The Republican insurgents were "20 men who call themselves 'Republicans'—and it doesn't make men Republicans to call them so, as 'by their fruits we shall know them'—these score of men, I say, wanted to throw down 200 Republicans—that is, they were perfectly content to substitute for one big 'czar' 20 little 'czars.'"[71]

## Progressives and party democracy: "By their fruits we shall know them"

The debates over party control of the legislative process and, in the end, the vote to strip Cannon of his chairmanship of the Rules Committee ushered in a Congress of weak parties, strong committees, and increasingly independent members that would characterize Congress for another half century. The battle against Cannonism was embedded in the "irreducibly ideological" partisan debates of the Progressive Era in which the value of and threats posed by strong party organizations were central points of contention.[72] With the defeat of Cannon, the insurgents felt they had succeeded in displacing the "tyrannical" and "czarist" rule of the era. To regulars, however, the bipartisan Democratic–Progressive alliance had succeeded only in leading the House into "chaos."

The House had, in fact, been in "chaos" since the 1908 election. Neither party could truly organize the chamber: Democrats were the minority and Republicans, with a narrow and divided majority, lacked effective control. Progressive insurgents held the balance of power between regular Republicans and the Democrats. But, if the regular Republican majority was insufficient to control the House, Cannon nevertheless refused voluntarily to permit the minority party or the minority within the Republican Conference to win control. Once his ruling on the Norris Resolution was overridden by the Progressive–Democratic alliance, Cannon took the unexpected step of inviting a motion to vacate the Speaker's chair and proceed to a new Speakership election. Some have portrayed this as an example of his greater commitment to "personal power" than to party responsibility, but these arguments hold Cannon to a particularly British view of the notion of party government rather than to Cannon's American view of party government.[73] Had Cannon recognized this as a vote of "no confidence," it was unclear who or what would emerge in the absence of his leadership. "The real truth," he argued, "is that there is no coherent Republican majority in the House of Representatives." Cannon challenged the Progressives and Democrats to formalize their alliance and to stand before the people by taking responsibility for controlling the House: "the real majority," he said, "ought to have the courage of its convictions, and logically meet the situation that confronts it ... so that power and responsibility may rest with the Democratic and insurgent Members who, by the last vote, evidently constitute a majority of this House."[74] A firm believer in an American style of party government, Cannon made the case for party democracy, but if the Progressive–Democratic alliance would not accept responsibility for ruling the House, he would.[75] He retained the office because most progressives were reluctant to turn the House over to Democrat Champ Clark and the "party of rebellion." Still, though he remained in the Speaker's Chair for the remainder of the sixty-first Congress, Cannon clearly had been defeated as had strong party organization and party responsibility which had been central to the governance philosophy of late nineteenth-century American politics.

The *ancien regime* had seen the political party as essential to the organization of a democracy in the nation as well as to the legislative branch charged with making policy for an increasingly complex and nationalizing economy and society. To Cannon and the Old Guard Republicans, only party could provide the collective responsibility and the safeguards against demagoguery necessary for the maintenance of both democracy and liberty.

By contrast, the emergent Progressive vision of American democracy that distrusted party organization and discounted its contributions enshrined instead a strong executive over legislative leadership, the individual politician's sense of the public good over the party platform, and the fragmentation of group politics and direct democracy over the collective responsibility of party in elections. The advance of the Progressive vision of American democracy and governance would be slow and uneven in the decades that followed, but few today would question that the Progressive idea of democracy has become the new American idea of democracy. It is, however, to our detriment that few question its wisdom and explore what was lost in the way of public accountability and responsible government as a result of the triumph of Progressive democracy.

# Notes

1   Thomas Brackett Reed, Republican of Maine, was the powerful Speaker of the House in the fifty-first, fifty-fourth, and fifty-fifth Congresses. His rules gave the Speaker the power to appoint committee chairs and members. He controlled which bills reached the floor for consideration and enjoyed near-arbitrary control over bill progress. Joseph Cooper and David W. Brady, "Institutional Context and Leadership Style: The House from Cannon to Rayburn," *American Political Science Review*, 75 (June 1981): 411–425, esp. 411–413.

2   Robert V. Remini, *The House: The History of the House of Representatives* (New York: HarperCollins, 2006), 268.

3   William Rea Gwinn, *Uncle Joe Cannon: Archfoe of Insurgency* (New York: Bookman Associates, 1957), 25. Gwinn's book is atypical in its serious examination of Cannon's political thought and has had a major influence on my view of Cannon.

4   "Cannon Calls it a Flurry" *New York Times* October 31, 1907, 1; "Speaker Cannon on Panics and Other Things" *New York Times* December 1, 1907, 1. Given the massive amounts of government subsidies and protectionist policies already in place, Cannon was most definitely not making a case for laissez-faire.

5   Quoted in Kenneth W. Hechler, *Insurgency: Personalities and Politics of the Taft Era* (New York: Russell & Russell, 1964), 31.

6   Blair Bolles, *Tyrant from Illinois: Uncle Joe Cannon's Experiment with Personal Power* (New York: W.W. Norton, 1951); Gwinn, *Uncle Joe Cannon*, Scott William Rager, "Uncle Joe Cannon: The Brakeman of the House of Representatives, 1903–1911," in *Masters of the House*, eds. Roger H. Davidson, Susan Webb Hammond and Raymond W. Smock (Boulder: Westview Press, 1998), 63–89. The term "black beast" is from *The Autobiography of William Allen White* (New York: McMillan, 1946), 368.

7   Quoted in "Gompers Invades Cannon's District" *New York Times* September 8, 1908, 5.

8   Cannon, "Protection and Prosperity." Speech to the National Association of Manufacturers, in New York, May 18, 1910. Reprinted in *Congressional Record*, June 14, 1910, 8065–8069, 8066.

9   White, *The Autobiography of William Allen White*, 401.

10  Joseph G. Cannon, "Abraham Lincoln: Speech, the Chamber of Commerce, Pittsburg, Pennsylvania" February 12, 1910, reprinted in the *Congressional Record* 1910, Appendix, 15–19; and Cannon, "Protection and Prosperity,". See, too, an extended interview with Cannon in A. Maurice Low's "The Real Joseph G. Cannon" *Boston Globe* May 2, 1909, reprinted in the Appendix to the *Congressional Record*, 61st Congress, 107–110.

11  Sidney Milkis, *Political Parties & Constitutional Government: Remaking American Democracy* (Baltimore: Johns Hopkins University Press, 1999); Stephen Skowronek, *The Politics That Presidents Make* (Cambridge: Harvard University Press, 1993); and, Jerome M. Mileur, "The Legacy of Reform: Progressive Government, Regressive Politics." In Sidney M. Milkis and Jerome M. Mileur, eds., *Progressivisim and the New Democracy* (Amherst, MA: University of Massachusetts Press, 1999), 259–287.

12  Incredulous, Cannon later said simply, "Why, walnut was the principal hard wood timber of the Wabash valley," *Uncle Joe Cannon*, 26.

13  Cannon, "Abraham Lincoln," 17; see also, Cannon, "Protection and Prosperity," op cit., 8066.

14  Cannon, "Abraham Lincoln," 19.

15  See Walter Dean Burnham, "Party Systems and the Political Process," in *Current Crisis in American Politics*, ed. Walter Dean Burnham (New York: W.W. Norton & Company, 1982), 92–117; James L. Sundquist, *Dynamics of the Party System*, revised edition (Washington: Brookings Institution, 1983).

16 John Gerring, *Party Ideologies in America, 1828–1996* (Cambridge: Cambridge University Press, 1998), 6.

17 Cannon, "Abraham Lincoln," 19.

18 Cannon, "Protection and Prosperity," 8066.

19 David Sarasohn, "The Insurgent Republicans: Insurgent Image and Republican Reality," *Social Science History*, 3 (October 1979), 245–261, 254–257.

20 On the "grudging" nature of cooperation between the two, see Anne Firor Scott, "A Progressive Wind from the South, 1906–1913," *Journal of Southern History*, 29: 1 (February 1963), 53–70; Burnham, "Party Systems and the Political Process," 109.

21 Gerring, *Party Ideologies in America*, 74.

22 Cannon, "Protection and Prosperity," 8067.

23 Sundquist, *Dynamics of the Party System*, 107.

24 Gwinn, *Uncle Joe Cannon*, 18.

25 See Allan Peskin, "Who Were the Stalwarts? Who Were Their Rivals? Republican Factions in the Gilded Age," *Political Science Quarterly*, 99: 4 (Winter 1984–1985), 703–716.

26 Theodore Roosevelt as quoted in Lewis L. Gould, *The Presidency of Theodore Roosevelt* (Lawrence: University of Kansas Press, 1991), 277.

27 See Gwinn, *Uncle Joe Cannon*, 37–38.

28 Theodore Roosevelt to William Howard Taft, March 19, 1903, *The Letters of Theodore Roosevelt*, 450–451.

29 Signs of anti-Cannonism, muted at first, emerged in the 1906 elections with progressives criticizing the Speaker and even some regular Republicans asking that Cannon not campaign for them; Lewis L. Gould, *Reform and Regulation: American Politics, 1900–1916* (New York: Wiley & Sons, 1978), 66.

30 Theodore Roosevelt to James Watson, August 10, 1906; quoted in Gwinn, *Uncle Joe Cannon*, 116.

31 Plank quoted in "Denver Platform Not to Be Extreme," *New York Times* July 5, 1908.

32 Letter 200, "Records Re. Committee Assignments, 60th and 61st Congress," National Archives and Records Administration.

33 See the following *New York Times* articles: "Tawney Blames Democrats: Declares They Voted in Republican Primaries and Defeated Him" September 21, 1910, 2; "Parties in Kansas Fear Silent Vote" October 30,

1910, 11; "Boutell Defeated in Illinois Primary" September 16, 1910, 2;
"Revolt in Illinois Against Cannonism" October 9, 1909, 5; "Democrat
Elected By Heavy Majority" February 2, 1910, 1; "Vermont Democrats
Meet" July 15, 1910, 2; "Fowler Attacks Cannon" December 6, 1909, 2;
"Plan to Defeat Longworth: Insurgent Republicans Want Charles H. Jones
to Oppose Him" August 21, 1910, 3.

34  "Parties in Kansas Fear Silent Vote," *New York Times* October 30, 1910, 11.

35  Cannon, "Abraham Lincoln," 19.

36  Cannon, "Abraham Lincoln," 19.

37  Low, "The Real Joseph G. Cannon," 107.

38  In praise of party organization, Cannon said, "Take a single strand of
untwisted thread, and the infant but a day old by the movement of its
fingers would tear it asunder. If you twist it and make a beautiful cord,
twofold strong, threefold stronger, and fourfold not easily broken;"
Cannon, "Protection and Prosperity," 8066.

39  Cannon, "Protection and Prosperity," 8066.

40  Cannon, "Abraham Lincoln," 19.

41  See Tulis, *The Rhetorical Presidency* for a discussion of the long-standing
nature of this debate from the Founding era to Woodrow Wilson's defense
of presidential rhetorical leadership.

42  Cannon, "Protection and Prosperity," 8066; Cannon, "Abraham Lincoln,"
19; and, *Congressional Record*, 61–62, June 18, 1910, 8489.

43  Quoted in Low, "The Real Joseph G. Cannon," 107.

44  Cannon, "Protection and Prosperity," 8067.

45  Cannon, "Abraham Lincoln," 17.

46  Quoted in Low, "The Real Joseph G. Cannon," 108.

47  See, for example, Cooper and Brady, "Institutional Context and Leadership
Style," 416–417.

48  Gerring, *Party Ideologies in America, 1828–1996*, 6.

49  Keith Krehbiel and Alan Wiseman, "Joseph G. Cannon: Majoritarian
from Illinois," *Legislative Studies Quarterly*, 26:3 (August 2001), 357–389;
Charles O. Jones, "Joseph G. Cannon and Howard W. Smith: An Essay
on the Limits of Leadership in the House of Representatives," *Journal of
Politics*, 30: 3 (August 1968), 617–646; John D. Baker, "The Character of
the Congressional Revolution of 1910," *Journal of American History*, 60: 3
(December 1973), 679–691.

50 Cannon, "Protection and Prosperity," 8067.

51 Defectors included Cary, Cooper, Kopp, Lenroot, Morse, and Nelson of Wisconsin; Davis and Lindbergh of Minnesota; Hinshaw of Nebraska; Hubbard of Iowa; Murdock of Kansas; and Poindexter of Washington; this list is from the "Trunk Materials" Box 5, Folder "Records Re. Committee Assignments, 60th and 61st Congress," National Archives and Records Administration.

52 Quoted in Low, "The Real Joseph G. Cannon," 108.

53 *Congressional Record*, 61–62, June 18, 1910, 8488.

54 Quoted in Low, "The Real Joseph G. Cannon," 108.

55 Quoted in Low, "The Real Joseph G. Cannon," 108.

56 Indeed, even when it became clear that reforms weakening party control seemed likely to pass, just like regular Republican leaders outside Congress, Cannon and the House party leadership sought to preempt reform sentiment by offering their own watered-down reform. On such efforts in states, see Alan Ware, "Anti-Partism and Party Control of Political Reform in the United States: The Case of the Australian Ballot," *British Journal of Political Science*, 30 (2000), 1–29. Cannon followed the same preemptive pattern inside the House; the emergence of Calendar Wednesday in the sixtieth Congress, for example, was in effort to blunt a movement for a Calendar Tuesday. On this internal battle and its subsequent revision in the sixty-first Congress, see Chang-Wei Chiu, *The Speaker of the House of Representatives Since 1896* (New York: Columbia University Press, 1928), 228–236 and Hechler, *Insurgency*, 52–59.

57 Gerring, *Party Ideologies in America, 1828–1996*, 6.

58 *Congressional Record*, 61–62, March 18, 1910, 3414.

59 *Congressional Record*, 61–62, March 17, 1910, 3328.

60 *Congressional Record*, 61–62, March 17, 1910, 3304.

61 *Congressional Record*, 61–62, March 17, 1910, 3318–3122.

62 *Congressional Record*, 61–62, March 17, 1910, 3302.

63 *Congressional Record*, 61–62, March 17, 1910, 3303.

64 *Congressional Record*, 61–62, March 17, 1910, 3316.

65 *Congressional Record*, 61–62, March 17, 1910, 3303.

66 *Congressional Record*, 61–62, March 17, 1910, 3294.

67 *Congressional Record*, 61–62, March 17, 1910, 3333.

68 *Congressional Record*, 61–62, February 14, 1910, 1873–1874.

69  Gwinn, *Uncle Joe Cannon*, 249–250.

70  Cannon, "Protection and Prosperity," 8067.

71  Quoted in Low, "The Real Joseph G. Cannon," 108.

72  Gerring, *Party Ideologies in America*, 6.

73  Jones, for example, argues that "if Cannon was consistent with the party responsibility theory, he would have resigned, not because of his analysis of his personal weakness or strength or because of his view of whether he had made mistakes or not, but due to the simple fact that on a paramount issue, *he had been defeated*;" Jones, "Joseph G. Cannon and Howard W. Smith," 631–632.

74  *Congressional Record*, 61–62, March 19, 1910, 3437. Later he added, that he hoped that "when the polls close in November [1910] next you either give a Republican majority in the next Congress, which, having full power, you may hold responsible, or that you give our Democratic friends a full majority and full power;" Cannon, "Protection and Prosperity," 8067.

75  He said, "This is a government by the people acting through the representatives of a majority of the people. Results can not be had except by a majority, and in the House of Representatives a majority, being responsible, should have full power and should exercise that power; otherwise the majority is inefficient and does not perform its function. The office of the minority is to put the majority on its good behavior, advocating, in good faith, the policies which it professes, ever ready to take advantage of the mistakes of the majority party, and appeal to the country for its vindication ... The country believes that the Republican party has a majority of 44 in the House of Representatives at this time; yet such is not the case;" *Congressional Record*, 61–62, March 19, 1910, 3436–3437.

# 7

# Elihu Root: Balancing Constitutionalism and Democracy

Robert J. Lacey
*Iona College*

Most often remembered for his foreign-policy role at the dawn of American imperialism, Elihu Root (1845–1937) has become a footnote in the history of American political thought. Most students of politics dismiss the ideas of Root as hopelessly antiquated and reactionary and fail to take seriously his nuanced critique of Progressivism. This is unfortunate. His political thought may be more useful now than ever before, for we all live, perhaps unwittingly, in the shadow of Progressivism. With its unreflective faith in democracy as an end in itself, the Progressive worldview has become an enduring part of the American creed. It behooves us all to step back and question what we have accepted on faith. Anyone interested in reexamining the tenets of progressivism could hardly find a worthier intellectual companion than Elihu Root.

Perhaps most surprising is that Root, an archconservative by reputation, actually sympathized with many of the goals of Progressivism. Like many of his contemporaries, he was troubled by the growing inequities produced by the Gilded Age, and he called for measures that would improve the well-being of wage earners and curb the power of big business. He favored reforms that made governmental institutions more responsible to the people and less beholden to party bosses and moneyed interests. He supported governmental reforms, such as the regulation of campaign finance, which promised to improve the performance of representative institutions within the existing constitutional framework. He also saw merit in introducing direct democracy to extra-constitutional institutions, especially primary elections, which promised to check the nominating power of party bosses.

But Root opposed the Progressive call for direct-democracy measures that circumvented representative institutions in government by placing decision-making power right in the hands of the people. In accordance with his conservative principles, he insisted that reforms must bolster, not bypass, established representative institutions and the system of checks and balances. Root believed it was possible to strike a balance between popular sovereignty and individual rights only if representative institutions, after painstaking deliberation, addressed the needs of the people without surrendering to their momentary whims and passions. Both an incisive critic and a cautious supporter of Progressivism, Root offered an unusually well-balanced perspective on the dominant political movement of his time. The Progressive spirit inspired him to question the status quo and even influenced his thinking on a number of issues, but it never moved him to turn against the founding principles enshrined in the Constitution. Root would remain a trenchant opponent of Progressivism, despite his sympathy for many of its goals, because he disapproved of its attempts to alter the constitutional framework created by the founders.

Born and raised in the small town of Clinton in central New York, Root was the son of a professor of mathematics and science at Hamilton College. After receiving his undergraduate degree from Hamilton in 1864, Root made his way to New York City, where he studied law, passed the bar, and quickly established himself as a highly regarded trial attorney. Adding a number of businessmen and corporations to his client list, Root not only became wealthy but also began to associate with men of undeniable political and economic influence. He became active in the Republican Party, chiefly at the local and state levels, and was appointed by President Chester Arthur to serve as US Attorney for the Southern District of New York in 1883.

Root returned to private practice two years later but remained heavily involved in Republican Party activities. Within party circles, he earned a reputation as a bit of a Mugwump, championing a number of reforms—including primary elections, campaign finance reform, and civil-service reform—that he believed would weaken party bosses and thereby improve the effectiveness of representative government. He also expressed sympathy with some measures that would curb the excesses of capitalism, especially monopolistic practices, and improve modestly the well-being of workers and their families. Root responded to civic duty once again when he became a delegate to the 1894 Constitutional Convention of New York, but up to this point, he was the consummate party insider who worked contentedly from behind the scenes.

This changed when President William McKinley nominated Root to serve as Secretary of War in 1899, thrusting him into the national limelight and turning him into one of the most visible public figures in the country. Entering office in the wake of the Spanish-American War, Root immediately faced serious challenges, foremost of which was the occupation of the recently acquired territories, including the Philippines, Cuba, and Puerto Rico. The responsibility of managing the nascent American Empire became Root's principal concern, and his efforts earned him a considerable amount of criticism. His detractors attacked him for downplaying the atrocities committed against insurgents in the Philippines, opposing universal suffrage in all the occupied territories, and negotiating treaties that betrayed the promise of independence made to these countries. But his defenders were just as adamant and praised him for overseeing a civilized form of imperialism that gradually returned sovereignty to the people, but only surrendered the reins completely when they were ready to handle the responsibility of self-governance. Presidents McKinley and Theodore Roosevelt were especially impressed with Root's performance, applauding him for his administrative abilities in particular. His efforts to reorganize and modernize the armed forces laid the groundwork for the emergence of a military power that would play a larger role throughout the twentieth century. Only with great reluctance did TR let Root step down in 1904. A year later, he convinced Root to replace John Hay as Secretary of State.

During his four years as Secretary of State, Root negotiated 103 treaties, only three of which failed to be ratified by the Senate.[1] Many of these agreements created procedures for arbitration, which he deemed the most effective way of settling international disputes peacefully. He was the first Secretary of State to travel outside the country during his term in office, and he worked tirelessly to improve relations with countries throughout the world, particularly those in Latin America and East Asia. For his efforts to bring about international cooperation through the use of arbitration, he was awarded the Nobel Peace Prize in 1912. But perhaps his most important achievement as Secretary State was to temper the impetuous and bellicose nature of President Roosevelt. One of only a few people from whom TR would accept advice and candid criticism, Root exercised considerable influence over his boss. Roosevelt admitted to this when he called Root "the brutal friend to whom I pay the most attention." He often expressed his deep admiration for Root, once referring to him as "the greatest man that has arisen on either side of the Atlantic in my lifetime."[2]

TR and Root seemed to be an odd pair not just temperamentally but also ideologically. While the Rough Rider became known for his progressive policies, Root carried with him a reputation as a stalwart conservative, an apologist for the status quo and the prerogatives of the rich and powerful, and a pawn of Wall Street. William Howard Taft remarked that the differences between TR and Root were always overstated. "The fact is that while neither Root nor I ever got the credit for being the Progressive members of the last Cabinet," said Taft, "we were the most progressive and the two who usually aided and abetted President Roosevelt in what were called his radical policies."[3] Along with TR, Root supported trust-busting, further regulation of corporations and securities, corporate and inheritance taxes, campaign finance reform, and civil-service reform. When TR left the White House in 1909, Root assumed that his days of public service were behind him. But, without seeking the honor, his peers in the state legislature elected him to represent New York in the US Senate, where he served one term and widened his reputation as a stalwart conservative. He agreed with the Taft administration on most issues and, when Woodrow Wilson became president in 1913, found himself in the position of trying to defeat the legislative agenda of the Democrats. It was during this time that Root also had a falling out with TR which, for many of his contemporaries, merely confirmed his unequivocal hostility toward Progressive reform and the irreconcilable ideological differences between the two men. The story of their severed friendship, however, does not expose Root as a reactionary and indiscriminate opponent of Progressivism but rather as an insightful critic of its enthusiasm for direct democracy.

When it became clear in January 1912 that Roosevelt would seek the Republican Party nomination for the presidency, Root faced a dilemma: While his affection for and loyalty to Roosevelt ran deep, Root had already publicly endorsed President William H. Taft for a second term. Root had known TR for over twenty-five years and had served in his cabinet twice, first as Secretary of War from 1901 to 1904 and then as Secretary of State from 1905 to 1909. Despite TR's disappointment with his chosen successor and the inevitable grumblings from the progressive wing of the Republican Party, Root saw no reason why there should be any serious challenges to the incumbent president's nomination. Going back to the days when they served together under TR, Root had always admired Taft's legal mind and administrative abilities, and he considered the first term of the Taft presidency an overall success in its adherence to Republican principles. Torn by conflicting loyalties, he had to choose between his close friend and his party.

In the end, Root did what he thought was best for his party—and the country. The Roosevelt insurgency troubled Root because it deepened the divisions within the Republican Party and, even more distressing, reduced the chances of a Republican victory in the general election. On February 12, Root wrote a letter to Roosevelt, making an impassioned plea for party unity and urging the Rough Rider to consider how his ill-considered run for the presidency would affect his place in history. It was too late. TR had already set the wheels in motion, arranging for nine Republican governors to write a formal letter inviting him to seek the nomination for president. Dated three days before Root's appeal, the governors' letter gave TR the reason to run. On February 21, TR announced his candidacy while making his way to Columbus, Ohio, famously declaring, "My hat is in the ring." In the speech delivered later that day, Roosevelt expressed his support for the popular recall of state judges and judicial decisions. Although "we should be cautious about recalling the judge," said Roosevelt, "the people should have the right to recall [his] decision if they think it wrong. We should hold the judiciary in all respect; but it is both absurd and degrading to make a fetish of a judge or of any one else."[4] Once he heard about the speech Root knew that he had to oppose Roosevelt's presidential bid.

By attacking the notion of an independent judiciary, the Rough Rider had strayed too far into the Progressive camp. TR now embraced the view that judges must be answerable to popular opinion and that the people should have the final word on the meaning of the law. In doing so, Roosevelt aligned himself with the supporters of direct democracy, who believed that such measures as the recall, the initiative, and the compulsory referendum served as necessary correctives to the Founders' cumbersome and elitist institutional framework. Root disagreed wholeheartedly, insisting that an independent judiciary represented the last defense against majority tyranny. He praised the system of checks and balances for fostering deliberation and compromise, resisting the temporary whims and passions of the people, and effecting change incrementally.

The election placed a strain on their friendship, culminating in a complete break when TR accused Root of treachery at the Republican National Convention. Presiding as chairman of the convention, Root made a ruling that awarded the vast majority of contested delegates to Taft and thereby ensured the president's renomination. As the clear favorite of rank-and-file Republicans, Roosevelt cried foul and accused Root of betraying the popular will within the party. But, Root made his decision strictly in accordance with the convention rules, which at the time favored not popular will but incumbency. It was quite appropriate that Root would dash the presidential hopes of TR—and sever their friendship for good—by adhering to the rules despite overwhelming popular opinion. As will become abundantly clear, his political thought rested on a reverence for the rule of law and the institutions that order our lives.

## Government and politics in a changed America

Elihu Root admired the design of government devised by the framers and objected to the casual indifference of many Progressives toward the Constitution. Though a reputation as an unreconstructed conservative followed him from the moment he split with Roosevelt at the 1912 GOP convention, Root was never an entrenched opponent of change. Indeed, he sympathized with the need for reform, recognizing that the rapid pace at which the world was changing posed problems and challenges that our forefathers, living in a simpler time, could never have anticipated. He often remarked in public addresses that the modern industrial world had created a condition of interdependence that put even the most competent individual at the mercy of economic and social forces over which he had no control. These forces, Root argued in a speech at Princeton University, "greatly reduced the independence of personal and family life. In the eighteenth century life was simple. The producer and consumer were near together and could find each other. Every one who had an equivalent to give in property or service could readily secure the support of himself and his family without asking anything from government except the preservation of order." The familiar image of pastoral self-reliance, once a reality for so many Americans, could never be recaptured. "Today almost all Americans," Root concluded, "are dependent upon the action of a great number of others persons mostly unknown. Their food, clothes, fuel, light, water—all come from distant sources, of which they are in the main ignorant, through a vast, complicated machinery of production and distribution with which they have little direct relation. If anything occurs to interfere with the working of the machinery, the consumer is individually helpless."[5]

Root feared the unchecked growth of the national government, but he also understood the need for it. It had become increasingly obvious to the American people that "the local laws of the separate states … are inadequate for the due and just control of the business and activities which extend *throughout* all the states, and that such power of regulation and control is gradually passing into the hands of the National Government," he said in an address before the Pennsylvania Society in New York. "Sometimes by an assertion of the interstate commerce power, sometimes by an assertion of the taxing power, the National Government is taking up the performance of duties which under the changed conditions the separate states are no longer capable of adequately performing."[6]

Root believed it was the obligation of government to mitigate the excesses of the Gilded Age, especially the widening gap between the rich and the poor. He recognized that the concentration of wealth in the hands of the few defied any common-sense understanding of fairness, for it reduced an increasing number of working people to abject poverty. He also feared that the failure to address the injustices of capitalism would intensify conflicts between capital and labor. "We are now witnessing the natural and inevitable struggle for a fair division of this new and rapidly increasing wealth," Root told an audience at Yale University, adding that "the wage-worker should have his fair share in increase of wages and decrease in hours of labor." The capitalist had taken advantage of his powerful position to get "more than is fair," amassing "enormous fortunes without apparently violating any law" while generating "really no return whatever to the wealth of the community." Root was careful not to cast moral judgment on business leaders, for he understood that they acted in accordance with the incentive structure permitted by the law. In his view, the rules governing the activities of corporations had to "be changed so that unconscionable advantages cannot be lawfully obtained."[7]

It would be a mistake to make too much of Root's appeals to economic fairness. He never endorsed the labor movement or expressed heartfelt sympathy for the plight of the working class. He saw Progressive reforms that curbed the rapacity of big business mainly as a way to promote social harmony. Speaking to the Union League Club in New York City, Root struck a Burkean tone in suggesting that the Progressive reforms endorsed by TR were actually "the greatest conservative force for the protection of property and our institutions" because they prevented class warfare by promoting a fair balance between capital and labor. "There is a better way to deal with labor, and to keep it from rising into the tumult of the unregulated and resistless mob than by starving it, or by corrupting its leaders," he said. Root recognized that the preservation of what is worth keeping—such as property rights and individual liberty—required placating the laboring class, making accommodations that are far preferable to the alternative, namely "the tumult of the unregulated and resistless mob." If continually provoked by an unjust system, workers might lose their faith in the American creed and, with their numerical advantage, "pull down" the government in a fit of revolutionary fury.[8]

Root believed that government could bring an end to class strife in America only if there was a dramatic rise in civic engagement. In his view, "the burden and duty of government rest upon all men, and no man can retire to his business or his pleasures and ignore his right to share in government without shirking his duty," said Root. "The experiment of popular government cannot be successful unless the citizens of a country generally take part in the government. There is no man free from the responsibility."[9] All citizens in a free society, moreover, must discuss various issues of public interest not only with like-minded people but also with those who have different perspectives and opinions. Only through "discussion, information, sincere and earnest attempt to get at each others' minds and to learn as well as to teach among people with different environments, different specific interests and different points of view" will citizens arrive at a stable notion of the common good—or, as Root put it, a "common public opinion."[10]

Root's call for civic engagement seems to strike a Progressive chord with his suggestion that the failures of American democracy required more democracy. Unlike many of his Progressive contemporaries, however, Root did not call for more political engagement within the institutions of government. Instead, he urged people to fulfill their civic obligations as active participants in a major political party. The important role that political parties play in a democracy underscores why voting was not enough to satisfy the duties of citizenship. "Merely voting," said Root "is a small part of the political activity necessary to popular government. An election is only the final step of a long process by which the character of government is determined. The election records the result of the process; the real work of government is the process."[11] By the time someone votes, there are only two realistic candidates from whom to choose and a limited number of salient campaign issues on which to base his choice. Nominating candidates, setting agendas and policy priorities, and drafting platforms all occur long before any elections take place. In these earlier, and generally uncelebrated, stages of the political process, said Root, citizens have real opportunities for meaningful participation and a better chance of making a significant impact.[12]

Root did not share the antipathy many Progressives felt toward political parties but instead embraced the need for a "responsible parties" system. He believed that the refusal to engage in party politics "would bring our constitutional government to an immediate end, wreck our prosperity, and stop our progress." Indeed, he thought that democracy could not function without the existence of political parties, because they performed the necessary service of organizing people around general principles of government that offered voters a clear choice. He envisioned "two great political parties [that] oppose each other upon fundamental differences, the members of each differing in many respects among themselves upon minor questions but not allowing those differences to break up their party."[13] In other words, each major party comprised active citizens who transcended narrow self-interest and, after a considerable amount of debate and discussion, resolved their differences on smaller matters in order to arrive at a conception of the common good. On election day, voters got to choose the common good toward which they wanted government to work. The party that won control of the institutions of government would enact policies pursuant to that notion of the common good. When the majority party fell into disfavor with the voters, it would be punished at the polls in the next election.[14]

Root acknowledged that the responsible two-party system was a theoretical ideal to which American democracy did not always adhere in practice. He believed that the unalterable tendencies of human nature led parties to revert to a "lower type" in which general principles were replaced by selfishness and personal ambition, a tendency that machine politics encouraged by "turning elections into contests not over principle but for spoils."[15] Even more troubling to Root was that machine politics threatened to undermine constitutional democracy by creating an "invisible government" led by party bosses who exercised power without accountability or limits. "The party leader," said Root, "is elected by no one, accountable to no one, bound by no oath of office, removable by no one."[16] Elected officials were too often "subservient to the party leader" and did not answer to the people who elected them. Instead, they followed the commands of the party boss, "the real governing power" who operated "without legal responsibility" or "legal restrictions."[17] At the 1915 Constitutional Convention of New York, Root suggested that this concentration of power in the hands of the party leader smacked of "autocracy" and urged his fellow delegates to "restore power" to the public officials who were "elected by the people, accountable to the people, removable by the people."[18] To this end, he supported primary elections, civil-service reform, and campaign finance reform, which he saw as effective means of making parties committed to principle and government answerable to the people.

Root praised the "widespread pressure for direct primaries" which revealed the determination among rank-and-file party members "to secure a real expression of their own will in the selection of candidates."[19] Vesting in the people the power to nominate candidates for office, primaries deprived political bosses of perhaps their most important source of leverage over elected government officials. Once nominated by the rank and file of their party, government officials were no longer beholden to political bosses who concerned themselves primarily with distributing patronage and favors. Under the primary system, elected officials had a mandate to enact policies embraced by the party activists who nominated him. In various public addresses and private letters, Root made his support for the primary abundantly clear. "For my own part," he wrote, "I still think, as I said at the Saratoga Convention last summer, the representation of the Legislature would be improved and the confidence of the voters increased by a method of nomination which makes the members of the Legislature more directly responsible to the voters and less responsible to the managers of the political machinery."[20]

Unlike many Progressives, however, Root had no illusions that primaries would achieve all that was claimed for them. In his view, "no arrangement of machinery for bringing about nominations can be effective in securing popular control unless the people are willing to come to the primaries and vote." The evidence suggested that most people were not willing to take the time to attend to political matters. Nevertheless, he insisted that the people of New York deserved a "fair chance to control their own affairs" by voting in primary elections.[21] Curiously, Root never gave serious thought to the possible unintended consequences of primary elections, some of which he might have found even more troubling than the autocratic rule of party bosses.

Perhaps Root never mused over the long-term implications of the primary because he expected that a more effective method of nominating candidates would soon replace it. He wrote to a friend that he regarded the primary as a noble attempt "to get away from a bad old system" but also as "a stopping place through which the voters are passing on their way to some system which will be developed without the manifest evils of the primary."[22] He echoed this sentiment in his Princeton lectures, suggesting that the primary and related reforms are temporary measures that point to future advances. "None of these expedients is an end in itself," he said. "They are tentative, experimental. They are movements not towards something definite but away from something definite."[23] But, with nothing better on the horizon, he accepted primaries as an imperfect nominating system that represented an encouraging improvement over past practices.

Root also saw a number of reasons to be encouraged by civil-service reform, largely because, like the primary, it weakened party bosses. While the primary took away their nominating power, civil-service reform made merit the basis for obtaining "a great mass of governmental offices and employments" that in the past were doled out by bosses in exchange for political loyalty.[24] With less patronage to distribute, the boss did not enjoy the same leverage over most public employees, and thus his electoral influence would diminish. Root applauded this outcome, but his enthusiasm for civil-service reform went beyond his objection to party bosses. Indeed, his chief concern was that, because the patronage-based system placed loyal but unqualified people in public sector jobs, the quality of government services suffered. At the 1894 Constitutional Convention of New York, Root spoke in support of civil-service reform, quoting President Grant favorably as saying: "The present system does not secure the best men and not even fit men for public office." After having served as Secretary of War for nearly five years, Root knew from experience the value of civil-service reform. "[I]f it were not for the Civil Service Law," he wrote to a friend, "every head of a department of Washington would become a raving maniac in the course of a few months."[25]

Root also believed that campaign finance reform would serve the public interest. At the 1894 Convention, he voiced his support for an amendment that would empower the legislature to reduce the influence of money in politics and also ban corporations from giving money, directly or indirectly, to any political organization for the purpose of promoting the nomination or election of any candidate for public office. "Until that is done," he said, "there is absolutely no limit to corruption, no limit to the purchase of votes, no limit to the improper influence of voters, or of parties, or of party men." He was especially troubled by the influence that "moneyed interests" wielded over political parties and by extension the candidates they nominate for office. With parties becoming increasingly reliant on corporations and businessmen, he saw this proposed amendment as the only way to put an end to this "great crying evil of American politics."[26]

Root's support for a number of Progressive reforms showed that he was neither insensitive to the problems of his day nor unwilling to address them using the power of government. Unlike many Progressives, however, he insisted that reform should never defy the principles of government enshrined in the Constitution and that the amendment process should remain a last resort. Only when overwhelming evidence indicated that the solution to an existing problem demanded constitutional amendment should the reformer pursue that course of action. Every alternative had to be exhausted before taking such a radical step. Until then, the reformer had to seek improvements within constitutional parameters, however frustratingly slow that process may be. A great admirer of the Founding Fathers, Root agreed with their assessment that the sinful nature of human beings made necessary a constitution that placed limits on the power of government, slackened the pace of change, and protected individual rights. Nevertheless, he maintained that the American constitution could accommodate the demand for progress in the modern world—that reformers could pursue Progressive ends through Madisonian means.

## The assault on representative government

Root sympathized with many of the goals of Progressivism but could not accept the methods reformers proposed to achieve them. Progressives seemed to have given up on representative institutions and decided that the best way to reinvigorate American politics was to create mechanisms that enabled the people to circumvent established institutions by acting directly to achieve their ends through the initiative, referendum, and recall. Root disagreed, arguing that these cures were worse than the disease. In his view, the Progressive support for direct democracy rested on dubious assumptions about human nature and popular sovereignty. It is these fatal errors in judgment, Root concluded, that led Progressives to abandon their faith in representative institutions.

At the core of Root's critique of Progressivism was his fairly pessimistic view of human nature. Subscribing to what one of his biographers called a "Calvinistic insistence upon the depravity of human nature," he saw human beings as inherently wicked and wayward creatures.[27] He expressed this viewpoint in many speeches and private letters, but a few examples should suffice. At the 1912 Republican State Convention, he praised the founders for creating a government based on the proposition that "our natures are weak, prone to error, subject to fall into temptation and to be led astray by impulse."[28] In a speech on the Senate floor, Root declared that human beings were "fallible" and "prone to evil." In a letter to then-Secretary of State John Hay, he called man "a jealous and pernickety animal."[29] What made matters worse was the relative immutability of human nature. While Root believed that people were somewhat educable, he doubted that they could change significantly for the better. "Human nature does not change very much," he said. "The forces of evil are hard to control now as they always have been."[30] He observed, for example, that "personal selfishness and desire for personal aggrandizement are by no means eradicated from human nature."[31] In the end, Root believed that human beings were hopeless sinners who tried to walk a righteous path but all too often lost their way. No matter how hard they tried, most men were unable to stay on the straight and narrow.

The political implications of Root's views on human nature can be seen in his mistrust of democratic majorities. As we saw in the previous section, Root stressed the importance of civic engagement, but his pessimistic view of human nature led him to conclude that the common people should not wield political power directly. He shared with the founders a belief that "men are no more perfect in the mass than they are as individuals" and that groups can actually amplify the flaws of human nature. "They knew that indeed when men come together or act in great bodies free from the sense of personal responsibility, they will often do things that they would shrink from doing as individuals."[32] As part of a group each person enjoys the cover of anonymity and thus the freedom to act in accordance with his darkest impulses and prejudices. An aggregation of these impulses, especially among those people who belong to the unruly masses, can cause great mischief. "Popular will," he concluded, "cannot execute itself directly except through a mob."[33] Root pointed to the chaos that beset the democracies of antiquity, citing their instability and liability to constant change. It was well-known, said Root, that "the weakness of democratic government was its liability to change with the impulse and enthusiasm of the moment, and, through continual changes, to vary from extreme democracy … to oligarchy and dictatorship."[34] Root opposed direct democracy—that is, any measures that placed political power directly into the hands of the people—because he feared that it would inevitably degenerate into anarchy, whereupon the people would call upon a strongman to restore order.

Root also defended his opposition to direct democracy on the grounds that governments are created not to reflect the will of the majority but to protect the "inalienable Rights" of individuals. Like many conservatives before and after him, he expressed his fear of majority tyranny. "Government does not depend on consent," he argued. "The immutable laws of justice and humanity require that people shall have government, that the weak shall be protected, that cruelty and lust shall be restrained, whether there be consent or not."[35] Root certainly acknowledged the many benefits of government based on consent, but he made it clear that "rights are not derived from any majority."[36] Root came close to embracing natural-law theory with the suggestion that there are "immutable laws of justice and humanity" that precede politics, no matter the type of regime. But he never fully developed his ideas on this issue, perhaps recognizing that his references to inalienable rights and the immutable laws of justice conflicted with his rather pragmatic belief that "public opinion … comes the nearest to being the voice of God that man has ever attained" if formed after exhaustive deliberation.[37]

Nevertheless, Root was able to resolve the tension between individual rights and popular consent in his unwavering allegiance to the Constitution. In the Declaration of Independence, Jefferson seemed to suggest that no such tension existed, that the protection of inalienable rights required consent of the governed. But the framers of the Constitution thought it necessary to strike a balance between consent and rights, which they tried to do by filtering the popular will through a representative government that fragmented power, frustrated majorities, and fostered deliberation and compromise. Their aim was to create a government that answered to the people but did not heed their intemperate and impetuous demands. That is, they wanted cooler heads to prevail before government addressed the concerns of the people.

Progressive critics believed that the Founders went too far in the direction of protecting rights, giving rise to a dysfunctional government that had great difficulty addressing the needs of the people. Root acknowledged that the American political system made legislative action difficult, and he made no apologies for it. In fact, he liked it that way. He preferred a government that did not try to accomplish too much. As Root put it, "you will find that America has suffered not from too little, but from too much legislation; not from too much consideration, but from too hasty and inconsiderate action."[38]

One reason he preferred government that erred on the side of inaction was that he doubted its ability to resolve many of the problems facing modern society. Because of "how little ... it is possible for any government to do," it would behoove us to remember "that we cannot abolish all the evils of this world by statute."[39] Ours was a fallen world, teeming with sinful and selfish people who resisted efforts that threatened their interests. In the end, government could only be as good as the people whom it comprised and represented. Or, as Root said, "government must be imperfect because men are imperfect."[40] In his view, one could hardly expect an imperfect government to make the world a significantly better place. Like Plato's republic, the utopia envisioned by many ambitious reformers could exist only in heaven or in words.

The imperfection of men and government introduced another problem, according to Root. Any government that pursued an ambitious policy agenda was bound to encroach upon individual liberties. He argued that "it is not merely useless but injurious for government to attempt too much." While he acknowledged that "the new conditions" of modern life required "government with authority to interfere with the individual conduct of the citizen to a degree hitherto unknown in this country," he cautioned that such measures "should be jealously watched and restrained." Not only did Root fear that an ever-expanding government may become tyrannical, trampling on individual liberties and bringing misery to untold numbers of people, he also perceived a subtler harm. "The habit of undue interference by government in private affairs breeds the habit of undue reliance upon government in private affairs at the expense of individual initiative, energy, enterprise, courage, independent manhood," he said. "Weaken individual character among a people by comfortable reliance upon paternal government and a nation soon becomes incapable of free self-government and fit only to be governed."[41] With the rise of the administrative state, Root foresaw the transformation of active citizens into passive clients of the state. In exchange for guarantees of economic security and well-being, these clients offered their compliance and their abdication of self-government.

The genius of the Constitution, according to Root, was that it secured individual rights by placing limits on the power of government and making change cumbersome and slow. Even when popular majorities made impetuous demands, the government was bound by "eternal principles of justice" enshrined in the Constitution. These principles compelled government to follow the "rules of right conduct" that were critical to "the protection of liberty and justice and property and order, and made it practically impossible that impulse, the prejudice, the excitement, the frenzy of the moment shall carry our democracy into those excesses which have wrecked all our prototypes in history."[42]

Unrestrained democracy allowed the passions of the people to run amok, paving the way toward tyranny of the majority. The Constitution curbed the popular will by enumerating specific rights on which government could not encroach, fragmenting power into separate and distinct branches of government, reserving all powers not specifically vested in the national government to the states, and giving courts the authority to declare null and void all statutes and executive actions that exceeded constitutional limits. Root celebrated these features of the American constitutional regime in many of his public addresses, impressing upon his audiences his view that people could only be free when government operated under clearly defined limits, within a framework of rules and laws. As he puts it, "free government is impossible except through prescribed and established governmental institutions, which work out the ends of government through many separate agents, each doing his part in obedience to law."[43]

Root did not think that placing limits on the power of government made it dysfunctional or incapable of addressing the emerging problems of modern life. He believed that the Constitution was flexible, allowing the government to meet those challenges that the Founders could never have anticipated or abided. "Many interferences with contract and with property which would have been unjustifiable a century ago are demanded by the conditions which exist now and are permissible without violating any constitutional limitation," he said. "What will promote these objects the legislative power decides with large discretion, and the courts have no authority to review the exercise of that discretion."[44] So long as the courts exercised restraint and refrained from encroaching on the fairly broad constitutional authority of Congress, the government would be able to handle emerging problems effectively. Root even maintained that amending the Constitution would prove unnecessary, insisting that "the process of reform which has now begun, will go on to a successful end, in conformity to the Constitution as it is."[45] In other words, the Constitution did not erect impediments to reform.

Root thus believed that the Constitution struck an appropriate balance by creating limited but effective government, securing individual freedom while permitting reforms that improved the general welfare. Perhaps most crucial in maintaining this balance was representative government, which he called "the greatest gift of our race to the development of freedom."[46] Root saw representative government not only as a practical necessity given the sheer size of the United States and the complexity of modern problems but also as the best way to channel the behavior of political actors toward moderation, deliberation, and compromise. "[T]he only method by which intelligent legislation can be reached is the method of full discussion, comparison of views, modification and amendments of proposed legislation in the light of discussion and the contribution and conflict of many minds," said Root. "This process can be had only through the procedure of representative legislative bodies."[47] While representative bodies may work slowly, trying the patience of those who want immediate results, Root found the alternative far more frightening. "Remember that long discussion, free, open, unrestrained and unchecked discussion in representative assemblies under our form of representative government, is the substitute for war," he told a group of New York businessmen.[48]

Perhaps most worrisome about direct-democracy measures such as the initiative and the referendum was that they required people to give proposed laws an up-or-down vote without the opportunity to discuss the matter further or to put forward amendments. Voters did not have the benefit of working within an institution governed by rules and customs that promote decorum. Without due consideration for others, they cared only about satisfying their own interests. As a result, it was inevitable that direct democracy would produce unwise legislation and political unrest. "For this reason," Root said, "the attempt to legislate by calling upon the people by popular vote to say yes or no to complicated statutes must prove unsatisfactory and on the whole injurious."[49] What also troubled Root about the initiative and referendum was that they gave citizens the power of legislators without the responsibility. It was incumbent on lawmakers to deliberate, discuss, and compromise before casting their votes. The initiative and the referendum gave citizen-legislators immediate gratification, allowing them to forgo those arduous steps and skip right to the final act.

According to Root, anyone who truly understood the reasons for the failure of representative institutions would have seen why direct-democracy measures such as the initiative and the referendum were such a bad idea. The lackluster performance of representative institutions was, after all, the result of the failure of citizens to fulfill their civic obligations. They neither engaged in party politics so as to nominate worthy candidates for public office nor made wise voting choices at the polls. It was, therefore, illogical to expect that those very same disengaged citizens would somehow transform themselves and assume the even more burdensome and time-consuming responsibilities of direct democracy. "[T]he attempt to reform government by escaping from the duty of selecting honest and capable representatives, under the idea that the same voters who fail to perform that duty will faithfully perform the far more onerous and difficult duty of legislation," he said, "seems an exhibition of weakness rather than of progress."[50] For Root, a political system that relied on additional citizen participation in government could only generate more disappointing, if not disastrous, policy outcomes.

In the long run, Root believed, a system that gave preference to direct democracy would have an even more troubling consequence: a representative government with greatly diminished public standing. "There is moreover a serious danger to be apprehended from the attempt at legislation by the initiative and compulsory referendum, arising from its probable effect on the character of representative bodies," Root said. These direct-democracy measures were instituted in many states because of a growing distrust of legislatures for their alleged failure to represent the people faithfully. The same distrust led to additional constitutional reforms that placed "a great variety of minute limitations" on the power of legislative bodies, and "the legislative representatives who were formerly honored, are hampered, shorn of power, relieved of responsibility, discredited, and treated as unworthy of confidence."[51]

Progressives instituted these reforms in large part because, in their view, state legislatures had failed the public trust. The problem, however, was that the initiative, the referendum, and other reforms that limited the authority of state legislatures failed to cure the evils of the system and instead served only to make them even less capable of representing the people. Most Progressives saw these reforms as a supplement to representative institutions and as a useful way to improve their overall performance by keeping them honest. But Root insisted that the actual effect was quite the opposite. Stripped of power, prestige, and credibility by these measures, state legislatures would attract fewer worthy men to serve in their hallowed chambers and, as a result, would find it even more difficult to regain the public trust.

For similar reasons, Root opposed the Seventeenth Amendment, which established the direct election of US Senators. Root commonly associated the direct election of Senators with the initiative and the referendum because it was yet another "expression of distrust for representative government," especially of state legislatures, to which the Constitution had given the power to elect US Senators. "[W]hat is to become of the state legislatures if we follow the principles of this resolution?" Root asked his colleagues in the Senate. "You can never develop competent and trusted bodies of public servants by expressing distrust of them, by taking power away from them, by holding them up to the world as being unworthy of confidence."[52] As with the initiative and the referendum, the direct election of Senators sent a clear signal that state legislatures could not be trusted with any serious responsibility.

Root believed that the same faulty reasoning used to justify the initiative and referendum also lay behind the Seventeenth Amendment. State legislators may have deserved the contempt with which they were often held, but they were elected by the people. And, if the people were not competent enough to elect good men to fill the seats of the state legislature, there was no reason to think they would do a better job selecting men to serve in the Senate. Indeed, underlying the proposal to elect senators directly was an illogical "proposition that the people who cannot elect honest men from their own neighbors can elect honest men to the Senate of the United States."[53]

Root predicted that the people would quickly prove their incompetence in electing Senators. No longer would the Senate have "the service of a large class of citizens who are specially qualified by character and training to render a peculiar kind of service specially needed for the purposes of the Senate; men who by lives of experience and effort have attained the respect of their fellow-citizens." Distinguished men of this sort "undertake the burdens of public office" as a "patriotic duty;" they would never "subject themselves to the disagreeable incidents, the labor, the strife, the personalities of political campaign." In their place would emerge men who coveted a seat in the Senate and stooped to all manner of demagoguery and electioneering in their efforts to win the prize. Ultimately, the Senate "will cease to be a deliberative body if every Senator has to convince, to explain to the great body of the people of his state every act he performs and every concession he makes."[54]

Particularly exasperating to Root was the fact that the Seventeenth Amendment was unnecessary. Indeed, the main problem to which its proponents often called attention required only a simple statutory remedy. In 1866, Congress passed a law that required state legislatures to elect a US Senator by a majority, which often led to a deadlock when several candidates vied for the position. Understandably, the long delays before the state legislature managed to fill a vacant seat in the Senate weakened public confidence in its ability to perform its constitutional duty. Root argued that Congress could easily restore the public trust in state legislatures by repealing the 1866 law and allowing state legislatures to elect Senators expeditiously with a plurality vote.[55] It made little sense to force state legislatures to go through multiple rounds of balloting before a majority could reach an agreement when popular elections typically applied a simple plurality—or "first past the post"—voting system. Given this easy fix, reformers could not justify taking away the constitutional authority of representative institutions. A statute had created the problem; another statute could have solved it.

This was but another example of Root's insistence that reforms, if necessary, should always strengthen existing institutions and improve their performance—and should avoid altering the Constitution whenever possible. Many of the measures discussed earlier—including the direct primary, campaign finance reform, and civil-service reform—received his support largely because he thought that they would bolster both Congress and state legislatures. Root gave serious consideration to any proposed reforms that refined the machinery of government, so long as they did not undermine representative institutions or any other constitutional principles. At the 1915 Constitutional Convention of New York, for example, he used his influence as chairman to push for a number of reforms, including the short ballot, the reorganization and consolidation of executive departments, an executive-driven budget, and simplified court procedures. Root saw these measures as attempts to protect "representative government against the attacks launched upon it by the advocates of direct government with their proposals for the initiative, the referendum and the recall."[56] Root argued that his reform proposals accomplished what many progressives wanted without undermining representative institutions.

Root's support for the short ballot was a case in point. By reducing the number of statewide elected offices, the short ballot would not only ease the burden on voters but also weaken party bosses and the invisible government over which they presided with near impunity. In lieu of elections, the governor would appoint people to these executive positions and make sure that their job performances reflected well on his administration. Under the existing system, in which multiple executive officers had to be elected, the political boss who nominated and supported them exercised his leverage by demanding that they use their positions to spend money and dole out patronage in support of the party organization. The short ballot, then, weakened the party boss and held the executive branch more accountable to the people—and it achieved this goal while shoring up the system of representative government. The whole point of the short ballot, said Root, was "to destroy autocracy and restore power so far as may be to the men elected by the people, accountable to the people, removable by the people."[57] While Root's goal here was consistent with Progressive values, his means were likewise consistent with constitutional principles.

Root also proved his loyalty to constitutional principles in his fight against the recall. As noted earlier, he had a falling out with Theodore Roosevelt after the ex-president exhibited a flagrant disregard for constitutionalism by throwing his support behind the recall of judges and judicial decisions. This use of the recall alarmed Root because it not only compromised the independence of the courts but also effectively took away their ability to exercise judicial review. Afraid of losing their jobs if they made an unpopular decision, judges would become cowardly creatures who capitulated to majority opinion. "Under the recall a judge may be brought to the bar of public judgment immediately upon the rendering of a particular decision which excites public interest and he will be subject to punishment if that decision is unpopular," said Root. "Instead of independent and courageous judges we shall have timid and time-serving judges. That highest duty of the judicial power to extend the protection of the law to the weak, the friendless, the unpopular, will in a great measure fail."[58] Even more troubling to him was that judges would be afraid to exercise judicial review when unconstitutional statutes and executive actions enjoyed widespread popularity. Abandoning its constitutional authority in this way would leave majorities and the other branches of government unchecked.[59]

For these reasons, Root insisted that the recall of either judges or their decisions "would strike at the very foundation of our system of government." He feared that the recall would bring about "a reversion to the system of the ancient republics where the state was everything and the individual nothing except as a part of the state, and where liberty perished." And he deemed it "a repudiation of the fundamental principle of Anglo-Saxon liberty which we inherit and maintain, for it is the very soul of our political institutions that they protect the individual against the majority."[60] As he saw it, the recall of judges or their decisions nullified the Constitution, turning it into merely an advisory document whose principles our government was no longer compelled to follow. In so doing, it created a state that "regarded the individual only as a member of the state," that dismissed the idea that the individual was entitled to "the right to life, to liberty, to the pursuit of happiness, and that government is not the source of these rights, but is the instrument for the preservation and promotion of them."[61] In the end, a state left unchecked by the courts would serve at the pleasure of a majority that knew no bounds and never hesitated to trample on the rights of those who stood in its path.

# Conclusion

Progressives in the early twentieth century often attacked Root for his opposition to many of their proposed reforms. They considered him a shill for Wall Street, an apologist for rich and powerful business elites, an agent of American imperialism, and an enemy of any kind of meaningful reform that would improve the lives of everyday Americans. While such accusations were unfair, it is certainly true that Root did not feel the sense of urgency that motivated many of his Progressive contemporaries. He inhabited a world of privilege teeming with political, economic, and social elites and had little contact with people who toiled in sweatshops and factories, lived in squalid urban tenements, subsisted meagerly as southern sharecroppers, or experienced any other kind of hardship. It was easy for him to warn against impetuous change when he enjoyed the benefits of the current system.

It should come as no surprise, then, that Root was sometimes on the wrong side of history. He opposed extending suffrage to women on the grounds that the competitive aspect of politics was destructive to their feminine nature.[62] He also showed little concern for the plight of African Americans, never voicing his opposition to racial discrimination and segregation, and he actually endorsed the racist theories of prominent eugenicist Madison Grant.[63] Finally, although he considered himself a defender of individual rights, Root betrayed an alarming nationalism during World War I when he called those who expressed dissent "traitors to the United States" and, in a statement that would make even Dick Cheney blush, claimed that some antiwar journalists "deserve conviction and execution."[64]

His disappointing record on some issues notwithstanding, it would be a mistake to characterize Root as a reactionary who resisted reform and progress at every turn. He recognized the need for a more active government that would solve problems arising from new social and economic conditions and an interdependent world. He also endorsed the reform of extra-constitutional institutions such as political parties and the fine-tuning of government machinery. His criticism of the Progressives rested primarily on constitutional principles, never on an aversion to—or a lack of sympathy for—their objectives. He welcomed reform efforts so long as they remained respectful of constitutional limits, and he insisted that any change worth having must be able to run the gauntlet of the admittedly cumbersome American political system. Root accepted the inevitability of change but insisted that its agents should proceed slowly and cautiously, taking pains to preserve those traditions and practices that hitherto had served people so well. "Growth," he wrote to a friend, "is the law of life and the perennial problem is how to hold fast to what is good and essential and at the same time substitute new growth for dead matter."[65] While he appreciated the Progressives' concern about various social and economic problems and their desire for finding an immediate cure, Root believed that it was always advisable to be patient. For a remedy hastily administered would probably end up doing more harm than the original evil.

As Root saw it, the Progressive call for direct democracy—ill-conceived and altogether harmful—was born of this kind of impatience. Progressives championed the initiative, the referendum, and the recall as effective means by which the people could circumvent what reformers saw as woefully corrupt political institutions, thus making government more responsive to their policy aims and holding public officials to account. Root anticipated far different results, the worst of which were majority tyranny and class warfare.

Some of Root's fears have come to pass, as demagoguery has become a pervasive feature of American democracy and the electorate has exhibited an alarming inability to cut through the noise of postmodern life to distinguish fact from fiction, reality from fantasy, and object from simulacrum. Today, we inhabit a world in which even presidents make decisions based on what the political satirist Stephen Colbert calls "truthiness"—truth claims that people arrive at intuitively, without regard for hard evidence or logic. Given the Orwellian character of our times, it may be time to reconsider what Root had to say about the dangers of unfettered democracy and about the role that institutions can play in creating more responsible government.

# Notes

1   Philip C. Jessup, *Elihu Root* (Vol. 1) (New York: Dodd, Mead and Company, 1938), 452.

2   Theodore Roosevelt quoted in Jessup, *Elihu Root* (Vol. 1), 422–423.

3   William H. Taft quoted in Jessup, *Elihu Root* (Vol. 2), 229.

4   Theodore Roosevelt, "A Charter of Democracy," February 21, 1912. Columbus, OH.

5   Elihu Root, "Experiments in Government" (April 15, 1915), *Addresses on Government and Citizenship* (Cambridge: Harvard University Press, 1916), 80.

6   Root, "Speech at the Dinner of the Pennsylvania Society in New York" (December 12, 1906), *Addresses on Government and Citizenship*, 367.

7   Root, "The Citizen's Part in Government" (May 1907), *Addresses on Government and Citizenship*, 70–72. It is worth noting that Root also condemned the actions of labor organizations that served to "put up prices, restrict production, and drive out competition" (72).

8   Root quoted in Jessup, *Elihu Root* (Vol. 1), 416.

9   Root, "The Citizen's Part in Government" (May 1907), *Addresses on Government and Citizenship*, 18.

10  Root, "Importance of Seeking Reform Through State Governments, Remarks at the Tenth Annual Dinner of the National Civic Federation" (November 23, 1909), *Addresses on Government and Citizenship*, 375.

11  Root, "The Citizen's Part in Government" (May 1907), *Addresses on Government and Citizenship*, 23.

12  Root, "The Citizen's Part in Government" (May 1907), *Addresses on Government and Citizenship*, 33.

13  Root, "The Citizen's Part in Government" (May 1907), *Addresses on Government and Citizenship*, 47.

14  Root, "The Citizen's Part in Government" (May 1907), *Addresses on Government and Citizenship*, 47–50. Root envisioned a system of responsible government that anticipated the recommendations of the APSA Committee on Political Parties in "Toward a More Responsible Two-Party System: A Report of the Committee on Political Parties," *American Political Science Review* 44 (1950).

15  Root, "The Citizen's Part in Government" (May 1907), *Addresses on Government and Citizenship*, 48.

16  Root, "Invisible Government, Speech on the Short Ballot Amendment" (August 30, 1915), *Addresses on Government and Citizenship*, 202.

17  Root, "The Citizen's Part in Government" (May 1907), *Addresses on Government and Citizenship*, 54–55.

18  Root, "Invisible Government, Speech on the Short Ballot Amendment" (August 30, 1915), *Addresses on Government and Citizenship*, 202.

19  Root, "The Citizen's Part in Government" (May 1907), *Addresses on Government and Citizenship*, 59.

20  Letter from Elihu Root to Timothy Woodruff (March 19, 1910) quoted in Jessup, *Elihu Root* (Vol. 2), 154.

21  Letter from Elihu Root to State Senator John Raines (April 13, 1909) quoted in Jessup, *Elihu Root* (Vol. 2), 149–150.

22  Letter from Elihu Root to William C. Church (1915) quoted in Jessup, *Elihu Root* (Vol. 2), 150.

23  Root, "Experiments in Government" (April 15, 1913), *Addresses on Government and Citizenship*, 89.

24  Root, "The Citizen's Part in Government" (May 1907), *Addresses on Government and Citizenship*, 58–59.

25  Root quoted in Jessup, *Elihu Root* (Vol. 1), 230.

26  Root, "The Political Use of Money" (September 3, 1894), *Addresses on Government and Citizenship*, 142–144.

27  Richard W. Leopold, *Elihu Root and the Conservative Tradition* (Boston: Little, Brown and Company, 1954), 74.

28  Root, "The Recall of Judges, Remarks in the Republican State Convention at Rochester" (April 10, 1912), *Addresses on Government and Citizenship*, 406.

29  Root, "The Arizona Constitution and the Recall of Judges" (August 7, 1911), *Addresses on Government and Citizenship*, 399; Elihu Root to John Hay quoted in Jessup, Elihu Root (Vol. 1), 350.

30  Root, "Experiments in Government" (April 15, 1913), *Addresses on Government and Citizenship*, 88.

31  Root, "The Citizen's Part in Government" (May 1907), *Addresses on Government and Citizenship*, 48.

32  Root, "The Recall of Judges, Remarks in the Republican State Convention at Rochester" (April 10, 1912), *Addresses on Government and Citizenship*, 406.

33  Root, "Experiments in Government" (April 15, 1913), *Addresses on Government and Citizenship*, 83.

34  Root, "Direct Election of Senators, Address in the Senate of the United States" (February 10, 1911), *Addresses on Government and Citizenship*, 260.

35  Root quoted in Jessup, *Elihu Root* (Vol. 1), 332.

36  Root, "Essentials of the Constitution" (April 16, 1913), *Addresses on Government and Citizenship*, 112.

37  Root, "Importance of Seeking Reform Through State Governments, Remarks at the Tenth Annual Dinner of the National Civic Federation" (November 23, 1909), *Addresses on Government and Citizenship*, 375.

38  Root, "Direct Election of Senators, Address in the Senate of the United States" (February 10, 1911), *Addresses on Government and Citizenship,* 275.

39  Root, "Experiments in Government" (April 15, 1913), *Addresses on Government and Citizenship,* 84–85.

40  Root, "Experiments in Government" (April 15, 1913), *Addresses on Government and Citizenship,* 86.

41  Root, "Experiments in Government" (April 15, 1913), *Addresses on Government and Citizenship,* 85–86.

42  Root, "The Direct Election of Senators" (February 10, 1911), *Addresses on Government and Citizenship,* 260–261.

43  Root, "Experiments in Government" (April 15, 1913), *Addresses on Government and Citizenship,* 83.

44  Root, "Essentials of the Constitution" (April 16, 1913), *Addresses on Government and Citizenship,* 115.

45  Root, "Direct Election of Senators" (February 10, 1911), *Addresses on Government and Citizenship,* 274.

46  Root, "The New York Constitution and Representative Government, Address Before the Economic Club of New York" (October 25, 1915), *Addresses on Government and Citizenship,* 228.

47  Root, "Experiments in Government" (April 15, 1913), *Addresses on Government and Citizenship,* 95.

48  Root, "The Business Men and the Constitutional Convention, Address before the Merchants' Association of New York" (March 25, 1915), *Addresses on Government and Citizenship,* 159.

49  Root, "Experiments in Government" (April 15, 1913), *Addresses on Government and Citizenship,* 95.

50  Root, "Experiments in Government" (April 15, 1913), *Addresses on Government and Citizenship,* 97.

51  Root, "Experiments in Government" (April 15, 1913), *Addresses on Government and Citizenship,* 96–97.

52  Root, "Direct Election of Senators" (February 10, 1911), *Addresses on Government and Citizenship,* 269–270.

53  Root, "Direct Election of Senators" (February 10, 1911), *Addresses on Government and Citizenship,* 271.

54  Root, "Direct Election of Senators" (February 10, 1911), *Addresses on Government and Citizenship,* 275–277.

55 Root, "Direct Election of Senators" (February 10, 1911), *Addresses on Government and Citizenship*, 264.

56 Jessup, *Elihu Root* (Vol. 2), 296.

57 Root, "Invisible Government, Speech on the Short Ballot Amendment" (August 30, 1915), *Addresses on Government and Citizenship*, 202.

58 Root, "Essentials of the Constitution" (April 16, 1913), *Addresses on Government and Citizenship*, 110–111.

59 Root, "Essentials of the Constitution" (April 16, 1913), *Addresses on Government and Citizenship*, 107.

60 Root, "Essentials of the Constitution" (April 16, 1913), *Addresses on Government and Citizenship*, 112. See also Root, "The Arizona Constitution and the Recall of Judges, Address in the Senate of the United States" (August 7, 1911), *Addresses on Government and Citizenship*, 394–402.

61 Root, "Essentials of the Constitution" (April 16, 1913), *Addresses on Government and Citizenship*, 98.

62 Elihu Root at the 1894 Constitutional Convention of New York in Jessup, *Elihu Root* (Vol. 1), 178.

63 Leopold, *Elihu Root and the Conservative Tradition*, 170–171.

64 Root quoted in Jessup, *Elihu Root* (Vol. 2), 328, 331.

65 Root quoted in Jessup, *Elihu Root* (Vol. 2), 503.

# 8

# Eugene V. Debs: Champion of *Social* Democracy

Jerome M. Mileur
*University of Massachusetts Amherst*

Progressivism was in large part a fight for power between factions within the Republican Party, its call for direct democracy as much a weapon as a principle. It sprouted at the turn of the twentieth century from soil well-tilled in the nineteenth by reform movements such as the Greenback, Farmer-Labor, and People's or Populist Party. It shared roots with the movements for civil-service and ballot reform and was fertilized by the new Muckraking journalism in magazines such as *McClure's* that came to prominence in the 1890s. Politically, Robert La Follette and Theodore Roosevelt were its great champions whose pursuit of power for themselves ultimately split the Republican Party both in Wisconsin, La Follette's home, and in the nation by TR's 1912 bid for the presidency. The critics of direct democracy were primarily Republicans, although not exclusively so as the example of Henry Jones Ford attests as does that of Eugene Debs. The latter emerged from the Socialist Left to challenge Progressivism for its shallow understanding of economics and consequent inadequacies as a reform movement. His criticism was also grounded in a different tradition of American thought than that of other critics.

Eugene Victor Debs was born November 5, 1855, in Terre Haute, Indiana, of immigrant parents from the Alsace region of France. His father, Daniel, had been raised in a prominent family whose members were leaders in banking, commerce, and public affairs. Daniel was schooled in Paris and Germany where he acquired a love for idealist and romantic philosophers such as Johann Goethe, Friedrich Schiller, and Victor Hugo. Attracted to the arts and enamored with the revolutions that swept Europe in the 1840s, he turned away from his family's commercial interests and, in 1849, emigrated to the United States, arriving almost penniless. Over the next several years, he married and moved his family West, settling finally in Terre Haute, Indiana, a raw frontier town with a sizable French community. Daniel struggled financially, working at menial jobs until his wife opened a grocery store in their home, after which their fortunes improved.

The Civil War divided the citizens of Terre Haute, as it did in much of southern Midwest, where loyalties lay with both North and South. The war and politics were regular topics of family conversation, and Eugene grew up sharing his parents' loyalty to the Union. Schools in Terre Haute were poor, but Daniel Debs nonetheless stressed importance of education, having named his first son for romantic writers he admired, Eugene Sue and Victor Hugo. He owned two books, the works of Schiller and Hugo's *Les Miserables*, and Eugene devoured both. From Schiller, he acquired an aesthetic sense that the good was beautiful and that human freedom was the greatest of life's objectives. Eugene was especially attracted to Schiller's poem, *The Hostage*, a tale of friendship set in ancient Greece in which the lead character, after trying and failing to kill the tyrant, is sentenced to death but is given a brief stay to attend a family wedding when a friend agrees to take his place to be executed if he does not return. The first then struggles against great obstacles to return just in time to save his friend. Both are brought before the tyrant who, shamed by his action, acknowledges the moral value of fidelity, spares both, and asks to be their friend. But, it was *Les Miserables* to which the young Eugene was most devoted. A tale of social misery and injustice set in France in the 1830s: its hero Jean Valjean, born into poverty, steals bread to feed his family, is imprisoned, and after his release leads a tormented life until redeemed by a small girl and a priest. It became a lifelong lesson and guide for him, a story that Debs read many times and often recommended to others.

Eugene was a good student but, against the wishes of his parents, he quit school at the age of fourteen when a postwar recession put financial strains on his family, which by then included two sisters and a brother. He took a job in the Vandalia railroad car shops, first as a painter and car cleaner, later as a fireman. Although not in school, his education continued at home. His father gave him Voltaire's *Philosophical Dictionary* and talked often with him about the French Revolution in which his ancestors had sided with the Republicans. With savings from his job, Eugene purchased a copy of *appleton's encyclopedia* from which he learned about the American Revolution. "The revolutionary history of the United States and France stirred me deeply," Debs later recalled, "its heroes and martyrs becoming my idols," none more so than Thomas Jefferson and Thomas Paine.[1] Debs's practical education also began with his entry into the world of working men. After four years, he left his job as a locomotive fireman for a position as billing clerk for the largest wholesale grocery company in the Midwest where he remained for another four years, during which time he attended a local business school at night. In 1885, the Brotherhood of Locomotive Firemen, mainly a fraternal organization, established a lodge in Terre Haute, of which Debs was a founding member, though he was no longer a railroad employee. By 1880, he had become its secretary-treasurer and editor of its magazine. He also joined with other young men to form a speakers program, the Occidental Club, which brought many prominent lecturers to the city with whom Eugene was able to spend time, Wendell Phillips and Robert Ingersoll among them. In these years, Eugene was increasingly prominent in the public life of Terre Haute. He was elected city clerk in 1879 as a Democrat, reelected in 1881 and, in 1885, won a term in the Indiana General Assembly.

Debs's experience with the Brotherhood of Locomotive Firemen led him to conclude that workers should be organized on an industrial basis rather than by trade or craft, and in 1893, he organized the American Railway Union (ARU) that enrolled primarily unskilled workers but was open to skilled ones as well. The following year, the ARU conducted a successful strike against the Great Northern Railway, of which the Vandalia line had become a part. It brought national attention to Debs. In the same year, members of the ARU in Chicago struck the Pullman Palace Car Company to protest severe cuts in their wages. Debs was reluctant to become involved but did so as the boycott of Pullman cars spread from the Chicago area to St. Louis and beyond. The company sought help from the federal government, obtaining an injunction against the strike on the grounds that it obstructed the US Mail. Despite the objections of Illinois Governor Peter Altgeld, President Grover Cleveland sent federal troops to Chicago to enforce the injunction. Cleveland's action provoked violence in which thirteen strikers died, led to thousands more being blacklisted, and damaged property worth millions of dollars. Debs and other union leaders were indicted for violating the injunction, found guilty, and sent to prison for six months during which time he was flooded with letters and literature from socialists around the country.

In prison, Debs became acquainted with Milwaukee Socialist leader, Victor Berger, who introduced him to *Das Kapital* and the theories of Karl Marx. While Debs never became a doctrinaire Marxist, he was impressed with much of what he found in *Kapital*: the economic interpretation of history, the theory of society as divided into social classes, the indictment of capitalism for oppressing the working class, and the inevitably of revolution in which workers would seize the means of production and produce a more fair and just society. Debs also read the utopian musings of Edward Bellamy, the single-tax theory of Henry George, the popularized Marxism of Karl Kautsky, the non-Marxist Fabian socialism of Robert Blatchford, and Laurence Gronlund's proposal for a cooperative commonwealth, which set forth a plan for socialism under American conditions. Gronlund conceived the state as a social organism with a "corporate oneness" and a "corporate individuality" that softened doctrinaire Marxist conceptions of class consciousness and protected individual freedom.[2]

After his six months in Woodstock Prison ended in 1895, Debs's political associations fluctuated as he sifted through the labor-oriented reformist politics that filled the final years of the nineteenth century. A Democrat in his Terre Haute years, Debs joined the Populist Party 1892, which he saw as an authentically mass-based reformist organization. In 1896, he endorsed the Populist-turned-Democrat William Jennings Bryan for president. It was his defeat that led Debs to declare unequivocally for socialism. In 1898, he turned his back on both of the major parties, denouncing them as captives of the corporations and led the ARU into a loose alliance with two socialist organizations, the Brotherhood of the Cooperative Commonwealth and Social Democracy of America, to form the Socialist Labor Party. The alliance proved to be unstable and fractured two years later when Debs joined fellow Midwesterner Victor Berger and New York Socialist Morris Hillquit to found the Social Democratic Party, which nominated Debs for president in 1900. But, it too was tormented by factional fights between radicals and moderates and, in 1904, split when the moderates defected to become the core of a new Socialist Party of America which put Debs forward as its presidential candidate that year and again in both 1908 and 1912. Through it all, Debs remained convinced that the cooperative commonwealth, an egalitarian community in which property was owned by all, was the way for socialism to end corporate control of economic and political power and secure the individual liberty promised by the nation's founders.

Factionalism was a continuing frustration for the Socialist movement throughout Debs's lifetime. He hated these fratricidal struggles which he attributed to differences in tactics rather than to philosophy.[3] Debs and Berger themselves had several tactical disagreements, an ongoing one being whether to ground socialism in trade or craft unions such as those in the American Federation of Labor or industrial unions such as the ARU that included all workers, unskilled as well as skilled, in a single union. They nonetheless remained allies for electoral purposes when Debs was nominated for president in 1900 by the Social Democratic Party and, in 1904, by the American Socialist Party. Tactical differences persisted for Debs, who in 1905 joined with Big Bill Haywood and Daniel De Leon to found the International Workers of the World (IWW), which was organized along industrial lines. This antagonized not only Victor Berger and Morris Hillquit, but also and especially Samuel Gompers, president of the American Federation of Labor, who declared war on socialism in all of its forms. Despite strains, the several divisions within Socialism once again stood together behind Debs as the American Socialist Party candidate for president in both 1908 and 1912.

The popularity of socialism peaked in 1911–1912 when the party enrollment surpassed 120,000 paid members and Debs polled 6 percent of the vote in the presidential contest.[4] It declined thereafter, weakened by Woodrow Wilson's New Freedom that incorporated portions of the socialist platform and by the defection of the IWW from the Socialist Party which took a quarter of the party membership with it. It was, however, World War I and its aftermath that dealt a near-fatal blow to both Socialism and Progressivism, neither of which again achieved the political success it had known before the war. Debs opposed American entry into the war and continued to speak against it once the nation had entered the conflict. In 1918, he was convicted of violating the Espionage Act, sentenced to ten years in prison, serving until his sentence was commuted by President Warren Harding on Christmas Day 1921. While in prison, Debs was again nominated for president by the Socialist Party in 1920, won 3.5 percent of the vote, and, until his death in 1926, remained "the preeminent symbol of American resistance to corporate capitalism."[5]

## The making of a socialist

Eugene Debs was not an intellectual, but he was an intelligent man, widely read and a free thinker, who lived his life in a realm of ideology and political discourse in which he maintained an independence of thought that, while principled, was never dogmatic. As a child, he embraced his father's love for the idealism and romanticism of French and German artists and philosophers, which profoundly shaped the devotion to humanity that underlay his thought and action as an adult. He had his first encounter with Marxism in his early forties. He admired its class theory as a historical explanation of social and economic conflict, but while this became a central component of his thought thereafter, he never accepted its determinism or even socialism as an end in itself. "I am for socialism," he said, "because I am for humanity," which to Debs meant achieving the freedom that would enable individuals to realize their full human potential.[6] Ending private ownership of production was but a means to a larger goal, not an end in itself, because he understood that public control of the economy could become as tyrannical as private control. A true revolution required a fundamental change in the hearts and minds of individuals. In this respect, his vision was more messianic than socialist.

Debs was not a theoretician. Indeed, he had no patience for theorists in the Socialist movement, especially the dogmatists, who were in his opinion the primary contributors to the factionalism he disdained. Debs was instead an evangelist in both mind and style, a riveting speaker who used knowledge instrumentally to educate the masses and convert them to socialism. In this, he sought an American idiom that drew heavily from the nation's history and would be familiar to his audiences. The American founding was an epoch on which he relied repeatedly, casting the nation's founders as revolutionaries fighting a repressive regime to win their freedom. He celebrated the *Declaration of Independence* as the guarantor of liberty and the definition of what it meant to be an American. Debs thought it a radical document in its simultaneous recognition of the rights of individuals and the equality of all men. Thomas Jefferson was preeminent in his pantheon of heroes in which Thomas Paine, John Adams, and Patrick Henry were enshrined, as were latter-day rebels and free-thinkers like John Brown and Elijah Lovejoy. Debs was resolute in the belief that all virtuous change came from individuals who challenged the status quo on moral grounds and in the name of humanity, and he, like so many in his generation, placed Abraham Lincoln on a pedestal as the Great Emancipator.

For the most part, Debs was cool to reformers. He described Mugwump reforms in the 1880s as "the Yankee Doodleisms of the Boston savants," and faulted Edward Bellany's *Looking Backward* for its paternalistic attitude "which dwarfs out of sight the individual, while it indefinitely expands government control to absolutism."[7] He joined the Populist Party but disputed its claim to be "one" with working men because its membership included farmers who were employers. In his emphasis on working class' self-reliance, Nick Salvatore observes that Debs "edged paradoxically close to a rejection of all reform schemes that relied on non-workers."[8] Two socialists, Karl Kautsky and Laurence Gronlund, were most influential with Debs. A social democrat, Kautsky was an orthodox Marxist, more moderate than others, who was committed to electoral politics in the transition from capitalism to socialism in which a republic would be a stage. He also downplayed the importance Marx gave to revolutionary activity.[9] Debs agreed. Gronlund was a Danish émigré, Chicago lawyer, and Marxist, who believed the social, economic, and political conditions in the United States ideal for the establishment of a socialist state. His theory of a cooperative commonwealth was attractive to Debs in part because it was an American socialism that was less doctrinaire in its understanding of class consciousness and therefore less of a threat to individual freedom. Debs had embraced the idea of class consciousness but thought it "a good servant but a bad master."[10]

Debs believed a cooperative commonwealth, "adapted to the American people and to American conditions," was a native socialism that could be explained to workers in a historic political language they understood, one that justified revolution against oppression in the pursuit of liberty and equality.[11] He also sought a Christian Socialism with a biblical language familiar to workers in a predominantly Protestant nation that would provide the moral grounds on which he could fault the competitive capitalist system and defend a cooperative one. The first decade of the twentieth century was a time of religious revival in the United States (some called it a Third Awakening) driven in part by a new Social Gospel movement that was challenging an older laissez-faire Protestantism which defended the market economy with its disparities in wealth, had little to say about social injustice, and was content with private charity in dealing with the plight of the poor. Advocates of the Social Gospel believed that the old time religion was having an adverse effect on both the social and spiritual lives of the people. For them, the ministry of Jesus, as found more in his deeds than in the words of the Bible, was the best guide for the lives of both individuals and society.

Most Social Gospel ministers identified with the Progressives, but a number of them were members of the Socialist Party, the most notable being George Herron who gave a nominating speech for Debs in 1904. Herron came to national prominence in 1890 when he delivered a provocative lecture to the Minnesota Congregationalist Club, entitled "The Message of Jesus to Men of

Wealth." In it, he decried the existing social and religious order for placing a "premium on competition, self-interest, and material power" that "failed to secure morality and justice" because "it put the weak at the mercy of the strong and at the same time minimized the paramount Christian principles of stewardship and sacrifice." The day is coming, he declared, when "a truly Christian social order would exist on earth, the fulfillment in the here and now of God's Kingdom of Heaven," in which the ordering of all things "would be in accordance with His divine sanction."[12]

Debs was never orthodox in his religion, never the member of a church, but he was greatly influenced by religious thought and drew regularly on biblical stories. He found religious imagery well-suited to both his message and his charismatic style of public speaking. The vengeful God of the Old Testament and the angry Jesus of the New provided prophetic models that legitimized his critique of capitalism with no need to apologize for his often harsh and personal pronouncements. Debs believed that Americans were God's chosen people destined to create a New Jerusalem, which would be socialist, and he felt it was his mission to spread this good news. He embraced Herron's message and turned it into a yet more radical Socialist Christianity that he used to indict Progressivism for its tepid response to the oppression of workers in a capitalist economy. Citing Herron, Debs argued that "Cain was the author of the competitive theory," while "the cross of Jesus [was] its eternal denial."[13] For him, Jesus was the Supreme Leader, a very real historical figure engaged in advancing a truly sacred cause, namely the struggle of the poor against mammon. Debs depicts Jesus, Nick Salvatore writes, as having "organized a working class movement... for no other purpose than to destroy class rule and set up the common people as the sole and rightful inheritors of the earth." This revolutionist Jesus, in Debs's view, suffered a "farcical trial," was slain, a martyr to his class, then coopted by the ruling class and transformed into "the pious abstraction, the harmless theological divinity who died that John Pierpont Morgan could be 'washed in the blood of the lamb.'"[14]

Debs blended the language and images of Christianity with the revolutionary and class-conscious message of Socialism to produce an appeal to workers that joined their spiritual lives with their everyday experience in the workplace to form a powerful social critique which went beyond economics and politics to social and cultural institutions in an indictment that accused American churches of not only failing to deliver the true message of Jesus but also of being biased against labor. The labor movement, he asserted, represented the true spirit of Christianity because "every blow organized labor strikes for the emancipation of labor has the endorsement of Christ."[15] The Progressives may have bathed their national convention in *Onward Christian Soldiers* and put forward a candidate who proclaimed a "covenant" with the American people and a battle for Armageddon, but it was Debs who traveled the campaign trail daily embracing Jesus in a fight for the poor. Progressivism may have numbered more Social Gospel ministers and their progeny among its party members and public officials, but their new theology was far less radical than that of Debs who mobilized the historic Jesus in dramatic moral appeals on behalf of social democracy.[16] It was, nonetheless, the worldly goal of economic reform (the cooperative commonwealth) that dominated the Debs campaign, just as it was political reform (direct democracy) that dominated the Roosevelt campaign. But where TR was calling for a more pure democracy, Debs at times seemed to be calling for nothing less than God's Kingdom on Earth.

## Social democracy for America

As the Socialist Party candidate for president in 1912, Eugene Debs felt bound by the party's platform, though he had no hand in its writing. It was a far more radical document than anything proposed by the Democratic, Republican, or Progressive parties. A number of its planks were subsequently adopted by these parties, including proposals for a graduated income tax, equal suffrage for men, women, and residents of the District of Columbia, and creation of federal departments of labor and education, as well as a shorter work week and better safety inspections in factories and mines. The platform also included proposals for institutional reform aimed at achieving a more truly majoritarian democracy for which the Socialists alone stood. Included among these were the abolition of the US Senate, the adoption of proportional representation in elections for state and federal legislatures, election of the president and vice-president by direct vote of the people, abolition of the president's power to veto legislation, elimination of all federal district and circuit courts, and abolition of the Supreme Court's power of judicial review and that of state courts to issue injunctions. The platform also called for a convention for the purpose of revising the Constitution and endorsed a few of the direct-democracy reforms championed by the Progressives, principally the initiative, referendum, and recall, and went beyond the Progressives in calling for a national referendum.

The platform omitted any mention of the direct primary, but their opposition to it was apparent in the campaign.

Debs may have agreed with all of these proposals, but he did not speak or write often about many of them. When he did, his remarks were relegated for the most part to a secondary level of importance as was explicitly the case with the initiative, referendum, and recall. His campaign focused primarily on the preamble to the platform and on its call for changes in the workplace. Debs, who thirty-five years earlier had won public office as a Democrat, may have thought the more sweeping institutional reforms of government too radical for his audiences of working men, often rural and small town residents whom he best understood from his youth in Terre Haute and whose patriotism and love of country might have made any talk about changing the Constitution sound more threatening than reformist, especially with the war to save the Union still fresh in the public mind. The economic plight of workers was a more immediate concern, none of whom thought the Civil War had been fought to secure the power and profits of banks and corporations and who were more receptive to the broader socialist analysis of the economic causes of their distress and the reforms proposed for the workplace. His concentration on the economic dimension of socialism also fit his goal of educating voters about the virtues of a cooperative commonwealth as well as with his evangelical, often messianic, style as a speaker.

As in the platform, Debs denounced capitalism for having outgrown its historical function and become "incompetent and corrupt and the source of unspeakable misery and suffering to the whole working class." The nation had fallen under "the absolute control of a plutocracy" whose only interest was profits, which meant prosperity for the few, hardship and misery for the millions of wage earners for whom "life has become a desperate battle for mere existence."[17] Capitalism, Debs told audiences, was the cause of poverty, slums, crime, child labor and prostitution, as well as much of the disease and insanity that afflicted society. Moreover, government and the other political parties had become the servants of the capitalists, not of the people. The goal of socialism was to end capitalist domination of life in America by giving workers control over the means of production. In making his case, Debs recalled the American Revolution and the "spirit of '76," arguing that the overthrow of capitalism would vindicate "American principles of government, as proclaimed to the world in the *Declaration of Independence.*" It would restore the very soul of the Republic and give "to our civilization its crowning glory—the cooperative commonwealth."

"I like the Fourth of July," he added. "It breathes the spirit of revolution. On this day we affirm the ultimate triumph of Socialism."[18]

Debs most often spoke in generalities about the cooperative commonwealth.[19] He directed his appeals primarily to working-class voters but also urged middle-class Americans to be part of this new world as well.[20] He was firm in the conviction that education was required to school both classes in the principles of Socialism before the sweeping cultural changes that were required could be brought about. Debs's conception of democratic citizenship was more nuanced than that of the Progressives. A free individual was basic to both, but where Progressives like LaFollette felt that Americans already possessed the necessary qualities for citizenship in a democracy and needed only to be liberated from the constraints of party bosses and political machines, Debs believed that Americans of all classes needed further education to gain a proper understanding of democratic citizenship. More than simply freeing them from the oppression of capitalism, it was necessary for them to grasp the relationship between individual self-respect and a new collective identity, a relationship between the citizen and society akin to that between the individual and Jesus. "Patterning himself after generations of Protestant ministers," Salvatore observes, "Debs emphasized the centrality of individual conversion in constructing a collective identity."[21] "Voting for Socialism," he said repeatedly, "is not socialism any more than a menu is a meal."[22]

Citizenship, however, required more than education; it required that individuals realize their "manhood," that they take full responsibility for their lives and the conditions in which they found themselves.[23] For Debs, manhood referred to the moral qualities of the individual: personal honor, responsibility to one's duties, honesty, loyalty, and in general all of the Protestant values. But, manhood was not to be found in the absolute independence of the individual. Instead, it was to be found in mutual dependence. God had endowed humans with the intellectual faculties and the freedom of choice, placing all people on an equal footing after which, Debs argued, it was up to them to "work out their own salvation, their redemption and independence."[24] It was a message aimed primarily at workers telling them that they, and not just the capitalists, were responsible for their oppression, and that they had the capacity and moral obligation to take responsibility for their lives. He called upon them to recognize the brotherhood of all people and to pledge themselves to the common cause of bettering the lives of all by transforming society. The "most sacred and binding seal we know to civilized men is the pledge of honor," he told workers. "No man, with any moral scruples, would be able to contemplate without a keen feeling of shame, the record of a broken pledge.... Anyone who violates that obligation, strikes down his manhood with his own hand." Manhood, in Debs's view, had characterized the American revolutionaries, and he invoked it repeatedly to encourage a different kind of revolution.[25]


## Political parties and Socialism

Debs disagreed with most of the institutional reforms of government and politics favored by the Progressives, including their preference for a stronger presidency and an expanded bureaucracy, especially one staffed by experts which, to him, smacked of elitism. He confessed to "a prejudice against officialism" and "a dread of bureaucracy," the more so if it were at the national level of government. "I am a thorough believer in the rank and file," he wrote, "and in *ruling* from the *bottom up* instead of *being ruled* from the *top down*. The natural tendency of officials is to become bosses: "They come to imagine that they are indispensable and unconsciously shape their acts to keep themselves in office."[26] He saw the changes proposed by Progressives as only putting greater distance between workers and their governors, and he thought the direct-democracy reforms were no substitute for a closer physical proximity between voters and their representatives. In his experience, federal courts had delivered antilabor injunctions to halt strikes, and presidents had mobilized federal troops to enforce them. Debs had gone to prison for violating an injunction in the Pullman Strike of 1894, and he preferred to see more restrictions on the powers of both the president and the federal courts, not an expansion of their roles and control. Moreover, he did not share the Progressive confidence in public opinion as a guide or check upon government, because it would merely reflect the beliefs and values of the capitalist system.

Of the political reforms, the sharpest and most significant difference between Socialists and Progressives was about the direct primary, which for many Progressives, like LaFollette, was the essential change needed to break the control of the bosses over politics and restore power to the people. If parties were not an evil in themselves, their bosses were, and with their machines constituted a major impediment to the realization of an authentic citizen democracy. Socialists, on the other hand, were advocates for strong parties and opposed both the direct primary and nonpartisan forms of government, believing the claim that these would yield a more pure democracy to be itself pure fiction. Debs saw party organization and political campaigns as critical to the growth of socialism by building party membership and educating workers about the cause. His idea of a political party was like that of Edmund Burke: an organization whose members shared a common interest (Socialism in this case) and came together to advance it peacefully through political action. For now, he thought, electioneering was not primarily about winning office but was rather an opportunity to educate voters and convert them to Socialism. He wanted only those who understood and believed in socialism to vote for the party's candidates and was against compromises with nonsocialist groups merely to gain votes. He believed that the cultural shift necessary for socialism to replace capitalism required that voters be born again, as it were, in Socialism, and this could not be achieved by a political party built on the pluralist principle. "The Socialist Party is the party of the workers," he insisted, "organized to express in political terms their determination to break their fetters and rise to the dignity of free men."[27] Nonsocialists in the party only polluted the organization. Debs's concept of a socialist community was akin to that of the Puritan Jonathan Edwards, whom he admired, where residents of the Massachusetts Bay colony had to agree on fundamental spiritual beliefs and values before they were qualified to act as self-governing citizens on secular matters.[28]

Debs's friend and comrade, Victor Berger, was perhaps the most outspoken Socialist proponent of political parties, a champion of their importance in a democracy and a severe critic of those who blamed them for the social and economic ills workers faced. For Berger, who in 1910 was the first Socialist to be elected to Congress, parties were not the problem but were instead part of the solution. He and Debs agreed that political parties were absolutely essential to the Socialist movement because it was only through political action that the capitalist system could be overthrown without resort to violence. Unlike Debs, however, Berger believed in gradualism and thought it important that Socialists win election to public office, building party strength step-by-step, one office here, another there, and he was comfortable pursuing this objective through the bourgeoisie methods of compromise and deal-making with nonsocialists which Debs deplored. But, more than it being important to Socialist strategy, Berger held that political parties were an institution *essential* to democracy itself, arguing that "a democracy (the *rule* of the *demos*, the people)—or a republic (*res publica*, government by the people) is *impossible without political parties*."[29] In a democracy, citizens inevitably organized around issues that were of common interest to them, and in a representative democracy parties, must exist and function well if these issues were to be clearly defined, alternatives evaluated, and support built for decisions. "As long as we have democracy, and particularly, representative democracy," Berger insisted, "parties will be absolutely necessary for its expression," because in the absence of parties there would be only "anarchy or crude factionalism."[30]

The leader of a successful local Socialist Party in Milwaukee, Berger not only opposed but satirized Progressive support for nonpartisan local elections. They wanted to eliminate party labels from the ballot in municipal elections, he observed, but not in state or national elections. "If parties are such an evil in local elections, why are they not an evil in state elections?... And why not also banish parties from national tickets?" The truth, he continued, was that Progressives blamed the parties for corruption in the political system so as to avoid identifying the real cause of the nation's social and economic woes, namely capitalism. Parties were simply a scapegoat:

> The average bourgeois ideologist who is looking for some explanation of the political rottenness... would *under no circumstances* charge it to "businessmen in politics" and to legal graft. Such an opinion might interfere with the respect for himself, his best friends, and for capitalism in general.[31]

Reformers argued that, if the people would just do their civic duty, the problems with the parties could be fixed. But to Berger, this was naïve. Like other critics of the direct-democracy reforms, he maintained that nonpartisan elections would be candidate-centered, focused wholly on the character and personal attributes of the candidates, which would effectively "eliminate all principles and ideas from municipal elections." Removing parties from a central role in the political process would, Berger asserted, be an "Eldorado for boodlers, grafters and crooks" and "infinitely increase the chances of corruption" because "corporations and grafter would have to deal with individuals only instead of dealing with organizations." Nonpartisan elections would place a premium on money and give wealthy individuals nonparty groups more influence in elections. The result, Berger concluded, would be "absolute political anarchy" in which "nobody would be responsible to the people."[32]

The underlying cause of social and political corruption was not the political party as an institution, Berger and Debs agreed, but was instead because all of the parties, except the Socialists, were controlled by the capitalist forces whose dominance of the economic system extended to the political as well. Those who blamed political corruption on the parties were, to Berger, either cynical or dumb. They were thinking "in exactly the same way as the workman of old, who wanted to smash the machines because they thought the machines were responsible for their poverty, but it was not the machines that kept them poor. It was the capitalist ownership of the machines that was at fault." In precisely the same way, he added, "it is not the parties that are to blame for the political rottenness of our public life, but it is the *capitalist ownership of the ruling* parties."[33] Parties were inevitably the expression of class interests and, Burger concluded, any effort to suppress them was "*stupid*, reactionary and absolutely undemocratic" and also risked the possibility that "opinions and demands will be expressed through the bomb, the dagger, the pistol," or even "through bloody revolution."[34]

## The Progressive Party a fraud

The fundamental difference between Debs and the mainstream parties was the Socialist call for the radical transformation of the economy from private to social control. The Progressives, Democrats, and Republicans endorsed various plans for government regulation of corporations to mitigate the harsh treatment of women and children in the workplace and assure more healthy conditions for all, whereas the Socialists called for an end to private ownership of the means of production. Debs felt the other parties refused to recognize the corrupting effects of capitalism on all aspects of social and political life in America. The differences between them were nothing more than a reflection of "the conflicting interests of the privileged classes," none of which was of any interest to the working class. At bottom, he argued, they were all alike because they all "stand for capitalist class rule" and are one in "their opposition to Socialism," which is to say to "the emancipation of the working class from wage-slavery."[35]

In 1912, Debs aimed his sharpest and angriest criticism at the Progressive party, branding it the "party of progressive capitalism" that was "lavishly financed and shrewdly advertised" to appear that it stood for empowering the people when in fact it stood "for the rule of capitalism." It was, he declared, "a reactionary protest of the middle classes, built largely upon the personality of one man and not destined for permanence."[36] He was particularly incensed that Theodore Roosevelt had "stolen" the red flag of Socialism to give Progressivism the appearance of radicalism for no other purpose than to confuse voters. He ridiculed Roosevelt as "a charlatan, mountebank, and fraud," denouncing his Progressive promises and pledges as "the mouthings of a low and utterly unprincipled self seeker and demagogue."[37] Debs reminded audiences repeatedly that the Progressives, like the Democrats and Republicans, stood for "the private ownership by the capitalists of the productive machinery used by workers, so that the capitalists can continue to filch the wealth produced by the workers."[38] He attacked the Progressive program of political and regulatory reform as "flimsy doctrine," adding that direct-democracy reforms such as the initiative, referendum, and recall were but a small part of the Socialist plan. The battle came down to a choice between capitalism and socialism. "You must either vote for or against your own material interests as a wealth producer," he told audiences of workers, adding that "there is no political purgatory in this nation of ours despite the desperate efforts of so-called Progressive capitalist politicians to establish one. Socialism alone," he continued, "represents the material heaven of plenty for those who toil and the Socialist party alone offers the political means for attaining the heaven of economic plenty which the toil of the workers of the world provides."[39] A cooperative commonwealth could not be built upon a foundation of private property, he told them. It would come only with social democracy, not progressive democracy.

## Conclusion

"Unlike Roosevelt and Wilson, Debs was far more than a reformist," James Chace writes. "As a radical, he preached that the power held by capitalist America should be transferred to those who made the products that created wealth. At the same time, he called for an American citizenship that transcended class barriers, a brotherhood that he believed was "incarnate with the founding of the nation."[40] Debs drew his radicalism from authentically American sources: Jonathan Winthrop and the Puritan idea of community, Thomas Jefferson's assertion in the *Declaration of Independence* of the equality of all persons and the guarantee of their God-given rights, Thomas Paine's *Common Sense* justification for revolt against oppression, those in subsequent generations who fought that the least among them might enjoy what it meant to be an American, and Abraham Lincoln who liberated millions held in slavery. Debs rejected reform programs that did not put workers first, and he had faith in the power of the ballot that "took republican tradition seriously and stressed individual dignity and the power inherent in the concept of citizenship."[41]

Debs came to socialism not from bookish theories but from experience, from the refusal of owners to treat their employees with respect and decency, from that of a government which imprisoned him for joining worker protests against injustice and for exercising his own right of free speech, and from the readiness of capitalists and government to use violence to enforce their joint will. He was a Marxist whose class consciousness was "part of a high moral demand in the interests of society as a complete organism and not of one class only," and who shared the Christian belief in the divinity of Jesus as the standard moral conduct for both individuals and society, a conviction reinforced by the Social Gospel Movement.[42] His call for social democracy, while unsuccessful at the polls, influenced the politics of his time and beyond in the New Freedom of Woodrow Wilson and Franklin Roosevelt's call for a cooperative commonwealth in his 1932 campaign address to the Commonwealth Club of San Francisco.

Debs was unlike other critics of the Progressive direct-democracy reforms. His objections sprang from a more radical tradition in American politics and thought than the conservative constitutionalism upon which most critics founded their analyses. His was a deeper complaint that went to the fundamentals of the capitalist system whose failures Progressives claimed their reforms addressed but which Debs saw as serving mainly to sustain social injustices that were alien to the intent of the American founders. He never outgrew the romanticism and idealism of his father, which endowed him with a certain innocence but also with an impressive and often compelling passion. "When Debs says 'comrade' it is all right," New York journalist Heywood Broun observed. "He means it. That old man with the burning eyes actually believes that there can be such a thing as the brotherhood of man. And that's not the funniest part of it. As long as he's around I believe it myself."[43]

# Notes

1   Quoted in Ray Ginger, *The Bending Cross: A Biography of Eugene Victor Debs* (New Brunswick: Rutgers University, 1949), 25. This essay relied heavily on Chapters 1 and 2 of Ginger's work for biographical information about Debs.

2   Chushichi Tszuki, "Laurence Gronlund and American Socialism." http://en.wikipedia,org/wiki/Laurence_Gronlund.

3  Factional differences were also rooted in the nation's social and economic diversity: in ethnic, racial, and religious differences magnified by the new immigration in the final years of the late nineteenth and early twentieth centuries, in differences between industrial, craft, and agrarian organizations, as well as in differences between the conditions of life in older eastern cities and that in the younger municipalities and the agrarian expanses of the West.

4  In 1912, Socialist Party membership reached its highest level; the party ran full party slates in all states, and elected 1,200 of its candidates to public offices in 340 municipalities, including seventy-nine as mayors in twenty-four states. Sidney M. Milkis, *Theodore Roosevelt, the Progressive Party, and the transformation of American Democracy* (Lawrence: University Press of Kansas, 2009), 231, and Ronald Radosh, ed., *Debs* (Englewood Cliffs: Prentice-Hall, 1971), 4. for the first time, Socialists had full party slates in all of the states.

5  Nick Salvatore, *Eugene V Debs* (Urbana: University of Illinois, 1984), 301.

6  Quoted in Salvatore, *Eugene V Debs*, 161–162.

7  Quoted in Salvatore, *Eugene V Debs*, 101.

8  Quoted in Salvatore, *Eugene V Debs*, 101.

9  See Karl Kautsky: "The Rise and Fall of Orthodox Marxism," *Socialism Unbound*, ed. Stephen Eric Bronner (New York: Routledge, 1990), 31–52.

10  Salvatore, *Eugene V Debs*, 165. See also P. E. Maher, "Laurence Gronlund: Contributions to American Socialism," *The Western Political Quarterly*, 15 (December 1962), 618–624.

11  Quote from Jean Y. Tussey, *Eugene V Debs Speaks* (New York: Pathfinder Press, 1970), 190.

12  http://en.wikipedia.org//wiki/George_D._Herron, p. 2.

13  Salvatore, *Eugene V Debs*, 131.

14  Debs quoted, Salvatore, *Eugene V Debs*, 311–312.

15  Salvatore, *Eugene V Debs*, 104.

16  See Robert M. Crunden, *Ministers of Reform: The Progressives' Achievement in American Civilization 1889–1920* (New York: Basic Books, 1982).

17  1912 Platform of the Socialist Party.

18  Debs quoted in Chace, *1912: Wilson, Roosevelt*, 82 and 87.

19  The Socialist Party platform provided in great detail the extent of public ownership being proposed. It would include collective ownership of

railroads, steamship lines, telegraph, telephone, and other means of transportation and communication, as well as grain elevators, stock yards, and related industries, the banking and currency system, and extension of the public domain to include mines, quarries, forests and water power, and the conservation of natural resources for the benefit of all.

20  Milkis, *Theodore Roosevelt, the Progressive Party*, 229.

21  Salvatore, *Eugene V Debs*, 231.

22  Quoted in Tussey, *Eugene V. Debs Speaks*, 180.

23  For Debs, "manhood" was a gender neutral term, for he believed in equal rights for women as called for in the Socialist Party platform. His audiences were predominantly men and "being a man" had a familiar and acceptable meaning in his time, but he intended the term "manhood" to include women much as the term "mankind" did.

24  Quoted in Salvatore, *Eugene V Debs*, 163.

25  Salvatore, *Eugene V Debs*, 46.

26  Debs, "Sound Socialist Tactics," *International Socialist Review* (February 1912), reprinted in *Writings and Speeches of Eugene V. Debs* (New York: Hermitage Press, 1948), 355.

27  Debs quoted in Tussey, *Eugene V. Debs Speaks*, 176.

28  Chace observes that Debs's vision was "not unlike that of Governor John Winthrop of Massachusetts who, in 1630, declared that America should be as a city upon a hill, the eyes of all the people upon it." He might have noted that Debs's vision of how to achieve this was also akin to Winthrop. Chace, *1912: Wilson, Roosevelt*, 87.

29  Victor L. Berger. "Abolish Parties? What For?," *Berger's Broadsides* (Milwaukee: Social-Democrat Publishing Company, 1912), 188. Italics in original.

30  Berger, "Abolish Parties? What For?," 188.

31  Berger, "Abolish Parties? What For?," 187–188. Italics in original.

32  Berger, "Abolish Parties? What For?," 191.

33  Berger, "Abolish Parties? What For?," 190. Italics in original.

34  Berger, "Abolish Parties? What For?," 189.

35  Quoted in Radosh, *Debs*, 55, 57, and 32.

36  Milkis, *Theodore Roosevelt, the Progressive Party*, 62.

37  http://en.wikipedia.org/wiki/United_States_presidential_election,_1912, p. 6.

38  Debs, "Socialist Politics," *International Socialist Review, 1911*, reprinted in
     Radosh, *Debs*, 57.
39  Quote from Milkis, *Theodore Roosevelt, the Progressive Party*, 235.
40  Chace, *1912: Wilson, Roosevelt*, 68.
41  Salvatore, *Eugene V Debs*, 148–149.
42  Salvatore, *Eugene V Debs*, 165.
43  Quoted in Chace, *1912: Wilson, Roosevelt*, 68.

# 9

# Laboratories of Reform: Wisconsin and Oregon

Jerome M. Mileur
*University of Massachusetts Amherst*

Lonce H. Bailey
*Shippensburg University*

Progressivism as a reform movement was intellectually national in its reach, enjoying widespread support of scholars, especially those in the new social sciences, and of journalists, especially those who wrote for popular magazines such as *McClure's*. But, politically, the battles for direct democracy were not fought nationally but rather on the turf of state and municipal governments because the administration of elections is a power reserved by the Constitution to the states. With the exception of the direct election of United States Senators, ratified in 1913 as an amendment to the federal Constitution, none of the contests for direct democracy and direct government reforms involved the federal government, though to be sure reform of politics at the lower levels of government inevitably had an impact on the politics in the nation. Less than a decade after their introduction, presidential primaries in the states played a central role in Theodore Roosevelt's strategy in challenging the renomination of William Howard Taft for president in 1912. It threw the Republican National Convention of that year into a turmoil that split the party and led to the election of the Democrat Woodrow Wilson as president.[1]

In the first dozen years of the twentieth century, northern cities from the East coast through the Midwest were swept by municipal reform movements. Progressives won election as Mayor in Boston, New York, Jersey City, Philadelphia, Cleveland, Toledo, Cincinnati, Minneapolis, Kansas City, and Denver. They won governorships in Missouri, Iowa, and Wisconsin, and state legislatures in the upper Midwest, including plains states, regularly sent

Progressives to the US Senate.[2] In California, led by reform-minded newspaper owners and editors, Progressives broke the hold of the Southern Pacific Railroad on state government and elected Hiram Johnson as Governor.[3] All of these contests grew from local issues and concerns, many of them more economic than political, but all shared both the spirit and reforms of the time. Two states, however, stood out in the drive for political reform: Wisconsin where Robert La Follette battled for the direct primary and Oregon where William U'Ren led the fight for the initiative and referendum. Both gained national prominence as leaders of the Progressive movement, and their states became models of reform for others. The movements for reform in all of these states sparked heated contests, pitting power against power in fights for control of the Republican Party as well as of state government. The battles in Wisconsin and Oregon, however, differed from that in California. For all the uncompromising, moralistic, and hard-ball tactics of the reformers, the contests in Wisconsin and Oregon featured serious debates between opponents over conceptions of the proper organization of government and politics.

## Wisconsin

In 1904 Wisconsin became the first state to adopt the direct primary for the nomination of candidates for all municipal, county, state, and national offices except president.[4] Approved by referendum, it was the product of a vigorous and sometimes unsavory campaign led by Governor Robert La Follette. Born in 1855, La Follette was an attorney, a graduate of the University of Wisconsin, and a three-term Republican member of Congress in the 1880s. In the early 1890s, he became a leader of a reform faction within the GOP, arguing that the party had abandoned the ideals of its antislavery origins and become the tool of corporate and financial interests. Passed over twice for the party's gubernatorial nomination, he won it finally in 1900 as part of a "unity" ticket that brought all factions of the party together. He promised to be a "safe" choice, but once in office he disavowed pledges made to business and other traditional party constituencies, denounced them as "corruptionists" and promised to return politics to the "first principles of democracy" by restoring power to the people. He built his own personal machine, enlisting those who swore absolute allegiance to him and dismissing others who, albeit Progressive in their sympathies, were unwilling to subject themselves unquestioningly to his executive authority.[5] Many Republican leaders felt betrayed by La Follette, were angered when he castigated them as the handmaidens of business and other self-serving interests, and broke with the governor.

The direct primary was not the cause of the split in the Wisconsin GOP, but it nonetheless became a central issue in the intra-party struggle that followed when the governor insisted on its adoption as the only way to assure that the people could combat the evils that were seen as the causes of corruption in state politics. The primary was not a new idea (it had been used in Milwaukee County since 1891), but its extension to all offices in the state was new. With no groundswell for change and no evidence that the caucus-convention system had failed or was unpopular with rank-and-file voters, party regulars or "stalwarts" denounced La Follette's proposal as radical and "populistic." They argued that what the governor's real objective was not popular control of politics but rather a system he could dominate as the "boss" of his own political machine. La Follette refused any compromise. Initially, the stalwarts defeated his proposal in the legislature, but in 1903, the assembly approved to the primary with the stipulation that it be submitted as a referendum question to give voters the final say.

The 1904 Republican state convention was the first battleground and proved to be one of the most tumultuous party gathering in Wisconsin history, an affront to any notion of democracy. It was, however, La Follette supporters, not the party regulars, who were the offenders, manipulating the rules to deny duly elected regulars their seats as delegates, seating others as delegates with no credentials other than their loyalty to the governor, and using physical force to block access to the convention to anyone of whom they did not approve. Their machinations transformed the convention from one with a stalwart majority into one with a La Follette majority, prompting party regulars to withdraw and hold a separate convention. The two met simultaneously, and each nominated a full slate of GOP candidates for state and national offices.[6] The question of which slate of candidates should be on the ballot as the Republican ticket went to the state supreme court where the chief justice, a La Follette appointee, ruled in favor of the governor's slate. In the general election, the governor was returned to office, albeit by a substantially reduced margin, and the direct primary was approved by a yet smaller margin as almost half of those voting for governor did not cast ballots on the referendum question.

## Leaders of rival Republican factions

Emanuel Philipp emerged from the bitter intra-party fight at the 1904 Republican convention as a statewide leader of the stalwart faction and the most determined, articulate, and thoughtful critic of the direct primary and other reforms advanced by La Follette. Born on the eve of the Civil War in March 1861 in a thinly populated area just over an hour northwest of the state capitol, the Philipp family moved to nearby Sauk City a year later when his father, Luzi, a Swiss immigrant, joined a Wisconsin infantry company to fight for the Union cause. Emanuel was raised in the self-reliant spirit of the frontier, honest and hard-working, and from his father gained a sense of responsibility to the community and nation. Six years older than Philipp, La Follette also grew up in rural Wisconsin, but at age one lost his father and had a difficult childhood with a stepfather. Philipp was an excellent student of Sauk City high school, graduated at age seventeen and taught for three years in nearby rural schools. After high school, La Follette attended the University of Wisconsin where he was an undistinguished student but was greatly influenced on issues of morality, ethics, and social justice by the institution's president John Bascom, who became something of a surrogate father to him.

At age twenty-four, La Follete became an attorney, while Philipp at twenty left teaching and moved to Madison to study telegraphy which led to a job with the Chicago and North Western Railway and a career in business. He rose to the post of freight manager for the railroad before departing for a comparable position with the Schlitz Brewing Company. He moved again to the American Refrigerator Transit Company and Union Pacific Railroad before establishing his own refrigerator car company in1903. Over the next decade, he built it into one of the largest and most successful refrigerator car companies in the country. In the 1890s, regulatory and taxation issues involving railroads and breweries brought Philipp regularly to the state capitol where he was drawn into Republican politics, identifying with the party regulars. La Follette had gone into politics almost immediately upon joining the bar in 1879, winning election as Dane County district attorney in 1880 followed by three terms in the US House of Representatives from 1885 to 1890. Defeated for reelection, La Follette became an increasingly harsh critic of the ethical shortcomings of regular Republicans. He launched an insurgency that challenged them for control of the GOP and led ultimately to his election as governor in 1900.

Intellectually, Philipp and La Follette were very different. Philipp's formal education ended with high school, but he continued to read widely, acquainting himself with the intellectual conservatism of Edmund Burke, David Hume, and Thomas Carlyle, as well as with the thought of the American founders and Abraham Lincoln as well as with Darwinian science. Meanwhile, La Follette, for the most part, appears to have found the moral teachings of President Bascom sufficient unto his needs. Philipp was more pragmatic and analytical in his approach to politics, focused more on reasonable accommodation of differences than was La Follette whose orientation was more ideological and centered largely on promoting his cause and career above all else. La Follette evinced little interest in political history or philosophy and was decidedly more moralistic and self-righteous than Philipp with a view of politics as a contest between good and evil. He regularly vilified any who disagreed with him as enemies of the public good, "sinners" in the eyes of an angry god, all the while painting himself as the champion of virtue. Harsh in assailing political bosses and machine politics, La Follette built, arguably, the most ruthless and efficient political machine Wisconsin had ever known. To achieve his ends, he ignored primary election results, subordinated political principles and ethical standards, undermined the careers of fellow Progressives, and blamed his enemies for the factionalism and other problems facing the Republican Party.[7] Regularly accused of being dictatorial, no criticism stuck. He was the "Teflon" politician long before Teflon was invented.

La Follette responded to the continuing criticism of his reform program with attacks that cast Philipp and other regulars as venal grafters, unscrupulous hacks, and servants of greed, offering no evidence other than their failure to support his reform program.[8] As governor, La Follette shunned many within his own party, including many who had supported his candidacy in 1900, and surrounded himself instead with a small, tight-knit group of loyalists who would do his bidding on all matters. His indifference to the party platform led stalwarts like Philipp to view him, Herbert Margulies writes, "not as a misguided zealot or a foolish visionary, but as a conscious hypocrite [and] a charlatan who would scruple at nothing to gain his ends."[9]

## Emanuel Philipp: Critic of direct democracy

After a decade of contentious politics and spirited debate, both Emanuel Philipp and Robert La Follette wrote books dealing with the intra-party battles of the

GOP. In *Political Reform in Wisconsin*, Philipp faults the La Follette reform program, with respect to taxation and railroad regulation, as well as the direct primary. In both its account of state politics and its style, the work stands in sharp contrast to La Follette's *Autobiography*, written in anticipation of his 1912 presidential bid.[10] Both are partisan in tone, but Philipp writes in the third person, does not mention himself, and is careful to document claims he makes and speeches he cites. La Follette, on the other hand, writes in the first person, casts himself in heroic terms as the sole champion of reform, and never lets facts get in the way of his story.

Emanuel Philipp was a conservative, but one who believed that conservatism should be grounded in a fixed, yet not rigid, set of values that were embedded in institutional arrangements, social and governmental, and whose "practical" application was open to experimentation and change. He shared James Madison's pessimistic view of human nature (that men are not angels) and believed that society influenced human behavior as much or more than did individual will. Like Madison, he was suspicious of theory and believed that reason grounded in experience was the best guide to sensible and workable change. He averred utopianism, preferring prudent men of action who shunned abstract thought in discussions of reform. To Philipp, a statesman should be disposed to preserve while also being open to change that would lead to gradual improvements in institutional arrangements. With Lincoln as his example, he believed a statesman should look backward in order to move forward, preserving the good while discarding the bad. For him, politics was a "science" that eschewed dogmatic approaches in favor of experiments aimed at devising more effective methods of governance. Constructive change in his view evolved from centuries of experience that informed and guided adjustments to new conditions. It was foolhardy to dismantle traditional structures of society or politics on grounds of some theory. Indeed, Burke's view of the French Revolution was seen by Philipp as a case study in how radical and untested change could do more to destroy a good world than create a better one. It framed his perception of utopian theories as a threat not only to the status quo but also to the orderly progress he thought essential for a stable polity.

Philipp was a philosophical conservative in the tradition of Edmund Burke whose thought he admired and who he often quoted. Like Burke, he believed society to be fundamental, the product of history and experience, and the repository of wisdom and virtue. Government and politics were natural outgrowths of the social organism and not of the individual. His objection to the radicalism of La Follette's abrupt and sweeping direct primary reform derived from his conviction that sensible and workable change should be organic. It should evolve rationally with concern for the well-being of the whole, not with that of individual parts. He was not opposed to change, but thought it should be achieved in the manner of the scientist whose methods tested propositions experimentally before adjusting theory and practice to new conditions or situations. Philipp was more conservative than La Follette, but far less so than the more ideological right-wingers in the GOP who feared change. He was opposed to change for the sake of change and despised what he saw as La Follette's demagogic appeals and hateful attacks on opponents.

Philipp's moderation may be seen in his view of the direct primary. Milwaukee County, where he served as Republican Party chair in1900, had used it for a decade. In so large a city, it was a more practical than the caucus as a method for involving party members in making political decisions. But, unlike La Follete's reform which swept all before it, the use of the primary in Milwaukee had evolved naturally by adapting to conditions in a large city in a way that preserved the caucus-convention system of nominations. Philipp had expected that the example of Milwaukee would serve to guide election reform in the state. His fierce objection to the La Follette reform lay in its "one-size-fits-all" approach that imposed primaries statewide on all communities regardless of size or local preference. The La Follette approach violated Philipp's understanding of the electoral system as an integral part of a larger organism which was the constitutional system. There was, moreover, no apparent need for the sweeping change as there was no evidence of public unhappiness with the party convention system or any sense in the mass electorate that the existing system had failed them. The reform was grounded wholly in theory. The use of the direct primary for every office in the state was, Philipp argued, a radical departure that would disrupt, if not destroy, an electoral system whose operation was satisfactory to everyone except La Follette and his handful of insurgents more intent upon political opportunity for themselves than for the welfare of the people.

Philipp saw the party convention as an institution that had grown naturally within the framework of constitutional politics in Wisconsin and, while requiring occasional adjustment as in the case of Milwaukee, it remained the preferable electoral arrangement for the state. He presented the case for party convention with succinct conviction:

> Government by parties and government of parties by the members of parties themselves are essential to the perpetuity of our institutions. Government by

individuals, however able, inevitably spells despotism. Party responsibility on the one hand and a wise distribution of powers between the co-ordinate branches of the government on the other are the means by which the necessary checks and balances are provided for the protection of our rights and as a guaranty of our liberties.

The overthrow of parties through the ascendency of the individual destroys party responsibility. Party organization and party leaders disappear with party principles, and individuals take their places with organized personal followings bearing the motto, "Anything to win," as their most sacred principle. The discussion of real principles is lost in the public exchange of bitter personalities.[11]

A system of statewide primaries, Philipp argued, placed a premium on personal politics by encouraging individuals to seek office on their own initiative, which would in turn lead to the disintegration of party organization and the loss of "real representative government" that only parties could assure. It would also produce a sharp increase in the cost of elections. In Milwaukee alone, he records, candidates for office in 1908 spent more than six times as much as their counterparts ten years earlier.[12] The direct primary also changed the source from which campaign money came. He calculated that, in 1898, one-third of all money spent in campaigns had been contributed through ward committees, whereas, in 1908, none came from ward committees because they no longer existed. The ward committees had "disappeared with the political parties they were organized to support and assist." Instead of ward committees "composed of business and professional men whose sole aim [was] to work for the triumph of party principles in which they believe," there were now "personal organizations, or clubs, designed to advance the political fortunes of some favorite leaders and made up for the most part of followers who hoped to profit by the success of those leaders."[13] Under the old system, the party could be held accountable for the actions of those elected in its name, and candidates were chosen by the party with that in mind. Officeholders were answerable to their parties which had provided most of the campaign workers and much of the money for their election.

In the party convention system, candidates were insulated by their party from direct influence by financial contributors, but not so in the primaries where political money went directly to the individual seeking an office. While there may be no overt quid-pro-quo, Philipp notes, the recipient was nonetheless placed under an obligation that does not exist in the party system. There had been much concern about the influence of large corporations in politics, whose "most effective way" of wielding influence was through campaign donations. "The easiest way to use money in politics," Philipp argued, "is to place the individual officeholder under direct obligation to the contributor," and the primary election law offered an ideal opportunity for the use of money in this way.[14] Moreover, the primary system forced candidates to raise and spend more money because there were more competitors for office, thus greater uncertainty, and there was no money coming from the candidate's party.

By increasing the cost of pursuing public office, the direct primary made money far more important in state politics than had ever been the case. This not only gave an advantage as never before to corporations and other private organizations with money, but it also privileged wealthy candidates and disadvantaged those of moderate means. The party convention system had made it easier for aspirants of modest means to seek office, first, by confining electioneering for state office to a contest for delegates to the party convention and, second, by the parties themselves providing a substantial portion of the money needed in the general election. Under the primary system, Philipp estimated that a single mailing to reach *all* voters in the state (there was no party registration in Wisconsin, thus no sure way to identify only Republicans) would cost a candidate $35,000 in postage alone. Multiple mailings would be necessary for success, in addition to which a personal organization of paid professionals was required to handle all aspects of the campaign from obtaining signatures on nominating petitions to staffing offices and distributing literature, functions that under the party system had been handled by volunteer members of the now defunct ward committees.

The primary system was not only biased in favor of wealth, it also rewarded ambition more than teamwork. Personal ambition, not peer review through the political party, Philipp argued, had become the defining characteristic of making nominations through primaries. In this highly individualistic environment, it was every man for himself with little or no loyalty to one another or to the political party. This posed the question, he continued, of who or what was represented by those elected and of what this uncertainty meant for a genuinely representative system of democracy. The consequence of this was already apparent in the nation's capital, Philipp argued, where the state's congressional delegation had lost influence because party leaders could not know who or what they represented. In 1903, before adoption of the primary, six of Wisconsin's eleven members in the House of Representatives were chairmen of committees, and both Senators held leadership position in the upper chamber. By 1910, only one member of the state's delegation to the House held a chairmanship, and neither of its Senators was among the leaders of that body.

Reformers pointed at House Speaker Joe Cannon's rigid sense of party government to explain the state's loss of influence, blaming him for punishing members for their independence and refusal to do his bidding. But, Philipp dismissed this as "sheer nonsense," claiming instead that the state's delegation was ignored because it was unclear that they really represented the Republican Party and its program. "There is no political party in Wisconsin today," he argued, because each member was a party unto himself. "Each member represents an independent effort at the primary and the polls," and because there was no party convention to draw a platform, each "goes to Washington as an individual who has been elected on a platform made by himself."[15] Coming from a state in which candidates no longer appeal to the voter on the basis of party principles, it should be no surprise, he concluded, that those chosen were not entrusted with leadership in a system of party government.

Finally, advocates for the primary system had claimed that it would produce a better class of officeholders with more ability and influence than those chosen by political parties. Philipp saw the state's declining influence in Congress as evidence to the contrary. In addition, he pointed to the unprincipled behavior of many, including La Follette, who were champions of reform but did not hesitate to repudiate the results of primary elections when the outcomes did not accord with their desires. He noted specifically the case of an incumbent district attorney in Milwaukee County who had been prominent in the fight for the direct primary but, when defeated for renomination in 1906, denounced those who voted against him as grafters or friends of grafters and filed for office as an independent. He won reelection, but only after appealing to Democrats to cross party lines to vote for him. This was not an isolated example. In 1908, the speaker of the House of Representatives, another leader in the reform movement, was defeated for renomination when Democrats took Republican ballots in the state's open primary and cast them for his opponent. He too ran as an independent with La Follette's support but lost in the general election. Also in 1908, the incumbent US Senator was renominated in the Republican primary and won the general election. But, election to the Senate was still the responsibility of the state legislature where

La Follette supporters, with his blessing, refused to accept the decision of the voters and called instead for an investigation into the amount of money spent in the primary. An extended inquiry followed before the incumbent was returned to the Senate. The indifference of La Follete partisans to the results of the primary was apparent to all and added to the suspicion and disrespect of national party leaders for the state.

## A brood of political and social abuses

Four years of experience with the direct primary was enough for Emanuel Philipp to conclude that it has failed to "perform the miracles its friends claimed for it" and had instead "brought forth a brood of political and social abuses of the most serious character." Its use had exposed "positive disadvantages and grave evils" which he detailed in a lengthy bill of indictment.[16]

1. The personnel of the office holding class has not been improved; better, more capable, and cleaner men have not been elected to office; public officers are not more devoted to their duties; the civil service is not improved by the appointment of a better class of employees.
2. Public morals are not elevated by the change in the method of making nominations. Never before in the history of the state was so much money expended by candidates in campaigns as at present. Never before were there so many open charges of corruption and the unlawful use of money.
3. It has disorganized parties and built up personal political machines.
4. The members of the state legislature are split up into factions and there is no party responsibility for their acts, which has resulted in an endless amount of useless and some harmful legislation.
5. The primary contests have engendered so much bitterness that each election brings about a new alignment of personal political machines.
6. Nominations at the primaries no longer represent the will of the members of the parties making the nominations. The members of the minority party invariably vote in the primaries of the majority party. Republican candidates with personal machines make trades with Democrats and Socialists for votes in Republican primaries ....
7. Poor men and men of moderate means can not become candidates for office under the primary election law where there are contests, except on two conditions. They must face ruin or accept money from others to defray their necessary expenses. If they accept financial aid they assume obligations no public servant should incur.

8. The electors can not "vote directly for the men of their choice" at a primary election. They must vote for some man whose name appears on the primary ticket, and that ticket is made up of candidates who have circulated nomination papers ... They may all be ... objectionable to 90 per cent of the voters, but the voter must submit to make his choice from [these] self nominated primary candidates.

9. Never in the history of the state have the enmities engendered by political contests been so bitter as they are today. All pretense of the old good natured rivalry between parties has disappeared from the political arena. Charges of unlawful use of money, of a debauched public service, of actual bribery, of personal dishonesty and political trickery were common during the last session of the legislature.

10. Few, if any, intelligent men who take an interest in politics can be found in the state who will not readily admit that the law is not satisfactory and needs amendment ....

11. While no attempt has been made to compute the entire cost of the law in operation to the taxpayers of the state, counties and cities, no one will for a moment dispute the truth of the statement that it has been enormous and that no compensating benefit has resulted ....

12. The law gives a decided advantage to the man in office ... over the newcomer. The well advertised candidate, although he is an inferior person, will [also] get the nomination over a less advertised, but better equipped candidate.

13. The placing of names of candidates on primary tickets by petition has developed a new industry in this state during primary campaigns—the circulation of petitions for hire. The party clubs of former years have disappeared; in their places have appeared the mercenaries who secure names on petitions for a consideration ....

14. The abolition of all conventions, county, district and state has deprived the voters of parties the opportunity to get together, rub elbows and become acquainted. In conventions men from different sections of the state met and exchanged views. They explained the merits and abilities of the several candidates for office and they made "trades" to the advantage of the party ticket in most cases. The conventions were the schools of politics to which many young men went for their education and they had an educative value. All the advantages of this free intercourse and exchange of ideas and information disappeared with the abolition of the convention.

15. The provision for making platforms in conventions made of candidates for office is a confessed failure. Platforms made in that way do not represent the

principles of the party, but are mere "catch vote" affairs. Even the candidates who make them do not respect them for they go out into the field with platforms of their own ...

16. The law has not dethroned the political boss. If we ever had a real boss in Wisconsin before the primary law we have merely changed bosses.... The law complicates politics, and any law that does this widens the opportunity for manipulation and increases the activity of the boss....[17]

Philipp was convinced that many who had favored the primary no longer believed in it. "There are enough who openly and unequivocally condemn the law and the principle involved in it," he argued, "to indicate clearly what informed public sentiment in Wisconsin now is on this subject."[18] The "shortest and most satisfactory solution" to the many problems with the law, he advised, was to repeal it.[19] In its place, Philipp recommended that the legislature return to the example of the Milwaukee primary which had successfully incorporated the primary with the caucus and convention system in the making of nominations. In Milwaukee, primaries were closed to members of a political party; voters nominated candidates directly for local office and chose delegates to party conventions where nominations for higher offices were made. The logic was peer review: voters would know office seekers personally at the local level, whereas delegates to party conventions could more easily acquaint themselves with the character and qualifications of candidates seeking statewide offices.

Following the example of Milwaukee, Philipp noted, would revive local party clubs and organizations with their educative and other benefits and also restore a check on the use of money in politics, thereby reducing the advantage wealth gave to candidates and organizations. Most of all, it would rid the state of a bad law. "To do so will not be a step backward as some will claim," Philipp insisted, "but a step forward. There is nothing sacred about [the direct primary]. It is only a pretty theory that does not work out in practice." He concluded with an appeal to the highest of his political principles, arguing that repeal of the direct primary would "guarantee constitutional government and thereby perpetuate our republican institutions."[20]

In 1914, Wisconsin voters appeared to prove Philip correct in his belief that they were unhappy with the La Follette reforms when they rejected many of the referendum questions placed on the ballot by Progressive majorities in the state legislature, including one for the adoption of the initiative and referendum. They also elected Philipp as governor, ending more than a decade of Progressive control of the office. The vote, Robert Maxwell observed, "represented a full-scale revolt against La Follette progressivism," favoring a rejection and "not a mere modification" of his reforms.[21] Progressives, however, retained majorities in the state legislature, and voters were never given the opportunity to vote directly on the question of repealing the direct primary law.

# Oregon

In the 1890s, Oregon was alive with reformers, older Mugwumps and newer Populists, battling against a powerful collusion between business and political interests that were seen as agents of corruption in state politics. The state came to the forefront as a leader in the movement toward direct citizen government through the "Oregon Plan" for the initiative, referendum, and recall that became a model for other states. Inspired by their use in Switzerland and impressed by James Sullivan's 1892 book *Direct Legislation by the Citizenship Through the Initiative and Referendum*, William U'Ren emerged early in the 1890s as the leader of the direct-democracy movement in Oregon. Unlike Robert La Follette in Wisconsin, whose reformist impulse was seen by friend and foe alike as driven as much by ambition as principle, U'Ren was widely viewed as a democratic reformer with no ambition for public office whose sole objective was to cleanse state politics through a more direct role for citizens in its government and politics, but his drive, determination, and convictions were every bit the equal of La Follette.

Born in Wisconsin, U'Ren's parents were working-class Cornish immigrants, his father a socialist and strong union man, and his mother a follower of John Wesley who raised her four children in an atmosphere of mysticism and devotion to God. William moved to Colorado at seventeen where he worked as a common laborer while studying law at night. At twenty-one, he passed the bar and practiced in law in Colorado for several years before migrating to Oregon in 1890 where he continued to practice law. U'Ren quickly became involved in reform politics, working initially with University of Oregon professor Alfred Bingham in a campaign that was successful in winning adoption of the Australian or secret ballot, after which he directed his energies to the cause of direct government.

U'Ren and others saw the initiative and referendum as "cornerstones" for the other Progressive reforms because they provided a way around a state legislature seen by them as dominated by the big money of corporate interests funneled through political party bosses who controlled politics. Reformers regarded the state constitution as a product of political compromise, not as a hallowed document, and believed that, for the most part, its system of representative government impeded the changes needed to adapt governance to rapidly changing social and economic conditions. The aim of the reformers was not to destroy the constitution or its representative institutions, but rather to modify it in ways that placed greater trust in individuals and established a more direct relationship between citizens and their government. They were confident that this would strengthen these institutions and, in doing so, improve the performance of government.

Arguing for what he called the three legs of direct democracy, U'Ren first brought labor unions and the state's Farmer's Alliance together to form the Oregon Direct Legislation League for which he served as secretary. In 1894, he was chosen to chair the Populist Party convention in Oregon and won approval of the initiative, referendum, and recall as planks in the party platform. Two years later, he won election to the Oregon House of Representatives where he led a Populist minority in exploiting a split in the state Republican Party to deadlock the body and prevent it from obtaining the quorum needed to organize. He demanded approval of these reforms as the price for his yielding, but the tactic failed to win the necessary legislative support. U'Ren left the legislature and returned to the Direct Legislation League, which he reorganized by broadening its base to include bankers, members of the state bar association, and the editor of the state's leading newspaper, *The Oregonian*. In 1902, this coalition pressured the legislature into placing a constitutional amendment on the ballot authorizing the initiative and referendum, which was adopted overwhelmingly by a popular vote of more than ten-to-one. Two years later, Oregon became the first state to use the initiative when voters approved a direct primary law.

In the first decade of the twentieth century, the initiative and referendum spread to Oregon's neighbors, California and Washington, as well as across the northern tier of states bordering Canada. In Oregon, U'Ren had become a political dynamo, leading or supporting a series of successful initiatives that extended the initiative and referendum to local levels of government, adopted the recall for elected officials at all levels, gave the vote to women, established the first presidential primary in the United States, created a system for the popular election of US Senators by requiring legislators to vote for the candidate who won the state primary for the office, and won passage of a corrupt practices act to regulate political money. He was not always successful, failing to win approval for a unicameral legislature or to establish a system of proportional representation and weighted voting in the legislature. An editorial in *The Oregonian* recognized his influence, describing him as "the most fearsome public figure in the state" and calling him the fourth branch of state government, adding that it was "an open question which exerts the most power."[22] Another commentator at the time called U'Ren the "high priest of Oregon radicalism," while more recently Robert Johnson depicts him as the "mechanic" of direct democracy and "the most robust national symbol of populist democracy during the first decades of the twentieth century."[23]

## Critics of the initiative and referendum

Following adoption of the initiative in1904, the number of questions on the Oregon ballot grew with each election, numbering thirty-two in 1910 and thirty-seven in 1912. Over three-fourths of them were rejected, as voters seemed to weary of the initiative, and criticism grew about the reform. Members of the State Bar Association spoke against it more and more, but nowhere was criticism sharper than in the state's leading newspaper, *The Oregonian*, which had supported U'Ren and the initiative in 1902. By 1908, it had reversed itself and, with the bitterness of a scorned lover, campaigned aggressively against it, declaring that the initiative had fallen into the hands of "faddists, sophists, schemers, doctrinaires of all sorts" and that it encouraged "every group of hobbyists, every lot of people burning with whimsical notions to propose initiative measures." Collectively, they had the practical effect of "abolishing the Constitution and laws altogether" and of reducing state government to near irrelevance. Calling the initiative a "crank's paradise," *The Oregonian* fretted that the reform was bringing national criticism upon the state and declared bluntly: "It was not intended that representative government should be abolished by the new system; but it has been abolished."[24]

The Oregon Plan also became a target of criticism for Progressive reformers nationally, many of whom questioned its effects, doubted its utility, and disputed the claim that it would restore citizens to their rightful place of authority in a popular democracy. Among the critics was Herbert Croly, author of *The Promise of American Life* that was so admired by Theodore Roosevelt who acknowledged a debt to it in his 1912 direct-democracy campaign for president. Croly doubted that the promises made by supporters of the initiative and referendum could be realized and feared that the reform might in fact become only another impediment to government action, especially if it were adopted nationally. The question, he wrote, was whether giving citizens the ultimate determination of public policy would "liberate the expression of the popular will or finally and effectively paralyze its expression."[25] He rejected the claim that direct government would "reinvigorate" representative institutions, arguing that it would instead weaken the existing system by creating an altogether new method for "delegating popular political authority." Croly cited Oregon as an example, noting that the effect of the reform "has not been the reinvigoration of representative government but its increased debilitation" because the tendency of Oregon voters "has been to make the legislature an increasingly negligible factor in the law-making power of the state." On this point, he cites the observations of University of Oregon professor, Allen H. Eaton, who found that, under the new system, "there is a strong tendency on the part of the legislature to shift responsibility to the people" with the result that "there is an apparently widening gulf between the people and the legislature."[26]

Croly also argued that, claims of reformers notwithstanding, direct government empowers minorities and in operation validates minority rule. "None but an idolater," he asserted, "could believe for one moment that the initiative and referendum … are instruments of majority rule," because "the proportion of the people who act … is never a majority."[27] Indeed, the vote on these questions is notoriously low as compared to that for candidates for public office. "At its highest," he continued, "the vote on a proposed law is rarely over eighty per cent, not of the registered vote, but of the vote for governor, and it frequently falls below twenty-five per cent."[28] He had no doubt that those in Oregon who voted on ballot questions had paid more attention to the issue than had others in the mass public and, in that sense, were better qualified to pass judgment. But, no "sincere democrat" could justify a supposedly democratic process on these terms. "Democracy," he asserted, "is not government by peculiarly qualified people or by a peculiarly qualified part of the people. It is or should be government in which the largest possible proportion of the adult citizenship … participates."[29] This was not the case in Oregon.

Croly's harshest criticism was reserved for the effect of direct government on the education of voters and on deliberation in the making of public policy. In a legislative body, proposals could be discussed in detail by members with differing views and, within reason, amended to accommodate this diversity of sincere but conflicting opinions. But voters could not deliberate about ballot questions. They could only approve or disapprove of them, and that,

Croly argued, was the "great weakness" of the initiative. It failed to provide a political education for voters, because there was no opportunity for ballot questions to receive "that thorough ventilation and discussion which tends to inform and illuminate popular opinion."[30] On their own, voters might form intelligent judgments, but the questions were often obscured by many provisions in which the average voter had little interest or understanding. This discouraged a discussion that would be truly educational. A true democracy should be organized, Croly concluded, "so as to stimulate the liveliest possible political interest over the widest practicable political area," but the initiative and referendum "fail absolutely to contribute to the accomplishment of this necessary democratic purpose."[31]

Croly was not the only prominent Progressive to question the initiative and referendum; political scientist Woodrow Wilson, then president of Princeton University, had deep reservations about direct government as well. Because they enabled voters to bypass legislatures, he thought them debilitating to both representative government and politics as a deliberative activity. The initiative gave voice to those who "have merely formed an independent, that is, an isolated opinion, and have not entered into common counsel." There was no opportunity to consult with those of different opinions, no opportunity to accommodate ideas that might improve legislation. The initiative in effect substituted a quantitative democracy for a qualitative one. "Common counsel is not aggregate counsel," Wilson argued. "It is not a sum in addition, counting heads. It is compounded out of many views in actual contact; is a living thing made out of the vital substance of many minds, many personalities, many experiences; and it can be made up only by the vital contacts of actual conference, only in face to face debate, only by word of mouth and the direct clash of mind with mind."[32]

The legislative process, he continued, was an educational process in which members came to appreciate "how honestly and with what force of genuine character ... or with what convincing array of practical arguments opposite views may be held." It was not that a representative, in the course of making policy choices, was unfaithful to promises made on the stump, but rather that he had learned more and understood better than could possibly have been the case at the time of his election. Consequently, his actions may stray somewhat from campaign promises, but his decision would be the product of greater wisdom and not a loss of conviction. There was, to be sure, Wilson conceded, ample evidence that citizens were losing confidence in their legislatures and as a consequence were understandably taking seriously the radical suggestions for change made by those who advocated adoption of the initiative and referendum. But, direct democracy, he argued, meant "the virtual abandonment of the representative principle." It meant a fundamental change in the nature of constitutional government in the United States.[33]

The president of Harvard University, A. Lawrence Lowell, a political scientist like Wilson, also had doubts about the initiative. In his study of state governments, which he called "the greatest of laboratories for experiments in direct legislation," he found that ballot questions of varied complexity extended across the full range of issues that legislatures commonly engaged and that their number had been growing at a rate he judged to be unmanageable for the considered judgment by citizens of a state. It was unlikely, he argued, that "the public could have a real opinion on all of them," adding that, "in a lamentable proportion of cases [the voter] acts upon an impression, a prejudice, or upon the advice of some person or party that he trusts."[34] Only a small fraction of the people appeared to act independently, yet "this is the assumption on which the initiative is based." More and more of the questions were rejected by voters, which Lowell concluded was a public recognition of "the popular incompetence to decide them, and on the principle that such measures ought not to be proposed in this way."[35] It might be possible to refine the process, narrowing its use to specific topics, but he was by no means confident that this could or would be done.

## Conservative voices

The initiative may have troubled many who were otherwise sympathetic to the Progressive agenda, but to conservatives who opposed the movement in its entirety, the initiative was a corruption of the nation's constitutional system. Among the harshest denunciations of the initiative was that of Ellis Paxson Olberholtzer, author of a comprehensive study of the growth and use of direct government forms in the United States through the first decade of the twentieth century, who concluded that these reforms posed a "grave crisis" for the representative system in America.[36] A native of Pennsylvania, born shortly after the Civil War in 1868, he was educated at the University of Pennsylvania where he earned a Ph.D. in 1893 after also studying at several European universities in Berlin, Heidelberg, and Paris. A journalist, Olberholtzer served on the editorial staff of the *Philadelphia Evening Telegraph*, as editor of *The Manufacturer*, and as literary and dramatic editor of the *Philadelphia Public Ledger*. He was best known, however, as a historian and editor of the twenty-volume American Crisis Biographies series.

Many of Olberholtzer's objections were familiar. The process of citizen petition had been made too easy: "Any charlatan, if he can obtain enough signers to his petition, can bring forward a plan for changing the Constitution." From 1898 to 1908, he found that no fewer than 472 constitutional questions had been submitted to voters in the various states, almost all of them amendments to state constitutions, which he saw as evidence that the people had not only gained ascendancy over legislatures but over the judiciary as well. He also believed that, rather than improving the performance of government, the Progressive reforms were more likely to make it worse by lowering the quality of those seeking public office. "Only the timid, shambling, ineffective men," he argues, "can come out of a system which strips public office of character and authority and makes it directly subservient to popular whim."[37]

But, more important was that Olberholtzer saw direct legislation as a fundamental change for the worst in the character of state governments, moving them away from the representative democracy preferred by the nation's founders toward a system of direct citizen government the founders rejected. The authors of the Constitution had embraced the historic distinction between a republic and a democracy: the former being a system of representative government intended to protect liberty and encourage civic virtue, the latter one of direct citizen governance that tended toward mob rule. John Adams, in Olberholtzer's view, had perfected the former, while the radical French democrat Jean Jacques Rousseau had given legitimacy to the latter as a "vague and fanciful appeal for a new political order" devoid of "monarchical forms."[38] He derided the reformers as wanting, like Rousseau, "to make themselves the citizens of a new Arcadia" in which they would "bring the state back to a condition as near as possible to that ideal original form in which the citizens met under an oak tree and made their own laws."[39]

Olberholtzer believed that the reformers had no interest in history or in the development of institutions. They were simply impatient, frustrated that government moved too slowly, and were prepared to set aside "our properly established system" of government and "put in place some other which promises to be speedier and less refractory in operation." Their primary interest was in change. Too often, it was change "only for the sake of change," though more often, he charged, it was to enact policies that "will work for the personal advantage of [the reformer] and of members of his social class."[40] The initiative and referendum, he opined, were nothing more than "bludgeons" with which to beat up on the slower moving parts of the system in order to do favors for the reformer's friends. The American founders had chosen a republican form of government to resist transient majorities and gusts of public opinion so that the state might "effectively perform the great tasks set for it to do, while at the same time owing the necessary responsibility to the people."[41]

Progressives saw many "evils" in government and politics in need of eradication, but Olberholtzer argued that all of them were of the people's own making. Yet, the proposed reforms gave those same people a more direct and influential role in the political process. By what logic, he asked, should we think that a people unable to judge wisely in the selection of representatives would be able to judge wisely in the making of public policy? Olberholtzer thought the reforms merely a facade intended to conceal the real purpose of Progressivism. Reformers overstated problems because it served a larger purpose: "politicians advocate 'reform for votes;' the editor, 'reform for circulation.'" But, most important by far were the "socialistic classes" who "raise up and dignify the 'plain people,' the common people," all the while defaming large corporations and the wealthy whom they charge with controlling legislatures, governors, and the courts. The reform movement, Olberholtzer believed, was in fact class warfare. It was what anyone familiar with Aristotle's classification of constitutions would expect in a pure democracy and precisely what the nation's founders sought to avoid.[42]

A similar critique of Progressivism came from Charles M. Hollingsworth, who found ludicrous the claim of Oregon Senator Jonathan Bourne, an ally of U'Ren, that direct government reforms had guaranteed the people absolute control of government. Instead, these "pseudo-democratic reforms," he charged, were the first step toward arbitrary rule by a single individual. Citing the examples of Robert La Follette and Hiram Johnson, as well as U'Ren, who repeatedly claimed personal and largely exclusive credit for reforms made in their states, Hollingsworth charged that "what the 'progressive' reform movement really does is to provide ways and means by which a majority of the electorate may commission one man ... with plenary, unrestricted powers" to carry out a program of governance that he alone had promised. This may be government *for* the people, he observed, but it puts "a severe strain on the meaning of terms to call it, pre-eminently, government *of* the people or *by* the people, or apply to it the descriptive phrase, 'restoring government to the people.'"[43]

In a sweeping indictment, Hollingsworth charges that the initiative and referendum were neither progressive nor democratic and were very likely unconstitutional. The representative system, he argued, "marks the greatest advance of modern over ancient constitutional government," yet direct-government reforms repudiate it and seek to return the country to a system used when states were small in size. If this is "progress," he observed with disgust, the word has a very different meaning from the way it is used elsewhere. No scientist would think that returning to conditions, methods, or systems of ancient times was progress. The American constitutional system was widely seen as marking a new era in the world's political progress, he argued, by advancing from arbitrary to free government. Making the system more popular does not, in itself, advance the cause of free government, but rather sets the stage for its demise. In the name of reform, Progressives were "inaugurating what was the last modification of the ancient popular systems of government before their final downfall and disappearance."[44]

Hollingsworth also rejects the claim that direct government was more democratic than the representative system. Indeed, he denied that Progressivism was a democratic movement, arguing that it was instead a class movement, a prelude to socialism, which was "avowedly in the interest of the 'plain people,' the 'common people,' the 'masses,' who have comparatively little wealth ... and against those who own or control large accumulations of wealth." Its aim was *economic*, not political. The real goal of the reformers, he believed, was to exclude the smaller class with large economic interests from having any voice in government; and he dismissed all claims which took the opposite view that the movement would disproportionately benefit the large economic interests.[45] Reformers aspire to replace party bosses with "leaders of the people," but this, he noted, was the literal meaning of the term "demagogue." Under such a regime, "in which all business [would be] administered by popular decrees," popularity and not the law would be supreme. This was neither democratic nor progressive and was instead "only a repetition of ancient history."[46]

Like others, Hollingsworth argued that the direct primary and direct government would not increase the power of the people as a whole but would instead empower ambitious individuals and nongovernmental groups. It was, however, the Progressive abridgement of a representative system of democracy that led Hollingsworth to his most damning accusation that the direct government reforms of the Progressives were unconstitutional. The Constitution guaranteed a republican form of government to all the states, and a republican government had since the time of Aristotle meant a representative system of government. The Progressive reforms, in Hollingsworth's opinion, would so erode representation as to violate this guarantee, as well as the nation's sacred pledge of allegiance to the United States of America and to the republic for which it stood. This was not a new charge. The constitutional guarantee of republican government had been raised nationally a year earlier when President William Howard Taft vetoed the constitution proposed by the Arizona territory in its application for statehood.

## Arizona and the recall

The debate over direct government arrived on the national stage in 1910 when Arizona applied for statehood proposing a constitution that included a provision for the recall of judges. Congress approved it, but President William Howard Taft did not. In his veto message, the president argued that giving voters the power to recall state judges violated the provision in the federal Constitution that guaranteed all states a republican form of government. Taft did not dwell on the meaning of "republican" government but focused instead on the importance of an independent judiciary. The Constitution, he noted, provided for separate branches of government with the legislative and executive being democratic, filled by election, responsive to public opinion, and accountable to the people. The judiciary, however, was different. Its members were appointed and were responsible to the law, not to the people or to public opinion. This required that judges be protected from the momentary passions of voters. Taft argued that this division of government had provided "great security" for free institutions, and that this security was "only firm and assured when the judicial branch is independent and impartial." Judges, he insisted, "must decide every question which comes before them according to law and justice" without regard for public opinion.[47]

Proponents of direct government protested the president's action, arguing that the Arizona constitution had been ratified by popular vote and that the residents of the territory should be able to decide for themselves the form that popular government would take in their state.[48] Framers of the Arizona constitution acknowledged that the Oregon Plan had guided their work, and they asked one of its architects, Senator Bourne, for his opinion about their proposal. Claiming that "Oregon has evolved the best system of popular government in the world," Bourne assured Arizonans that they had been wise to incorporate constitutional provisions that enabled them to hold public officials immediately accountable. He urged that the principle of governing themselves directly was too important to be surrendered to any man who "happens to occupy temporarily the office of President." "Dictation from one man in Washington," he counseled, "should be as distasteful to the people of Arizona as dictation from London was to the American colonists."[49]

An outraged Charles Hollingsworth denounced Bourne, ridiculing his "unbounded pretensions" in challenging the rightful authority of a man "who 'happens'—by the free choice of the whole nation—to be president of the United States and who was acting to enforce the constitutional guarantee of republican government for all states." He thought it contemptible that Bourne should equate the actions of the president with those of George III. Bourne had also urged the people of Arizona to forego statehood rather than accede to the demands of the president. Hollingsworth thought this suggestion "so impractical and utterly unstatesmanlike as to be ridiculous and childish" and found it appalling that Bourne and reformers like him believed that government-by-the-people could be "carried to the point of entirely disregarding the official authority of the Chief Executive of the Nation."[50] He saw this as yet further evidence that Bourne and those like him were radicals intent upon subverting constitutional government in America.

President Taft won the battle. Arizona changed its constitution to drop the recall provision. But he lost the war. Subsequent to its admission to the Union, Arizona amended its constitution to include a provision for the recall of judges. Through it all, the constitutional question about the meaning of "republican" government was never engaged. It appears to have become an afterthought in the more immediate debate over the merits of the initiative and referendum. In the end, the term republican lost its distinctive association with representation in the vocabulary of politics and became simply interchangeable in meaning with democracy. It was among several political concepts whose historic meanings changed during the Progressive era with unintended and, for the most part, unexamined consequences.

# Notes

1    Milkis, *Theodore Roosevelt, the Progressive Party, and the Transformation of American Democracy*, Chapter 3. Also Doris Kearns Goodwin, *The Bully*

*Pulpit* (New York: Simon & Schuster, 2013), 686. The *New York Times*, noting that 1912 was the first use of primaries in a presidential contest, observed editorially, "We hope it may be our last. The spectacle presented by the fierce fight for the nomination is one … that should bring a blush of shame to the cheek of every American." The old system, the editorial continued, "was a rational, a seemly procedure," but under the new one "we are no longer a people, but a mob." Quoted in Goodwin, *The Bully Pulpit*, 695.

2   Russell B. Nye, *Midwestern Progressive Politics* (New York: Harper & Row, 1959), Chapter 5.

3   George E. Mowry, *The California Progressives* (Berkley, University of California, 1951), Chapters.

4   A presidential primary was added in 1912.

5   Robert S. Maxwell, *La Follette and the Rise of the Progressives in Wisconsin* (Madison: State Historical Society of Wisconsin, 1956), Chapter 5. See too David P. Thelen, *Robert La Follette and the Rise of Progressives in Wisconsin* (Boston: Little, Brown, 1976).

6   A lengthy account of convention is published on-line by the Wisconsin Historical Society at "Political Reform in Wisconsin: The Direct Primary," http://my.execpc.com/~fedsoc/phipol101.html (accessed December 12, 2014). The 1904 Republican National Convention rejected the delegates chosen by the La Follette convention and seated those chosen by the regulars. For La Follette's account of the 1904 convention, see his *Autobiography* (Madison: University of Wsconsin, 1960), 138–141.

7   Herbert F. Margulies, *The Decline of the Progressive Movement in Wisconsin 1890–1920* (Madison: State Historical Society of Wisconsin, 1968), 50.

8   In 1908, Philipp won a lawsuit for malicious libel against *McClure's* and Ray Stannard Baker for an article that drew directly on accusations made about him by Governor La Follette which the court found slanderous. Robert S. Maxwell, *Emanuel L. Philipp: Wisconsin Stalwart* (Madison: State Historical Society of Wisconsin, 1959), Chapter 5.

9   Margulies, *The Decline of the Progressive Movement in Wisconsin 1890–1920*, 50.

10  Emanuel L. Philipp, *Political Reform in Wisconsin* (Madison: State Historical Society of Wisconsin, 1973), reprint, and Robert M. La Follette, *Autobiography* (Madison: University of Wisconsin, 1963), reprint.

11  Stanley P. Caine and Roger E. Wyman, "Introduction," *Political Reform in Wisconsin*, 78 (1973).

12  Philipp details dramatic increases from 1898 to 1908 in the cost of elections for governor and other state executive offices, as well as for mayor of Milwaukee. Philipp, *Political Reform in Wisconsin*, 80–82.

13  Philipp, *Political Reform in Wisconsin*,79.

14  Philipp, *Political Reform in Wisconsin*, 80.

15  Philipp, *Political Reform in Wisconsin*, 87.

16  Philipp, *Political Reform in Wisconsin*, 89.

17  Philipp, *Political Reform in Wisconsin*, 89–91.

18  Philipp, *Political Reform in Wisconsin*, 89.

19  Philipp, *Political Reform in Wisconsin*, 92.

20  Philipp, *Political Reform in Wisconsin*, 94.

21  Maxwell, *Philipp: Wisconsin Stalwart*, 86.

22  http://oregonlive.com/O/index.ssf/2011/03/william_uren_gave_oregon_syste.html, 1 (accessed December 09, 2014).

23  Robert D. Johnston, *The Radical Middle Class* (Princeton: Princeton University, 2003), 127.

24  Quotes from Ellis Paxson Olberholtzer, *The Referendum in America* (New York: Charles Scribner's Sons, 1912), 505. In an address to the Oregon Bar Association, attorney Charles Carey, after reviewing the dangers posed by the methods of direct government, urged that restraints be placed upon them. Another Portland attorney and University of Oregon trustee, Frederick Holman, went farther, telling a Chicago audience that the initiative and referendum had been greatly abused, that questions were often loosely drawn, voters unable to make intelligent judgments on many of them, that as participation declined legislation was being adopted by a minority of voters, often against the best interests of the state, and that the state's constitution was being "freely changed with reckless regard." Olberholtzer, *The Referendum in America*, 503–505.

25  Herbert Croly, *Progressive Democracy* (New York: Macmillan, 1914), 256–257.

26  Croly, *Progressive Democracy*, 284. See too Allen H. Eaton, *The Oregon System* (Chicago: A. C. McClurg & Co., 1912), Chapter 16. Eaton is sympathetic to the initiative and referendum but feels that it has been used for purposes for which it was not intended and has not been all that

was promised, yet the principle good but the "machinery" is in need of perfection.

27  Croly, *Progressive Democracy*, 284.

28  Croly, *Progressive Democracy*, 306.

29  Croly, *Progressive Democracy*, 307.

30  Croly, *Progressive Democracy*, 308.

31  Croly, *Progressive Democracy*, 307.

32  Woodrow Wilson, *Constitutional Government in the United States* (New York: Columbia University, 1908), 104–105.

33  Wilson, *Constitutional Government in the United States*, 105. Wilson appears to have changed his mind during his 1916 bid for reelection as president. Faced with a Progressive Republican opponent, New York Governor Charles Evan Hughes, Wilson spoke favorably about the initiative in a campaign visit to Oregon.

34  A. Lawrence Lowell, *Public Opinion and Popular Government* (New York: Longmans, Green and Co., 1930), 209.

35  Lawrence Lowell, *Public Opinion and Popular Government*, 210–211.

36  Olberholtzer, *The Referendum in America*, 471. The work compares in great detail the statutory and constitutional provisions in all of the states that had adopted the initiative, referendum, and recall. Published originally in 1893, it was updated several times until a final edition appeared in 1912.

37  Olberholtzer, *The Referendum in America*, 477–478.

38  Olberholtzer, *The Referendum in America*, 471.

39  Olberholtzer, *The Referendum in America*, 467 and 500.

40  Olberholtzer, *The Referendum in America*, 492.

41  Olberholtzer, *The Referendum in America*, 472.

42  Olberholtzer, *The Referendum in America*, 475.

43  Charles M. Hollingsworth, "The So-Called Progressive Movement: Its Real Nature, Causes, and Significance," in *The Annals* (Philadelphia: Academy of Political and Social Sciences, September 1912), 30. Emphasis added. The editors have been unsuccessful in attempts to locate biographical information for Charles Hollingsworth. The invitation from the Academy to participate in a symposium on the initiative and referendum suggests that he was a scholar of some repute, as does his self-published volume on the Oregon Plan. Neither publication indicated an institutional affiliation.

44  Hollingsworth, "So-Called Progressive Movement", 34.

45  Charles M. Hollingsworth, *The "Oregon Plan": Is It A Political Panacea?*
    (Washington: by Charles M. Hollingsworth, 1911), 13.

46  Hollingsworth, "Hollingsworth, So-Called Progressive Movement", 35–36.
    Hollingsworth was no champion of democracy, but like Nicholas Murray
    Butler preferred a meritocracy.

47  Quoted in Delos F. Wilcox, *Government By All the People* (New York:
    Macmillan, 1912), 212–214.

48  This was of course the idea of popular sovereignty that Stephen Douglas
    had championed and Abraham Lincoln rejected in their pre-Civil War
    debates about slavery.

49  Quoted in Hollingsworth, *The "Oregon Plan,"* 7.

50  Hollingsworth, *The "Oregon Plan,"* 8–9.

# 10

# American Politics Remade

Jerome M. Mileur
*University of Massachusetts Amherst*

The storm of Progressivism began building in the final decades of the nineteenth century—Mugwumps in the East, Populists in the West—and blew across the nation in the first years of the twentieth century to transform the landscape of American politics. Older notions of limited government buttressed by laissez-faire attitudes were swept away by a nationalizing gale that left behind a more activist presidency and an enlarged bureaucracy at the center of the nation's governance, depositing ideas of congressional government in the dustbin of history. So too with the idea of party government. The older structure of partisan politics, of caucuses and conventions, was directly in the path of the fierce winds that hammered the political bosses and their machines. The storm hit with the fury of rectitude, leaving behind the tattered remains of representative democracy that were to be resurrected and given new life by the new institutions of "pure" democracy that promised to restore the power of the people as individuals to its rightful place in the governance of state and nation.

The Progressives saw the founders Constitution as outdated and an impediment to change. Their reforms, however, Thomas West argues, were not modest adjustments to facilitate a more effective response to new social and economic conditions but were instead "a total rejection in theory, and a partial rejection in practice of the principles and policies on which America has been founded." Jeffrey Sedgwick agrees, calling the Progressive moment a "second founding." The reformers abandoned the Natural Law foundation upon which the Constitution had rested, amending its carefully designed construction of representative institutions and intricate arrangement of checks and balances by appending a complex of direct-democracy and direct-government reforms.[1] The critics of Progressivism focused heavily on how these political reforms were likely to affect the operation of constitutional government as they knew it: the effect on representative institutions, on elections and party government, on the character of politics, on the role of political money and public opinion, and on leadership in government and politics.

By the twentieth century, the founders Constitution had undergone significant change with the expansion of executive power during the Jacksonian and Lincoln presidencies as well as the creation of a mass-based political party system and party government. Only the separation of presidential and vice-presidential voting in the Electoral College had entailed a constitutional or statutory action. All of the other changes had evolved naturally within the constitutional frame, and all were consistent with republican principles of governance. This changed after the Civil War. Before the war, with the exception of voter registration laws, there had been little statutory regulation of elections, and almost none of political parties which had grown up as extra-constitutional private associations. This changed in the decade of the 1880s with civil-service reform and adoption of Australian ballot laws.[2] The former sought to end the system of patronage that was central to the Jacksonian party system, while the latter provided government printed ballots that not only assured secrecy in voting, but also gave statutory definition to political parties, transforming them into quasi-public institutions.

Before the Civil War, informal changes in the methods of nomination and election to public office were driven by a growing spirit of populist democracy, especially in the newer western states where universal white male suffrage was the norm. Changes in the methods of campaigning and making nominations expanded the reach and depth of popular government but did not displace liberty as the primary purpose or objective (the telos) of constitutional government in America.[3] Democracy remained one dimension in a regime of mixed government as bequeathed to the nation by its founders. For those critical of the Progressive political reforms, "democracy" meant what it had to American statesmen since Jefferson: popular *control* of government. To Progressives, however, it meant the *direct rule* by the people. This idea of democracy was the rock upon which the Progressive program was built. The reformers, as Robert Lacey observes, had an "unreflective faith in democracy as an end in itself." Nonetheless, the Progressive notion of democracy went largely unquestioned and unchallenged by most of the critics, for whom defense of the founders Constitution was the overriding concern.[4] There is great irony here, for despite the obeisance Progressives paid to "Father Abraham," they turned their backs on Lincoln's understanding of democracy, embracing instead the more simple and simplistic idea popular sovereignty championed by his adversary, Stephen Douglas.

Popular sovereignty as the definition of democracy had been a centerpiece of the 1858 debates between Lincoln and Douglas. To the latter, democracy was simply majority rule, which led to his contention that the democratic solution for whether a territory would enter the Union as a free or slave state should be decided by majority vote of its residents. Lincoln agreed that popular sovereignty was an essential component of any definition of democracy, but that there was more to the idea of democracy in America than simply rule by a majority. In the American frame, he argued, democracy was limited by a higher law recognized in the nation's founding document, *The Declaration of Independence*, which held that all men were created equal and endowed by their Creator with certain inalienable rights. For Lincoln, the principles upon which the nation was founded were sacred. They preceded the Constitution, defined both the purpose and moral character of the new nation, and could not be overridden by simple majorities if the nation were to remain true to the principles to which its founders had dedicated it.

Like his political heroes, Henry Clay and Daniel Webster, Lincoln held a more nuanced understanding of democracy that was captured in the great prepositional trilogy of the Gettysburg Address as government of, by, and for the people. Not only did this parade of prepositions identify three different dimensions of democracy, but Lincoln's understanding of democracy was deepened further by the phrase "government *of* the people," which is a gerund with a double meaning. As the "love of God" meant both that Man loves God and that God loves Man, so too this dimension of Lincoln's definition meant that, while the people control the government, the government must also govern the people.[5] The system of representative democracy bequeathed the nation by its founders was a logical by-product of this definition whereas the Progressive embrace of Douglas's popular sovereignty was more congenial to their nostrum of direct citizen democracy.

## The case against direct forms of politics and governance

The critics of Progressive reforms were backward-looking in their assessments of direct democracy and direct government, much as the American founders had been backward-looking in justifying revolution and designing a Constitution.

The republican view of the founders was shaped by the history and experience of ancient Athens and Rome. They drew from the seventeenth-century Puritan Revolution in England for their notions of popular government, of citizenship, and of the rights that defined liberty. They produced a written declaration to explain and justify their separation from England, but the ideas in it, so its author said, were commonplace, not original to the document, and they produced a written constitution, an invention of sorts but one that drew heavily upon the ideas of Locke, Montesquieu, Machiavelli, and Aristotle, as well as from the American colonial experience under British rule. The only novelty in the Constitution was the creation of a federal system with two levels of sovereignty, but this too came from experience, not theory, born of practical necessity to win approval from states that had long existed as colonies, separate from one another and jealous of their identities and authority. The Progressives, their critics argued, approached reform not by the careful empiricism and inductive methods of James Madison and the American founders, and of the much admired English statesman Edmund Burke, but instead proceeded by deduction from an ideal of democracy that was based in part on a romantic image of town-hall democracy in the New England states.

In many ways, therefore, the critics represented the "last hurrah" for the American Founding. They were voices in defense of the Constitution, republican government, and representative institutions, presenting arguments that had been the staple of American political discourse from the founding through the Civil War. Most of them, like William Howard Taft, had a deep reverence for the Constitution. Some thought it an inspired document, the product of demigods; all saw it as the cornerstone in the historical development of America from which all else had followed. Some retained a belief in the Natural Law foundations of the Constitution, but most held an organic view of the Constitution and felt, as Henry Jones Ford did, that over time it had adapted well to calls for greater democracy, evolving through a process that was consistent with the new science of Darwin as well as with the example of the founders. Most of the critics shared Ford's view that the Constitution was a living thing whose orderly adaptation to change enabled the various parts of the body politic to adjust naturally and harmoniously to new conditions and practices. Lincoln was their model President, not only for his political leadership in having saved the Union and moral leadership in ending slavery, but also because he based all of his actions on the authority of the Constitution, even when some departed from previous understandings and practices. Lincoln understood the document to be a solemn compact that the dead had passed to the living and for which the living had the equally solemn duty to preserve so that it might pass unbroken to generations yet unborn. Most of the critics saw the Progressive reforms as a breach of this compact, as a dangerous departure from it that would leave behind an unfamiliar and untested Constitution, not a stronger one as the reformers claimed.

The Progressives did not share their critics' understanding of the historical movement to popular government as a steady evolution from the failures of ancient democracies through the rise of empires and monarchies to the Magna Charta and more liberal forms of government, culminating in the founding of the American Republic with its advanced frame of government. Indeed, the reformers seemed to view the present as a moment in an historical progression of moments that moved unsteadily in the direction of popular government, but with significant interruptions and misdirection. The slaughter of the Civil War was sufficient evidence for them that history was not an orderly or seamless process, and the failure of constitutional government to prevent it had reduced the founders from demigods to mere mortals. It was a perspective found in the work of Progressive historians like Charles Beard, whose economic interpretation of the Constitution was a less romantic and more cynical (Beard would have said, "more realistic") account of the motives and behavior of the Framers.[6] If history taught any lesson, it was, the historian Carl Becker observed, that history taught *no* lessons, while the political scientist Arthur Bentley, focusing on the behavior of public officials, concluded that all outcomes of government were the result of interest group interactions and pressures, not abstract values or ideals.[7]

Progressives and their critics alike embraced Darwinian science and found the Social Darwinism of Herbert Spencer repugnant. Progressives, however, thought the process of evolution too slow for a world of rapid social and economic change. Unlike Lincoln, who conceded that events had controlled him, the reformers believed that that Man, not Nature, should control both the direction and pace of change in government and politics and were confident that they could and would do so. Their critics, on the other hand, believed that change should be natural, that it should grow from and build upon experience, and that politics should proceed "scientifically" through experimentation. Change based on abstract theory could have excessively disruptive and even dangerous consequences. Critics like Elihu Root, who sympathized with the Progressive view that change in governance was desirable, nonetheless objected to many of their political reforms as being disconnected from history and insensitive to the "unintended consequences" that proposals might have for institutions of governance other than those targeted by the reformers.

It was the threat these reforms were seen as posing to republican government and the constitutional system of representative democracy that most alarmed the critics. They warned that direct government (the initiative in particular) would undermine the moderate and more qualitative politics in legislative bodies where those of varying opinions could engage each other in face-to-face discussions of their differences and adjust their views to accommodate the reasonable objections of others. A deliberative process of give-and-take would thus be displaced by one in which "the people," not their elected representatives, would make decisions and would do so with only a two-word vocabulary, "yes" and "no." A qualitative politics would thereby be replaced by a quantitative one in which deliberation was shunted aside and only numbers would be important. The claims of reformers notwithstanding, this was not a more democratic process, the critics insisted, but rather one open to manipulation and domination by elites who would control which questions were on the ballot and how they were framed. Moreover, experience with the initiative, albeit limited at the time, was that only a fraction (often a very small fraction) of those voting for candidates also voted on ballot questions. Progressive theories of empowering the people were a deceit, the critics insisted, because the real effect of direct government would be to diminish the power of the people, not increase it.

Reformers, however, insisted that the outcome of initiative elections was a valid measure of public opinion. Taft and others denied this, arguing that turnout in these elections was not representative of the mass electorate and that outcomes could be manipulated to produce the result sought by sponsors of an initiative. A strong advocate of representative institutions who regarded the Progressive worship of democracy as a fetish, Taft argued that the existing system was more truly "representative" of the people than were citizen plebiscites. Ford agreed with Taft, adding that direct forms of democracy made it more difficult to determine whom to blame for the actions of government. Legislators could not (or should not) be held responsible for decisions made by the people. Moreover, direct government made it easier for legislators to evade responsibility by referring decisions on controversial matters to a public referendum. For Ford, responsibility was essential in a democracy. In addition, Taft, Ford, and other critics feared that direct government posed a serious threat to civil liberties, especially to the freedoms of speech and religion, which they thought more secure in the hands of elected representatives than in those of the mob. The tyranny of the many, Taft argued in an echo of the founders, was as great a threat to individual liberties as that of any unrestrained monarch.[8]

The critics shared the Progressive preference for executive leadership but worried that the direct-government reforms which expanded executive power might so weaken legislative authority as to pose the threat of an "unrestrained monarch." Many feared that the combination of direct government and direct democracy created conditions ripe for demagogues. Pandering to public passions was the very essence of demagoguery, and abandoning constitutional constraints on the exercise of power in favor of mere popularity risked the rise of unprincipled individuals whose lust for office would be predicated on personality, their campaigns filled with irresponsible accusations and empty promises. The critics did not share the confidence of reformers in public opinion as a guide to governing or as a restraint on the excesses of ambition. Indeed, they thought it a feeble constraint, and most likely none at all, on the ambition of unscrupulous candidates skilled in the arts of popularity, who upon election could lay personal claim to being the "voice of the people."

Of the direct-government reforms, none provoked a more spirited opposition than the proposal for the recall of judges and judicial decisions. Nicholas Murray Butler called it "the most preposterous and more vicious" of the Progressive reforms. An independent judiciary was seen by almost all of the critics as the bedrock of a free constitutional democracy, with decisions removed as far as possible from influence by the public. Judges owed their duty to the Constitution and to the law, as William Howard Taft never tired of preaching, *not* to the people. In his 1912 presidential bid as candidate of the Progressive Party, Theodore Roosevelt was abandoned by close friends like Root, and even his son-in-law, Congressman Nicholas Longstreet, when he endorsed the idea of judicial recall. The founders had provided that justices of the Supreme Court be appointed for life, removable only by impeachment, so that they might be free from political pressures. Recall exposed judges to the political passions of the moment, thereby threatening not only the carefully balanced design of the Constitution but also the security of civil liberties. Taft feared that some Progressives did not regard individual rights as absolute and denounced that view as alien to the principles of the *Declaration of Independence*. The critics rallied as well to the defense of judicial review which they thought essential to both judicial independence and judicial power and as the ultimate protection for civil liberties.

Progressives and their critics were deeply divided in their respective views on the importance of politics in the nation's governance. Reformers tended to see it as a corrupt, boss-ridden, deal-making and unprincipled activity that was too often an impediment to good government. They believed that a nonpartisan civil service, staffed with experts and using scientific methods of management, would substantially reduce the role of politics by eliminating favoritism, patronage, and other unsavory influences in the administration of government. The direct primaries, the initiative and referendum, and the regulation of lobbying and campaign finance were expected to do much the same for legislatures by cleansing them of the forces of corruption, thereby restoring not only honesty and competence to the public service but also the ideal of the general good as the standard by which the people's business should be conducted. If Progressives did not condemn the activity of politics as such, they did denounce all things "political," which to their critics was a distinction without a difference.

All of the critics rallied to the defense of politics as inherent in and essential to free government, most believing that it had been built into the Constitution through the division of powers between three branches and two levels of government. The only way so fractured a construction could be made to work without one division tyrannizing over the others was through reasonable bargaining and compromise. The critics acknowledged the evils of the boss system, but thought reformers failed to appreciate the critical role that parties as institutions played in a democracy. They saw the political party as the principal institution through which the collective wishes of the people could find effective expression in the political arena. To be sure, parties were in need of reform, but not extinction. Albeit extra-constitutional, having emerged naturally to bridge the institutional gaps between the branches and divisions of government, the two-party system made it possible for government to function more effectively. Several of the critics—Woodrow Wilson, Elihu Root, and Eugene Debs among them—urged that the parties be reformed along lines that later became familiar to political scientists as the "responsible-parties model." Political parties, the critics insisted, were essential to democracy. Indeed, Root asserted that democracy could not function in the absence of parties. They may not have agreed with Joseph Cannon's idea of party government, but they certainly agreed with Lincoln's. They also agreed on the virtue of a two-party system as being the natural by-product of Man's nature in that there seemed always to be two sides to every public question, and they regarded nonpartisan forms as simply a fiction.

The critics were opposed to the direct primary for its adverse effect on political parties. In their view, primaries rendered parties irresponsible and ineffective as representative institutions. In taking candidate nominations away from the direct control of party members, the primary might strike a blow at bossism but would do so at the expense of parties as organizations by removing the principal incentive for citizens to participate in them. Emanuel Philipp noted that, after only four years and two cycles of primary elections in Wisconsin, an extensive party infrastructure based in municipalities and counties across the state had disappeared entirely and with it had gone cadres of workers as well as a principal source of financing for the campaigns of party candidates. No longer did thousands of citizens meet together in local caucuses and state conventions to discuss the selection of party candidates. Instead of having a voice in vetting prospective candidates in the early stages of the process, party members were left with nothing more than a vote at the end.[9] Voting alone, however, as Root observed, was not enough to satisfy the duties of citizenship in a democracy. Primaries provided no role for party members in setting the party agenda, determining policy priorities, or drafting a platform, all of which became the responsibility of candidates.

The party platform also lost its significance as a guide to and control over the way officials, elected in the name of the party, conducted themselves in office. With no peer review, candidates simply put themselves forward supported by personal organizations and campaigning on issues of their own selection. Instead of their being bound by the collective interests of the party, the party was left to live with the policy positions taken by those who won its primaries, who may or may not agree with one another or with the historic principles of the party. With no platform to which candidates were pledged, there could be no party responsibility for the actions of those chosen in the party's name. Responsibility was at the heart of Ford's notion of democratic governance, and the direct primary made this all but impossible. For him, the essence of democracy was that voters be able to *control* government and to do this required that they be able to assign responsibility for decisions that were made. Regular elections were sufficient to this end but only if voters knew whom to blame if they objected to the actions of the government.[10] The direct primary reduced the party to little more than a label, the winning of which was prerequisite for success in the general election, but the overall effect of which was to create an undisciplined system in which both representation and collective responsibility were muddled.

Beyond their effect on political parties, critics faulted primaries for changing the character of the nation's politics. All saw money as becoming vastly more important as primaries would multiply the number of candidates seeking various offices as well as double the number of elections, thereby doubling the cost to taxpayers for the administration of elections. Where campaigns had previously been financed primarily by the parties, they had now to be paid for from private sources as each hopeful pursued private contributions for themselves alone. This, the critics argued, gave a disproportionate advantage to wealthy candidates, to those with wealthy friends, and to private groups willing to donate sizable sums to candidates, tilting politics even more in favor of upper-class interests and against those of the working class and the poor. Some also complained that the primary would splinter politics in legislatures where members, elected as individuals, would be free agents and more willing to cross party lines, thereby adding to the difficulty for voters to know who was responsible for actions taken. For some, like Debs, primaries created an unprincipled politics in which personality and image would count for more than program, a system in which the building of an authentic mass-based politics would most likely be impossible. To others, the primaries threw the door wide open to demagogues.[11]

The reformers and their critics also had sharply different views of human nature and of the role of the people and public opinion in government. Direct democracy rested on an optimistic and, to its critics, dubious view that individuals were by nature virtuous and public spirited but had been corrupted by politics. Released from the corrupting influence of politics, their decisions on public questions would be in the interests of the general good. Indeed, some reformers claimed the pure voice of the people was the secular equivalent to the voice of God. The Progressives thus assumed human nature to be what they needed it to be to justify their reforms. The critics, on the other hand, retained the more pessimistic and, to them, more realistic Madisonian view that men were not angels. The new democracy, Taft among others insisted, would not change human nature. Ambition, not idealism, ruled Man's behavior, and popular government, if it were to preserve liberty and maintain order, had to protect the people from their baser instincts. This was best done through the founders system of representative institutions that could filter public opinion, mediate conflicting views, and be accountable to the people at regular elections. With the check provided by periodic elections, the people could control the actions of government; they need have no role in or responsibility for the actual administration of government. Ford put this view concisely: for policy making, elect; for administration, appoint. The Progressives, their critics believed, simply asked more of citizens than was realistic or necessary for a system of popular democracy. In the end, it left the people as a whole weaker, not stronger, in a regime ruled by minorities, not majorities, dominated by money.

## The legacy of reform[12]

The historian Richard Hofstadter has characterized Progressivism as a middle-class movement for reform.[13] At its core, this middle class embodied a professionalism new to American life—in law, medicine, education, and journalism—organized both nationally and in the states by associations with rules of conduct and ethical codes to guide and discipline the behavior of their members. These new professionals were in the first generation of Americans to reach adulthood following the Civil War. Almost none had been a combatant but all were familiar with the brutal consequences of the conflict and its aftermath, which led them to feel that something had gone awfully wrong in America to produce anything so terrible, something that neither the nation's Constitution nor its politicians had been able to prevent. Postwar America was also experiencing dramatic social and economic change: industrialization had transformed the economy, immigration had remade society, urbanization had changed the physical landscape, and westward expansion had redrawn the nation's geography. Yet, the nation's politics seemed mired in corruption and incapable of constructive response, more the problem than the solution in a phrase made popular in the 1960s.

Progressivism offered a broad program of political reforms that promised a more pure democracy in which the people would share responsibility for governance with their elected officials. These reforms resonated with the new college-trained professionals for whom it became both an agenda for and measure of good government. The Progressive case was championed by a number of charismatic leaders—Robert La Follette in Wisconsin, William d'Uren in Oregon, Hiram Johnson in California, and nationally by Theodore Roosevelt in his 1912 bid for the presidency. New magazines, especially *McClure's* with its cadre of Muckraking reporters like Lincoln Steffens, Ida Tarbell, and Ray Stannard Baker, also built support for Progressive reforms among its middle-class readers.[14] In addition, the growing presence of universities inhabited by historians and social scientists whose interests in society, the economy, and government were more practical and applied than theoretical provided scholarly backing for reform.[15] If Charles Beard at Columbia represented the new history, Richard Ely and John R. Commons at Wisconsin, Charles Merriam at Chicago, and Thorstein Veblen at Chicago and Stanford embodied the new reform-minded social sciences, while William James at Harvard offered the new "realistic" American philosophy of pragmatism. They were joined by social reformers like Lilian Wald in New York and Jane Addams in Chicago and their counterparts in education like John Dewey at Chicago.

. The critics enjoyed no comparable support. They had neither leaders as attractive nor spokesmen as articulate as those associated with reform.[16] The critics sounded like voices from an older America defending a political order that had proven inadequate to secure the Union and seemed unable or unwilling to deal with the nation's new agonies. Little wonder that Progressivism captured the hearts and minds of the new professional classes, as direct democracy and direct government triumphed. Since the 1970s, nominations for all offices at all levels of government have been made through primary elections, the last to succumb being the presidency when the mixed system for nominations that existed for a half century after World War I was displaced after the 1960s by Democratic Party reforms of the presidential selection process. The political parties have fallen victim to the primaries, as the reformers desired and their critics feared. The initiative and referendum have not spread as widely as primaries, but their impact on the nation's politics since the 1970s has been profound nonetheless, pushing government and politics away from the liberalism of Progressivism, the New Deal, and the Great Society toward the conservatism of Ronald Reagan and his heirs. Participatory democracy, the 1960s version of direct democracy and direct government, has produced many new avenues for direct citizen intervention in the administration of government, especially through the courts, and has done as much to check activist government as to guide it in constructive directions. It has led as well to the privatization of many public programs which, whatever the benefits, has complicated and confused responsibility for the conduct of the public's business.

With the spread of nonpartisan forms and a severely weakened party system, political movements that sprang from the mid-century rights revolution became the driving force for liberalism in the nation's politics, only to be repeatedly frustrated and at times overwhelmed as the interest-group liberalism, born of the New Deal, morphed into a new interest-group conservatism that came to prominence in the final decades of the twentieth century. Together, movement liberalism and movement conservatism have hardened into partisan divisions that have stalled and often stalemated federal action on public matters. Moreover, as the critics of Progressive political reforms foresaw, candidate-centered campaigns focused on personality more than program have become the norm in elections, making money vastly more important in almost every aspect of American politics and governance. In legislative bodies, fund-raising now not only consumes an inordinate amount of time but has also tilted both membership and agendas in the direction of wealth, marginalizing further the influence of the middle class and working poor, rendering them, more than minorities or women, the most underrepresented group in the nation's system of "representative" government.

There is perhaps no greater indictment of the Progressive reforms than that rendered by "the People," whom reformers claimed would be the great beneficiaries of their program. Instead, as the critics predicted, large numbers of Americans feel less rather than more powerful. They have retreated in great numbers from politics, participating less and less in elections with turnout in presidential contests drooping to barely over 50 percent of those eligible to vote, lower yet for mid-term and state elections, including ballot questions, and lower still in municipal contests. Negativism and cynicism about politics has spread throughout the population, while government, state as well as national, has become the primary target of criticism from right and left alike. In addition, the critics of Progressivism were prescient about the role that public opinion would play in the new democracy, mocking claims that it would be the true voice of the people. It has instead produced what pollster George Gallop has called a "polling democracy" in which, to a remarkable degree, deliberation about candidates, public policy, and the direction of government has been replaced by numbers.

In the late 1960s, as political protests released a new flood of participatory democracy into the nation's politics, the political scientist, E. E. Schattschneider, concluded that the "dream about direct democracy [was] at the root of most of the modern disenchantment with democracy."[17] Walter Lippmann, a prominent Progressive in the first decades of the twentieth century, shared Schattschneider's mid-century misgivings, arguing that these reforms had produced "a functional derangement in the relationship between the executive power on the one hand, the representative assemblies and the mass electorates on the other hand."[18] Nothing in these assessments was changed by the rise of movement politics in the 1960s, the Democratic Party reforms in the 1970s, or the rise of Reagan conservatism in the 1980s. As the twentieth century ended, Philip Ethington renewed the complaints of Schattschneider and Lippmann, observing that, "among the many ironies of the so-called Progressive Era, the saddest perhaps is the deep and enduring damage done to democracy," adding that the Progressive reforms had "institutionally empowered a theory of representation that virtually guaranteed an ethically barren public discourse."[19] The historian Michael McGerr agreed, writing that "progressivism created much of our contemporary political predicament."[20]

The direct-democracy and direct-government reforms of the Progressives have become, in the words of Arthur Lipow, "part of the natural political order in the United States" whose character and function, despite occasional objections by a Schatschneider, a Lippmann, an Ethington, or a McGerr, "have remained relatively invisible, like a piece of furniture which blends into the background until we stumble over it in the middle of the night." In a "truly amazing" way, Lipow continues, these reforms have given "direction and fundamental outline" to changes that have taken place since, yet "the myths about the *political reform side* of the movement have proven to be peculiarly resistant to critical historical analysis [and] remarkably free from serious ideological or organized political challenge."[21] That these reforms should remain largely unquestioned and their consequences unexamined seems the more remarkable in that history has shown those who opposed them to have been correct in most of their criticisms. Histories of the Progressive era commonly ignore these critics or dismiss them as "conservatives" who were against change and, by implication, allied with the bosses, special interests, and unrestrained capitalism. This has no doubt contributed to the disappearance of their arguments from contemporary debates about democracy and political reform, but this may have less to do with ideology than with the fact that the Progressive triumph reached beyond the realm of reform into the vocabulary of political discourse. It reconstructed the everyday language of politics in ways that have made it more difficult to challenge the "natural political order" that is the Progressive legacy.

Searching for an answer to the question of what makes change happen in American politics, E. E. Schattschneider examined how the meaning of political words changed over time and concluded that a political conversation from the Progressive era would seem strange if not incomprehensible to a fellow American a century earlier to whom a radical was a "primitive," an issue an "offspring," and a boss "a stud of raised work on a door frame." The same would have been true for a conversation between a mid-twentieth-century American and one from a century earlier for whom an ethnic was a "heathen," a career a "race course," and a pragmatist "a meddler." In assessing the reform proposals of the Progressives, their critics used political words, like "democracy," to mean what they had meant through more than a century of American life whereas the reformers did not. Moreover, they apparently failed to recognize these linguistic shifts and their importance to the Progressive case. Coming from an era in which the Constitution had been at the center of political debates, the critics concentrated on defending the framers Constitution and, for the most part, did not address the Progressive understanding of democracy which drove their program. By not challenging the reformers' idea of democracy, the critics ceded the crucial terrain upon which their battle was fought and lost.

A half century later, Schattschneider addressed the question of democracy's meaning, beginning from the premise that, "How people define democracy is important," and asking, what is it that "the people" *do* and *can do* in a democracy? He found that Americans had given two answers to this question: there was Jefferson's answer in the *Declaration of Independence* that democracy was "government by *consent of* the people," and another from the Progressives that it was "government *directly by* the people." These definitions, he observed, envisioned "profoundly different" roles for the people. "It is one thing for the people to govern," he wrote, "and it is something else to judge the leaders of government by the results they have achieved."[22] The latter was the definition widely accepted from the Revolution through the Civil War, and the one embraced by the critics of reform. The former was the Progressive redefinition of the term.

The origins of the Progressive definition, Schattschneider believed, came "somewhat lefthandedly" from Aristotle, who did not like democracy which he thought synonymous with mob rule. In Aristotle's classification of constitutions that was widely accepted by the American founders, a democracy was ruled in narrow selfish interests and was the corrupt form of popular government, whereas a republic was governed by a broader enlightened self-interest and was the good form. The difference was that between a mob and a public. Athenian democracy was a republic, as was Rome. In America, however, the New England town meeting provided the contrasting example of direct citizen democracy that over time became romanticized as the ideal democracy. It proved a reasonably effective form of government for the small, homogeneous communities in colonial New England whose populations were alike in ancestry, religion, and culture. As the colonies grew in size and diversity, town meetings became impracticable at all but the town level of government. By the time of the revolution and independence, the framers of the nation's new Constitution thought it clearly unworkable as a form of government for an expanded republic. It was the Frenchman John Jacques Rousseau who popularized the idea of direct citizen government as a form of democracy suitable to the governance of a nation. He was, in Schattschneider's view, "the father of the notion of an absolute, unlimited, magical, popular sovereignty," an idea that he dismissed as "the greatest oversimplification in the history of political thought." He acknowledged that Rousseau's idea promised "instant democracy, something for the taking *now*" and had "all the charm of immediacy and simplicity" but added that only the most passionate ideologues "have promised so much to so many." Yet, it is just this that the Progressives had promised.[23]

Democracy as "government by the people" provided reformers with a definition from which their direct-democracy and direct-government reforms followed as logical applications. But it did more: it changed the purpose of constitutional government in America. The overarching goal of the framers had been to secure liberty, but for the reformers, liberty was displaced by democracy as the overriding objective for the nation.[24] For them, democracy was no longer a component in a mixed regime. It became the regime itself, freed from its ancient association with class rule and civilized as a social virtue applicable to all. Liberty lost not only its preeminence but its independence as well. It became incorporated into democracy as individual liberties (civil rights) were joined with majority rule to become the operational definition of the term, which for a time was called "liberal democracy" but then simply "democracy."

At the same time, democracy was more than the purpose (the telos) of the American constitutional system. It was also the *method* by which a democratic polity was governed. It was understood as a *process* akin to the due process of law or the scientific method that sorted through the evidence of competing interests and was open to the participation of all in the resolution of differences.[25] In this new Progressive vocabulary, "democracy" became the term used to cover those public activities of bargaining and compromise that had from the time of Aristotle through Lincoln been called "politics," while politics became the "political"—the demands, pressures, ideologies, and influences that played upon and corrupted government. Politics thereby became an easy whipping boy for reformers. It was the subterranean realm of political parties wherein bosses pursued power for themselves, interest groups and their lobbyists sought special favors, and corporate money bought public officials, all operating largely out of the public eye. Rather than the guarantor of liberty in a free society, as the framers had understood the activity, politics was recast by scholars and reformers alike as a battle for power—a question of who gets what, when, and how.[26]

The definition of power also changed in the new Progressive lexicon. As with the shift from representative to direct democracy, reformers discarded the conventional notion of *political* power in favor of *will* power. The difference between these two concepts of power was delineated clearly by Thomas Hobbes who saw will power as inherent in the nature of Man while political power came into existence only with the formation of a state.[27] The former gave direction to the behavior of individuals; the latter was a check to protect civil society from the excesses of individual will. In his criticism of the Progressives, Ford focused on power and was explicit in asserting that it was an *institutional*, not an individual concept. Political power was located in and gave force to the organization of government, which in turn shaped the character and role of political activity (the exercise of will power) that occurred within. For Ford, as for the American founders, political power inhered in public offices, not in their occupants. Not so for the reformers, who argued that political power resided in the individual, conflating it with will power, and insisting that it was the release of this power from the institutional constraints of government that was essential to realizing a true democracy.

Democracy, politics, and power, as redefined by the Progressives, served both to justify and sustain their direct-democracy and direct-government reforms, much as the older definitions had done for the Constitution of the framers. Other terms also shifted in meaning in ways that further strengthened the conceptual fortress erected around the idea of Progressive democracy to make challenges to the Progressive ideal yet more problematic. By equating the term "republic" with "democracy," *representative* democracy lost its historic standing as a form of democracy separate and distinct from *direct* democracy. Instead, it was incorporated into the American system of democracy as government by the people wherein direct forms of citizen participation were privileged as being *more* democratic than representative forms. The idea of democracy as the popular "control" of government shifted as well, no longer meaning merely the power of the people to throw-the-rascals-out if unhappy with their performance but extended now to the direct involvement of citizens in the making and administration of public policy. "Self-government" remained a synonym for democracy, but acquired—indeed, required—a more immediate and activist role for the "self" (individual citizens) in their own governance.

In effect, the reformers and their critics were talking past one another, using the same words to be sure but with different meanings drawn from different times in the nation's history. The critics spoke an older language born of institutional understandings of government, politics, and power, while the reformers employed a new one drawn from Civil War debates and given depth and breadth by the new social sciences, especially psychology, and the new philosophy, pragmatism. Where the former was concerned with creating a constitutional order aimed at securing liberty and producing virtuous citizens, the latter sought to open the government and politics created by that constitutional order to the fuller participation of naturally virtuous citizens so that they might realize their full potential as human beings. The former designed institutions to blunt those aspects of human nature that could threaten liberty, whereas the latter aimed at breaking these barriers so that the true social and public-spirited nature of citizens could be freed to lead government and politics into the service of all in society. The former recognized a substantive tension between many of the elements in the Constitution of their design—liberty v. equality, majority rule v. minority rights, democracy v. politics—and saw their reconciliation, never permanent to be sure, as best achieved through a politics of deliberation that was also the best guarantor of a free society.[28] The latter instead wished many of these tensions away by redefining key political concepts—democracy, politics, power—as *processes* with little substantive content, the effect of which was to evade the tensions inherent in the older idea of democracy by establishing a constitutional framework with direct democracy and direct government as its institutional centerpieces.

Progressivism remade the Constitution and provided the nation with a new vocabulary by which to analyze and evaluate the performance of the government and politics thus created. This new reductionist lexicon explained and justified the reforms of direct democracy and direct government. It became the language of the new social sciences and history in universities whose expansion in size and social reach coincided with the era of reform at the end of the nineteenth and beginning of the twentieth centuries. The Progressive concepts of democracy, politics, and power came to govern the thought and work of scholars and journalists alike and have since remained hegemonic in the nation's political discourse. For all the frustrations and disappointments these concepts have produced in both governance and scholarship, their origin and history have gone largely unexamined. They are the modern "self-evident truths" that guide the minds of those who think or talk or write about American politics and who dominate the news media and the academy. It is this unquestioned link between language and reform forged by the Progressives that has made direct democracy and direct government, as Arthur Lipow laments, "peculiarly resistant to critical historical analysis."[29]

# Notes

1   Thomas West, "Progressivism and the Transformation of American Government," in *The Progressive Revolution in Politics and Political Science*, eds John Marini and Kent Masugi (Lanham: Rowman & Littlefield, 2005), 13–31. Ronald Pestritto argues that Progressives wanted to adjust the principles in the American Founding by abandoning the natural law foundations of the nation's original political order. http://nlnrac.org/critics/american-progressivism, 1 (accessed December 09, 2014). See too "Introduction," in *American Progressivism*, eds Ronald J. Pestritto and William J. Atto (Lanham: Rowan & Littlefield, 2008).

2   Ballots had previously been printed and distributed by political parties, but these laws provided that ballots be prepared by the government and that its officials administer elections. The statutory definition of a "political party" was necessary to determine those parties entitled to have their names and candidates printed on the official ballot.

3   Unlike the changes in political practice before the Civil War, adoption of ballot laws was driven primarily by an elite group of middle-class reformers—the Mugwumps—concerned mainly with the integrity of elections. At the time, they were seen as aimed not only at party bosses but also at the corrupting influence of the new immigrants who were widely viewed as not being as reliably "American" as were earlier generations.

4   The only real challenges to the Progressive idea of democracy came from the political extremes. The Socialist Eugene Debs derided it from the left as *capitalist* democracy that protected private property and the wealthy few. He argued instead for a *social* democracy that would truly empower the mass of the people in their own governance. Unlike others, his argument was not grounded on the Constitution but located instead in the more radical tradition of American thought that traced to the *Declaration of Independence*, Thomas Paine, and free thinkers who followed. Philosophical conservatives Charles Hollingsworth and Ellis

Paxson Olberholtzer denounced progressive democracy as *class* democracy that served the interests of the poor while dismissing those of the wealthy. For them, property rights were fundamental to all other guarantees in the Constitution and that a "true" democracy would be free from the bias of class. Like Aristotle, they saw a republic as the virtuous form of popular government and democracy as the corrupt form.

5    For a discussion of Lincoln's use of the prepositions to define the different dimensions of in the idea of democracy, see Mortimer J. Adler and William Gorman, "Reflections on the Gettysburg Address," *The New Yorker* (September 8, 1975), 42ff. It may be noted that Lincoln's use of "for" refers to the purpose of popular government and recalls Aristotle's classification of constitutions in which he distinguishes between a "republic" as a regime of the many governed by enlightened self-interest and "democracy" as a corrupt regime governed by the narrow self-interest. The framers accepted this Aristotelian distinction, which led to their embrace of republican government and their reservations about democracy.

6    Charles A. Beard, *An Economic Interpretation of the Constitution of the United States* (New York: Macmillan, 1935). See too Richard Hofstadter, *The Progressive Historians* (New York: Alfred A. Knopf, 1968), which deals with Frederick Jackson Turner and Vernon L. Parrington as well as Beard.

7    Carl Becker, *The Heavenly City of the Eighteenth Century Philosophers* (New Haven: Yale University, 1932); Arthur Bentley, *The Process of Government: A Study of Social Pressures* (Bloomington: Principia Press, 1949).

8    See David H. Burton, *The Learned Presidency* (Rutherford: Farleigh Dickinson University, 1988), 120–121.

9    Philipp and Taft approved the use of primaries for nominations at the local level but opposed their use for statewide and congressional nominations, arguing that local primaries should select delegates to a state party convention which would choose candidates for statewide and congressional offices.

10   Ford here echoes the view of Jefferson and Lincoln that democracy requires only that the people be able to *control* government, not that they make decision for or administer it. Like many Progressives, Ford favored a short ballot that removed all executive offices from election, save for governor, and, like the federal government, made them appointive, arguing that this

would simplify the assignment of responsibility by enabling voters to hold the chief executives responsible for the actions of government during their tenure. See too Beard, "The Ballot's Burden," 589–614.

11   In Wisconsin, a chorus of La Follette's critics deplored his use of the primary to paint himself publicly as the great reformer fighting to restore citizen democracy, whereas out of the public eye, he was a ruthless self-promoter who acted often like a petty authoritarian insisting that it was his way or the highway. See Philipp, *Political Reform in Wisconsin*; Maxwell, *La Follette and the Rise of the Progressives in Wisconsin*, esp. chap. 11.

12   For a related discussion, see Mileur, "The Legacy of Reform: Progressive Government, Regressive Politics," 259–287.

13   Richard Hofstadter, *The Age of Reform* (New York: Alfred Knopf, 1955).

14   Goodwin, *The Bully Pulpit*, chapters 7, 26, and 27.

15   Nye, *Midwestern Progressive Politics*, 137–151.

16   Norman Wilensky observes that, in 1912, Republicans who supported Taft and opposed Roosevelt were "among the least articulate of public men … neither eloquent nor intellectual." There were few authors or professors in their ranks and, despite viewing direct democracy as an "immediate danger" to political stability, never set forth a coherent credo in defense of their position. Wilensky, *Conservatives in the Progressive Era*, 13. George Mowry found the same in his study of Progressivism in California, noting that he could find no records left by those who supported the *status quo* or opposed reform. Mowry, *The California Progressives* (Chicago: Quadrangle Books, 1951), vi.

17   E. E. Schattschneider, *Two Hundred Million Americans in Search of A Government* (New York; Holt, Rinehart and Winston, 1969), 60.

18   Walter Lippmann, *Essays in The Public Philosophy* (Boston: Little, Brown and Company, 1955), 47. Lippmann elaborated on this functional derangement, arguing that "the people have acquired power they are incapable of exercising [while] the governments they elect have lost powers which they must recover if they are to govern. [T]he people are able to give and to withhold their consent to be governed … They can elect the government. They can remove it. They can approve or disapprove its performance. But they cannot administer the government. They cannot normally initiate and propose the necessary legislation. *A mass cannot govern*." 14 (ital. added). He also saw no reason to believe that

public opinion offered a solution, calling it bogus democracy to permit momentary opinion to compromise executive and legislative power. 33–34.

19 Philip J. Ethington, "The Metropolis and Multicultural Ethics: Direct Democracy Versus Deliberative Democracy in the Progressive Era," in *Progressivism and the New Democracy*, eds Sidney M. Milkis and Jerome M. Mileur (Amherst: University of Massachusetts Press, 1999), 192–193.

20 Michael McGerr, *A Fierce Discontent* (New York: Free Press, 2003), xiv.

21 Lipow, *Political Parties and Democracy*, 13. Italics added.

22 Schattschneider, *Two Hundred Million Americans in Search of a Government*, 58.

23 Schattschneider, *Two Hundred Million Americans in Search of a Government*, 60.

24 To the Progressive Woodrow Wilson, the greater goal was to make the world safe for democracy. Save for World War II, which was fought in the name of freedom, democracy has been the guiding star of American foreign policy since Wilson.

25 It is noteworthy that the Cold War reinforced this notion of democracy as a way to distinguish American democracy from the majoritarian claims to democracy of the Soviet Union.

26 Harold Lasswell among others saw the political science as the study of power. Harold Lasswell, *Power: Who Gets What, Where and How* (New York: P. Smith, 1950), reprint.

27 Thomas Hobbes, *Leviathan* (New York: Liberal Arts Press, 1958), Part I, 78–86 and 109–119. See too John Plamenatz, *Man and Society* (New York: McGraw-Hill, 1963), Part I, 135–136.

28 On the tension between politics and democracy, see Bernard Crick, *In Defence of Politics* (Chicago: University of Chicago, 1962), especially Chapter 3.

29 Lipow, *Political Parties*, 13.

# Contributors

**Lonce H. Bailey** is Assistant Professor in the Department of Political Science at Shippensburg University, United States, where he teaches course on US politics and public administration. He is the coeditor, along with Doug Harris, of *The Democratic Party; Documents Decoded* and *The Republican Party, Documents Decoded.* (2014) He also serves as the Academic Director for the US State Department's Study of the US Institute on American Politics and Political Thought, an academic institute for academics from overseas.

**Douglas B. Harris** is Associate Professor of Political Science at Loyola University Maryland. At Loyola, he has chaired the Political Science Department, directed the University's Honors Program, and is currently codirector of Messina, Loyola's first-year seminar program. He is coauthor of *The Austin-Boston Connection: Fifty Years of House Democratic Leadership* (2009) and coeditor of *Doing Archival Research in Political Science* (2012), *The Democratic Party: Documents Decoded* (2014), and *The Republican Party: Documents Decoded* (2014).

**Robert J. Lacey** is Associate Professor of Political Science at Iona College, United States. He is the author of *American Pragmatism and Democratic Faith (2007)* and is currently working on a book to be published by Bloomsbury about Edmund Burke and his intellectual heirs in modern American political thought.

**Jerome M. Mileur** is Emeritus Professor in the Department of Political Science at the University of Massachusetts Amherst, United States, where he taught courses on American politics and thought. He is coeditor, with Sidney Milkis, of *Progressivism and the New Democracy* (1999), *The New Deal and the Triumph of Liberalism* (2002), and *The Great Society and the High Tide of Liberalism* (2005).

**Paul Rego** is Associate Professor of Politics and International Relations at Messiah College, United States. His teaching and research interests include constitutional law, American political thought, and the American presidency. He is currently working on a book about the political thought of Lyman Trumbull, who served in the United States Senate from 1855 to 1873.

**Jeffrey L. Sedgwick** is Professor Emeritus of Political Science at the University of Massachusetts—Amherst. In his academic career, he has taught and written on a variety of aspects of American Government including American political thought and presidential leadership. He was appointed as the Director of the Bureau of Justice Statistics for the U.S. Department of Justice and in 2008 was appointed to serve as Assistant Attorney General for the Office of Justice Programs.

# Index